REA

ACPL ITEM
DISCARDED

Y0-ABY-437

BUILDING BETTER WEB SITES

A How-To-Do-It Manual for Librarians

NOTICE: If any part of these contents is lost or damaged, the Patron will be charged for the total cost of all items.

_____ Disk   _____ Video

_____ Cassette   _____ CD

_____ Text   _____ Other

Yuwu Song

Notice: Warning of Copyright Restrictions

The copyright law of the United States (Title 17 United States Code) governs the reproduction. distribution. adaptation. public performance. and public display of copyrighted material

Under certain conditions specified in law. non-profit libraries are authorized to lend. lease. or rent copies of computer programs to patrons on a nonprofit basis and for nonprofit purposes. Any person who makes an unauthorized copy or adaptation of the computer program. or redistributes the loan copy. or publicly performs or displays the computer program. except as permitted by the title 17 of the United Stated Code. may be liable for copyright infringement

This institution reserves the right to refuse to fulfill a loan request if. in its judgement. fulfillment of the request would lead to violation of the copyright law

HOW-TO-DO-IT MANUALS
FOR LIBRARIANS

NUMBER 123

NEAL-SCHUMAN PUBLISHERS, INC.
New York, London

MAR 0 3 2004

Don't miss the companion CD-ROM located on the inside back cover of this book!

Published by Neal-Schuman Publishers, Inc.
100 William Street, Suite 2004
New York, NY 10038

Copyright © 2003 by Yuwu Song

All rights reserved. Reproduction of this book, in whole or in part, excepting worksheets, without written permission of the publisher, is prohibited.

Printed and bound in the United States of America.

The paper used in this publication meets the minimum requirements of American National Standard for Information Sciences—Permanence of Paper for Printed Library Materials, ANZI Z39.48–1992. ∞

Library of Congress Cataloging-in-Publication Data

Song, Yuwu.
    Building better Web sites : a how-to-do-it manual for librarians / Yuwu Song.
        p. cm. — (How-do-do-it manuals for librarians ; no. 123)
    Includes bibliographical references and index.
    ISBN 1-55570-466-2 (alk. paper)
    1. Library Web sites—Design. 2. Web sites—Authoring programs. I. Title.
II. How-to-do-it manuals for libraries ; no. 123.

    Z674.75. W67 S66 2003
    005.7'2—dc21

                          2002035769

CONTENTS

LIST OF FIGURES

PREFACE

Over the last decade, library Web sites—both as public bulletin boards for the library itself and as gateways to large amounts of electronic information resources for patrons to access—have moved from novelty to necessity. For many, the library's Web site has become as familiar—and utilized—as the traditional in-person visit. Increasingly, many patrons prefer using the library's Web site instead of making the trip from home or office to the actual library building. Not only is it now clear that a first-rate Web site is essential for today's library, we must also consider that from now on, a Web site may be the *only* contact many patrons have with a library. *Building Better Web Sites: A How-to-do-it Manual for Librarians* addresses this urgent challenge.

Today's information society demands that librarians understand both the principles of remote library services and the techniques of creating and maintaining Web content. Those who work with library Web sites need varying degrees of knowledge about how Web pages are created, how interactive features are developed, and how multimedia elements and databases are made as well as familiarity with current Web development technologies. *Building Better Web Sites: A How-to-do-it Manual for Librarians* addresses both the principles and the techniques in one book. It is designed to show readers how to:

- create functional and appealing Web pages,
- develop and incorporate interactive features, and
- integrate multimedia elements and databases.

This volume focuses on the practical aspect of library Web site development, on structure and design rather than content and administration.

Building Better Web Sites examines the fundamental design principles for a library's site. Illustrated examples offer:

- diverse samples from different libraries,
- details on making construction plans,
- site goal definitions,
- site design options,
- site maintainance tips, and
- ways to increase traffic to and use of your site.

Chapter 1, "Building and Maintaining Better Sites," begins with a brief nontechnical introduction to the Web and the purposes of having a library Web site. It presents a process and specific advice for planning, designing, and developing a library Web site. For those who know they want to start a Web presence but are not sure where to begin, this chapter provides many useful hints and suggestions. It highlights various factors to be considered: defining the goal of your site and planning its content with the patron in mind; producing and promoting your site to your patrons; and keeping your site current. This chapter wraps up with a consideration of the actual creation process–how to organize all the materials collected into an appealing site that visitors can use comfortably.

Chapter 2, "Learning and Mastering HTML Basics," covers the nuts and bolts, just enough for you to get started on the Web. This chapter concentrates on how to code pages without unnecessary details on the coding language. It covers information on advanced HTML tags, and how to create tables, frames, and forms. For beginners, this chapter can be used as a tutorial, while, for advanced learners, it can be used as an HTML review and reference.

Chapter 3 "Moving Beyond HTML," covers design beyond simple HTML. It explores JavaScript and its applications, CSS, DHTML, and CGI. These concepts and tools bring special effects and interactivity (such as pop-up windows or online quizzes) to the Web site.

Chapter 4, "Designing Web Graphics," brings a site to life. Graphics enhance and illustrate resources and services—from background and mastheads, to navigational icons, to floor plans and maps. This chapter examines formats, compression, graphics tools, downloading rules, background images and color, imagemaps, animation, and simple 3-D text creation.

Chapter 5, "Exploring Inventive Web Formats and Multimedia," investigates the programs that create dynamic interfaces, interactive online tutorials, and exciting audio-visual capabilities. These applications can greatly extend content delivery and multimedia functions. This chapter embraces discussions of PDF, Microsoft Office formats, Flash, Shockwave, Authorware, video, QuickTime VR, audio, screen capturing software, and library multimedia applications and products.

Chapter 6, "Investigating Advanced Web Technologies," shows the way to craft more sophisticated sites featuring more interactivity, flexibility and functionality. It offers a more forward-looking "alphabet soup": XML, SMIL, SGML, and VRML. Database-driven Web sites appraise ASP, PHP, Cold Fusion, and JSP.

Chapter 7, "Planning for the Future of Building Better Web Sites," focuses on the trends and issues likely to impact library

Web site design expectations. It discusses networking, a portable Web, versatile interface modes, artificial intelligence and portals, dynamic creation of applications, sophisticated search tools, multimedia retrieval and management, media-based navigation, online language translation, digital libraries, and other freshly-imagined approaches and paradigms.

The "Appendixes" features five useful resources:

1. a list of organizations and institutions that prospective developers may find useful,
2. a quick-guide table of Web formats matching file extensions and descriptions to recommended display instructions,
3. a complete *Building Better Web Sites* glossary, defining terms from Adobe Acrobat to XML,
4. a Dreamweaver Tutorial, which provides a concise summary about the basics of the most popular and powerful Web authoring tool. It will provide the ability to create HTML pages without having to learn all the codes, or simplify the process for those who do the codes, and
5. a bibliography containing a list of useful books, articles, and Web sites to turn to for more detailed information on a variety of subjects such as HTML, CGI, Java, JavaScript, Imagemap, multimedia, and advanced Web design resources.

HOW TO USE THE CD-ROM

Open the CD-ROM by inserting the disk into your computer's "D" drive and click the""D" symbol to open, or open office documents, then select "D' drive.

The companion CD-ROM, located in the inside back cover of *Building Better Web Sites: A How-to-do-it Manual for Librarians* provides "one-click-away" access to source codes for applications and page templates. (These will help beginners get their site off to a quick start, or at least, they will lead readers to further explore these sample sites or applications to see how innovative ideas described were actually implemented.) They include:

*   HTML code for a simple page, form, table, and frame, library Web site design examples,
*   JavaScript/DHTML applications,
*   CGI sample code,
*   Web-based videos,
*   XML examples,
*   SMIL applications,
*   Java animations,

- Flash animations,
- applications created with Web-based programs, etc.

To enhance the learning experience, the *Building Better Web Sites* CD-ROM links each figure so they can be viewed in their final, authentic form—on the computer screen. Figures can be easily seen on a laptop or PC.

There are two ways to look at the figures.

1. To view while read or to review figures in one continuous scroll, open the folder of the chapter number, select the folder marked "Figures." Open the HTML file (often the Netscape or Explorer file) with the file name like FiguresChap01.htm.
2. If you prefer to only view a specific figure, follow the exact directions after this CD-ROM symbol

embedded above the individual figure.

Note:

Whenever possible, real Web sites are hyperlinked so you can connect to them directly from the CD-ROM.

My hope is that this manual meets two needs. First it identifies library challenges and offers specific solutions and software to solve these problems. Second it examines the myriad software options available and then matches them with their wisest uses.

My goal is to build bridges—from an idea for a Web site to the realization of one, and from perfunctory starter sites to spectacular sites.

ACKNOWLEDGMENTS

I thankfully acknowledge the support by my wife, Qunying Li. I express my heartfelt thanks to Charles Harmon for his encouragement and input on this project, which led me to start working on the book and produce an improved final version. I also appreciate the timely assistance of Michael Kelley, Kevin Allison, and Gary Albert in the process of the project. Last but not the least, I greatly acknowledge all the help given to me by the following individuals: Scott Herrington, John Barnard, Annie Platoff, Jennie Duvernay, Tom Luxon, Karl Bridges, and Jason Francois.

1 BUILDING AND MAINTAINING BETTER LIBRARY WEB SITES

INTRODUCTION

WHAT IS THE WEB?

As one of the services on the Internet, the Web (World Wide Web) is composed of millions of Web sites interconnected on a global computer network. With about ten million sites on the Web in January 2000 (and about 25 million by the end of the year and a hundred million by 2002), users have more choices than ever before. Web sites consist of Web pages, which hold various kinds of electronic files and documents including text, graphics, animation, sound, video, other types of multimedia, and program or application files. One of the most useful features of the Web is interactivity. For example, a Web page may include hyperlinks. A user can click the link and move to another part on the same page, other pages on the same site, or another site on the Web. Hyperlinks enable users to retrieve information in any order they prefer. The main activities of users visiting a Web site are reading text, listening to audio files, or viewing images, animation, and video. In addition, they can interact with the interface of the Web.

Usually, a Web site is referred to as a collection of connected Web pages (electronic files, documents) placed on the same server. The Web pages are linked together in a meaningful way for the display of information. For a Web site, the top-level page is the homepage, which provides a general overview of the Web site. For each Web site there is a unique address, called Uniform Resource Locator (URL). The major tool used to develop Web pages is Hypertext Markup Language (HTML), a language for creating codes for data presentation. Web browsers such as Netscape and Internet Explorer read and interpret HTML, and display the data in the way HTML specifies.

THE LIMITATION OF THE WEB

A Web page is different from a magazine or newspaper page, a TV show, or any other existing form of communication. Compared to them, the Web has many limitations in what can be shown. The World Wide Web, sometimes referred to as the World

Wide Wait, can be as swift to navigate as the expressway is during the height of rush hour traffic. Due to the limited traffic flow on the computer network, it would take minutes to transmit the equivalent of one high-quality, full-color magazine page across the Web via an average modem connection. And it will be a long time before the Web can deal with the kind of sound and motion people see on TV.

WHAT IS WEB DEVELOPMENT IN A LIBRARY ENVIRONMENT?

Web development in a library setting is a unique blend of information selection, organization, publishing, user interface design, and technology. Many reasons exist why libraries need a Web presence. They range from presenting local information about the library to creating new library services and resources. The library Web site helps the users to find information about resources, services, collections, news, policies, and staff of the library. It creates an integrated and coherent library-wide Web environment responsive to the users' information and access needs. The development of Web technologies made it possible for libraries to extend their services beyond the libraries' physical walls. They can use Web sites as gateways to reach out to their users and bring them in. Like a business site, a library site should be designed to attract new patrons (customers), give information about products and services, do market research, and provide patron support. The design of Web sites in a library setting will become of growing importance to librarians as both a way to organize information and resources for effective retrieval and a way to promote their services.

In this book, we will discuss general principles as well as techniques of library Web site design. We will also provide numerous examples from library sites detailing styles, contents, and technologies that can be incorporated into your Web site. Selected from public, academic, and special libraries, these examples clearly demonstrate the range of possibilities in the creation of a site that will serve the library patrons well.

Generally, there are five phases in library Web site development and maintenance processes:

- Planning
- Site Structure Development
- Production
- Publishing
- Promoting and Maintaining

PLANNING

There are many things to ponder when you are going to build a library Web site. Who is the typical user? What kind of contents should you put online? What type of design, layout, and navigation should you pursue? With what kind of Web connection will your typical user be accessing the site? What new forms of interactivity should be used? What kind of new technologies should be used? How do you promote and maintain the site?

It is necessary to start with a plan, which explains how to decide on an approach, a project timeline, and Web-related policies. And more important, you need to form a Web team to do the job. In order to form a Web team, you need to define the mission statement, objectives, and development and management structure. You will need to make decisions on personnel. The following are some sample components for a Web team.

MISSION STATEMENT

A mission statement provides some basic guidelines for you to develop your Web site. Here is an example.

The library Web site supports the informational needs of the patrons. To achieve this goal, we select, acquire, organize, and preserve materials and provide access to them through:

- Conducting systematic organization (such as cataloging and indexing)
- Providing access to all kinds of electronic resources (online catalogs, search engines, and commercial and noncommercial databases)
- Offering instruction of effective utilization and evaluation of these resources
- Promoting and marketing the library resources and services

After considering the goal, specific objectives can be formulated:

- Developing a user-centered library Web site, which is easy for patrons to navigate and get information
- Creating an effective development and management structure that promotes, maintains, and improves the library Web site

PERSONNEL

The team should be composed of librarians who can provide content and who are familiar with library resources, services, and the profession in general. It should also have technical specialists with Web skills such as graphic design, programming, systems administration, and so on. Smaller institutions may prefer to use out-sourcing (hiring external consultants for specific projects or tasks) because they may not have the luxury to form a team. However, from the following discussions, they still can learn something about the basic tasks, required skills, and administrative support for a major project.

TEAM LEADER'S RESPONSIBILITIES

The team leader is responsible for:

- Coordination
- Overall management

This person should have a wide range of talents including project management expertise, Web development and site management proficiency, people skills, and computer training experience.

TEAM RESPONSIBILITIES

As for the Web team, its major responsibilities include:

- Deciding the organization and content of the site.
- Designing information architecture, templates, and style guides.
- Gathering, editing, and putting online materials from content providers.
- Writing policies and procedures related to the site.
- Developing and maintaining the site.
- Managing the site's infrastructure and appearance.
- User-testing the site for improvement.
- Establishing a channel for users to report problems and make suggestions for changes.
- Forming advisory or working groups for Web projects and directing their activities.
- Coordinating with internal and external representatives for Web development for issues regarding changes and compliance with the policies and procedures.
- Enforcing the Web policies.

It may not be necessary that all team members are proficient in a particular Web skill such as CGI programming or a particular

Web design tool; however, it is necessary that they have basic computer skills.

ADVISORY AND WORKING GROUPS

The Web team may choose to form long-term or ad hoc groups to address some of its concerns and carry out some of its objectives.

- Content development
- Navigation
- Design
- Development
- Maintenance
- Promoting and publicizing
- Cataloging
- E-resources and e-journals
- Digital library projects
- Library staff (nonpublic) pages
- Library portal
- Database-driven Web sites
- Staff online training
- Online instruction
- Online services
- Remote access and authentication
- Usability testing
- ADA compliance
- Copyright issues
- Investigating new tools and technologies
- Workstations
- Special projects

There are a few things one should take into consideration. One is the appreciation and the backing of your administration for the Web project. Due to its cross-organizational nature, a Web development and management team requires top-down support from the institution's leaders who understand and appreciate the value of empowering a group to bring about the successful implementation of a Web project. As for the working environment, all team participants need access to computers and the Web-editing software from their own workstations. For more sophisticated hardware and software such as a video-editing platform, you may need a special workstation or a lab for work sessions.

CONCEPT DEFINED

The best preparation for creating a library homepage is for site developers to spend some time examining the homepages of similar libraries. This activity will give designers an indication of the basic concept of a library Web site, what works and what does not, what is interesting to the patrons and what is not, and what features make a homepage easy and pleasant to use. Before you define the whole concept for your library Web development project, you need to know who your viewers are. You have to identify your visitors and their needs.

Audience Identification and Needs Analysis

You should explicitly identify the Web site's intended audience. You should also get information of patrons' needs from interviews, questionnaires, or conduct needs analysis. The identification of potential Web visitors and the analysis of users' needs will establish what your services should be, and it will also help you to make decisions about the site design, resource allocation, and maintenance. Before you do the analysis, you may want to get some basic information such as:

- Who are the users?
- How many?
- Where are they?
- What information and resources do they want?
- What services do they want?
- How can they access your site?

Take an academic library Web site, for example; one major characteristic is the multiplicity of users and information needs in the academic institution. A library site needs to provide an interface accommodating the different needs, academic disciplines, and capabilities of the many and varied users. The majority of the patrons are students, faculty, and staff within the institution. The secondary user population includes other peer institutions both nationally and internationally, and the general public.

Only by getting and evaluating the information above would you be able to answer these questions:

- Why should you have a Web site?
- What are your goals?
- What resources and services do you want to provide?
- How should the Web site be developed and maintained?
- What is your vision for the future?

With these questions answered, you have pretty much come to know what your Web site should look like. Based on this information, you can develop a creative brief covering what you want to accomplish.

CONSENSUS, POLICIES, AND INVOLVEMENT OF USERS

You need to reach consensus among library staff and library departments as to the purpose of the library Web site. Some librarians think of the Web site as a gateway to additional resources on various kinds of subject areas. Others hold that the Web is a communications tool for their major users, and yet others look upon its primary purpose as to provide information about the innovative online services, collections, and other resources and projects. You need to formulate a policy to guide the design and development team on matters such as content selection, information architecture, interface design, development, evaluation, maintenance, and promotion.

Developing effective user-centered library Web sites will demand that systems design, development, and implementation be based in use and done collaboratively with library users or "customers." With the help of the users you should evaluate Web page designs either during or after their design and implementation. It is important to take into consideration the actions needed to move from the analysis of what is, to the design of something innovative, spending time for the testing of ideas before the Web site architecture becomes fixed. You need to know what your customers want, and to what extent the library Web site will provide products and services. This can be done through intensive research, user survey, usability inspection and evaluation. You may want to develop a consistent question and answer method for several user groups, using two or more groups of evaluators conducting independent evaluations. And they would identify the usability problems of a particular design and test the site a few times in its developmental life cycle. This would ensure an unbiased assessment of a library Web site development. For more details, also check the section of usability testing in this chapter.

BUDGETS AND PROJECT TIMELINE

Last but not least, a detailed budget plan and schedule should be set for work on different phases of the project. The budget plan and schedule can be developed based on tasks to be accomplished: such as overall planning, content selection, information architecture, interface design, development, and so on. For a visual display of the first phase, take a look at Figure 1–1, Phase 1: Planning.

Figure 1–1 Phase 1: Planning

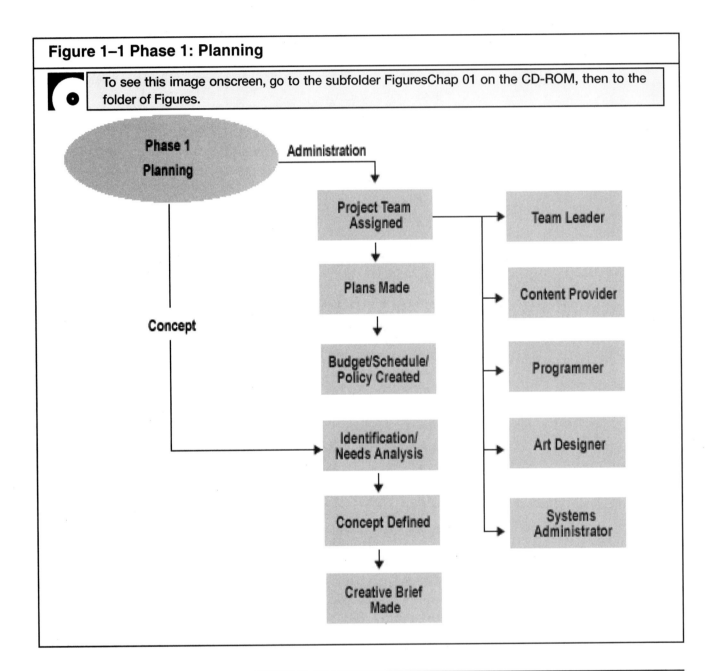

To see this image onscreen, go to the subfolder FiguresChap 01 on the CD-ROM, then to the folder of Figures.

SITE STRUCTURE DEVELOPMENT

Before you design and develop the general architecture of the Web site and the interface, you need to identify and select contents and review the technical needs.

CONTENT OVERVIEW

Like printed materials, you don't select everything that is available. You evaluate first. After that you choose the most valuable information for your patrons.

Contents for the Sites

By a glance at some library Web sites, you will see what most libraries put online:

- Information about the library
  - Hours of operation
  - Location
  - Library rules and policies
  - Mission statement
  - Contact information
  - Personnel directories
  - Photograph or drawing of the library
  - Information about the library such as operation, personnel, and annual report
  - News about the library or library activities
  - Calendar of special events
- Internal sources of information
  - Online catalog
  - Indexes
  - Other types of resources
- External sources
  - Selected sources on the Internet
  - Sources about the local area/region
  - Links to local authorities' homepages
- Library services
  - Online renewal
  - Recall
  - Interlibrary loan
  - Online reference
  - Suggestions
- Patron assistance
  - Help
  - Guides
  - Tutorials
- Other information resources
  - Subject directories
  - Training materials
  - Book reviews
  - Lists of recommended books
  - Book club choices

- Special collections of resources maintained by the library
- Information about Internet access and policies at the library
- Links or pages for specific audience (faculty, students, staff, children, young adults, and so on)

But for your library site, you should conduct content search and selection based on the identification of your audience and users' needs analysis. After deciding on the main content, you should organize them into smaller sections, with headings and subheadings.

What Should Be on the Library Web Site Front Page?

The front page is the door to your library site. It should consist of:

- Title of the site
- Library's logo
- Content of the Web site
- Date the Web site was created
- Date last updated
- Copyright information
- A link to the institution's homepage (if applicable, for example, a school's homepage)
- Contact information for the library (e-mail address, postal address, phone, and fax number)
- A link to a plain-text version of your site if you used technologies that made your site inaccessible for some users

REVIEWING THE DESIGN PRINCIPLES AND TECHNICAL NEEDS

Identity

One of the first things you should consider for your information architecture and interface design is to create a site identity. The library's name and logo are no doubt the most obvious identity components. Another important identity component is page layout. Web pages with a similar design can enhance the identity. The writing style of the Web documents will also help users to distinguish your site from others. With these identity components put in place, users will immediately recognize them as belonging to the library Web site.

It should be noted that your library Web site might be part of a larger institutional Web site. The parent institution site will no doubt influence the design of the library site identity. For example, the academic library Web site is sometimes restricted by the design conventions of the school's site. In this case, you may want to use similar fonts, colors, styles, graphics, and other page components in order to match the look and feel of the larger site.

Simplicity vs. Bells and Whistles

Whatever you decide to do as a library Web site designer, it cannot be stressed enough that consideration be given to the type of site you are developing and the type of people who may be viewing it. Adult library users might be more interested in simplicity and functionality than in bells and whistles. For this kind of audience, you may need to make each page as simple as possible. To be simple but not simplistic is the key for good information architecture and interface design. Simple layout, simple design, conservative colors, and uncluttered structure make the Web site easy to read, navigate, and understand. Dancing texts, bright colors, fancy background, animated GIFs, mouse-over, or Flash do not mean instant and universal appeal for this type of audience. But for kids and young adults, bells and whistles may be enticing and engaging.

Text

As far as text is concerned, you should understand that most people usually don't like to scroll down a lot to read your text on one screen. So it is necessary to break up text into smaller chunks of information. Try to avoid long paragraphs of text, especially text put together without a break, a heading, or some graphics. It is difficult to read long paragraphs in printed form, let alone to read on a computer screen. Keep paragraphs to five or six sentences. Resist the temptation to overdo styles such as too many headers, too many italicized or bold words. If possible, you should replace lengthy textual descriptions of things with icons and graphics.

Fonts

If you want to use a text font different from the default, make sure that the font is one that is standard on viewers' machines. The widely used fonts include Arial and Times New Roman.

Links

Links are very important components of a page. There are a few things you should pay attention to. To make navigation easier, you should avoid putting too many links on any individual page because that will have your visitors getting lost quickly. You also should avoid putting too many links next to each other. Try to make links simple. Links made up of lots of words look clumsy and awkward. They create a "wall of blue." Always try to avoid putting links in the middle of a paragraph, unless it is absolutely necessary. If you send the readers somewhere else before they finish reading your text, they might be lost and unable to come back since they might follow links after links in different paragraphs in different pages.

There are links, which look like regular text and you don't know that they are links until you mouse over and see the little hand icon. This kind of link may confuse users. Some Imagemaps or graphics-based links also confuse users. Unless you are just curious or stoned out of your mind, you might not think to click on these images or to even roll your mouse pointer over them to see if there is any information. It is hard for people to know that you want them to make choices unless you let them see it or make it clear that rolling a mouse pointer over the images will reveal informative text or a link. To facilitate navigation, it is a good idea to make your links predictable and make links look like links (distinguishable from text and graphics). You can use buttons, different fonts and colors, or place them in a more prominent position.

For certain links, descriptive information about them is needed. In some libraries' Web sites, we see a page full of links to search engines without depiction. This is definitely not a good practice because unless the users know something about the search engines, the names of the search engines mean nothing to them.

You should make sure that in every page there is a link leading to the site's home page. This will help facilitate navigation because no matter where you are, you will always find a way home.

Colors

Color is vital to making a Web page user friendly. Novice designers often tend to overuse colored text and backgrounds. The rule of thumb here is: use no more than four colors per site. Library sites for kids are exceptions. Use your own judgment to decide what kinds of text colors are appropriate. Try to avoid dark, elaborate, or patterned backgrounds because they distract the viewers from the task at hand and make reading difficult. For Web site background, plain colors are by far the most preferred. They are better than others if you have a lot of text, which requires sustained attention. There are three key words, which you should consider when using colors: conservative, useful, and appropriate.

Consistency

Consistency is essential in interface design. Always remember to integrate the look and feel of your pages. You should use consistent navigation scheme, design structure, and terminology across pages. The layout should be consistent in terms of the use of fonts, colors, graphics, and so on. For instance, you should always place repeated graphics in the same location on each page. To ensure consistency, you may want to create a template for team members working on the Web project. The template is designed to maintain a consistency of style, look, and function. It contains the basic information of a page: header, footer, navigation set, contact information, and other identity components such as the library name and logo. The graphic below is a screen shot of a Web page template of Arizona State University Libraries.

Figure 1–2 ASU Libraries Web Page Template

To see this image onscreen, go to the subfolder FiguresChap 01 on the CD-ROM, then to the folder of Figures.

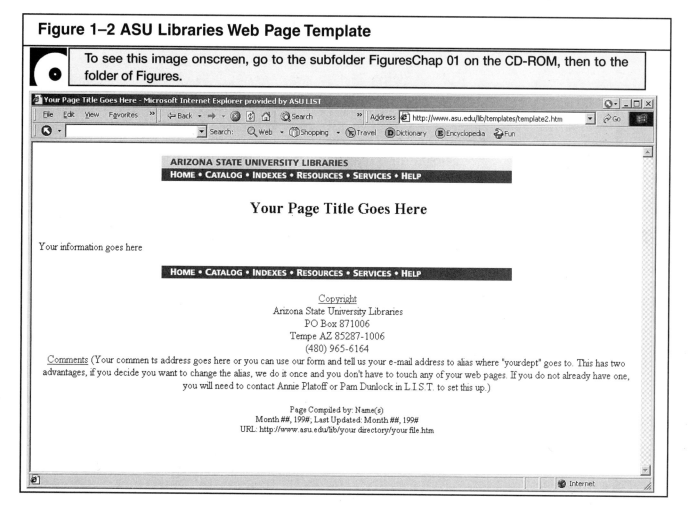

Computers, Platforms, and Browsers

Since not all machines and software are created equal, you should consider alternate computers, platforms, and browsers because your site may look different on computers different than your own. It is important for you to know the facts that:

- People use different computers.
  IBM compatible PCs may dominate the world market, but there are millions of people who use the Internet via a different platform. Apples still make up 12 percent of the market. WebTV is also growing in popularity.
- People use different browsers.
  More than 25 percent of people use something other than Internet Explorer such as Netscape, Opera, and WebTV when cruising the Internet. Because browsers are developed in different ways, each browser has new HTML tags that it supports. In addition to upgrades to the latest HTML standard, there are proprietary tags for features supported only by a particular browser. For example, Internet Explorer 5 and above supports XML tags and SMIL-like tags, which can be used to play online slides, while Netscape 6 does not. XML technologies and XML-enabled features are really attractive. You can use these new features if you are sure about the browsers your visitors use; for example, you can specify a particular browser for Intranet users. But if you do not know your user groups and the browsers they use, you should take certain things into consideration before you use these new features:

1. Do both Netscape and Internet Explorer currently support this feature?
2. Do you really need this new feature to enhance your site or do you use it for the purpose of showing off?
3. What percentage of the users will use the browser that supports the new features? Is it worth your effort to have this feature for only a small number of the users?
4. Do you have to create and maintain special versions of your pages for different browsers?

- People use different versions of browsers.
  Different browser versions will display your pages differently. And newer versions aren't always better. For example, Netscape 6 cannot handle the DHTML while Netscape 4 renders the same page perfectly.
- Computers have different screen sizes.
  A different screen size can change the way your page appears. Keeping the page width manageable is useful. The page that looks great on a 1024 x 768 screen may not look so when viewed on a smaller screen because some important information on the right side of the page is off the screen. It is very frustrating when you have to scroll left or right to view a page on the screen. Today's screen size is 800 by 600 pixels. But some people still use computer monitors with the old 640-by-480-pixel layout.

Figure 1–3 Three Different Screen Sizes

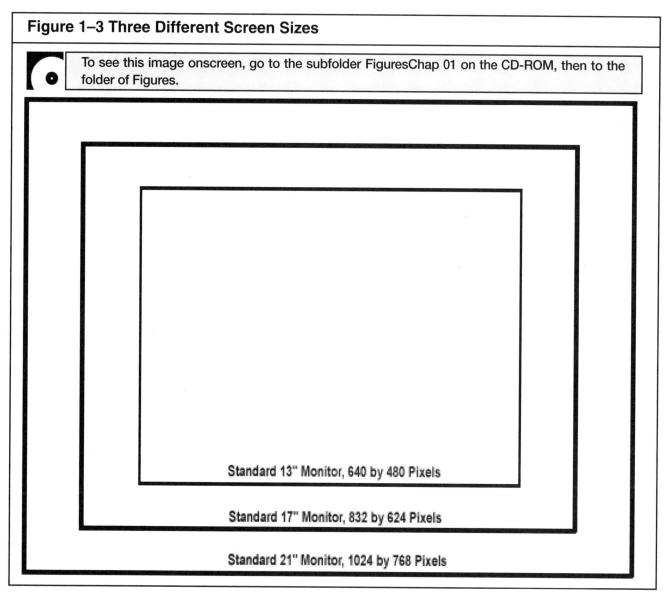

To see this image onscreen, go to the subfolder FiguresChap 01 on the CD-ROM, then to the folder of Figures.

Standard 13" Monitor, 640 by 480 Pixels

Standard 17" Monitor, 832 by 624 Pixels

Standard 21" Monitor, 1024 by 768 Pixels

Since viewers have a variety of screen sizes and it is still years ahead before most people use 1024 x 768 (resolutions) monitors, you should design for the most common denominator screen size: 640 x 480. This will ensure that users won't scroll to the right-hand side to see the whole page. When possible, also try to design your site in such a way that your homepage will not require scrolling vertically.

It is always a good practice to check your site on different computers with different systems and browsers to see how it looks and make changes accordingly. For different browsers, at least you need to check how your site appears on the Big Two: Netscape and Internet Explorer. One popular Web site NetMechanic provides a program, Browser-photo, which helps you to check how your site looks on different machines. The Web address is: *www.netmechanic.com/browser-photo/tour/BrowserList.htm.*

All of these factors above may affect how your site looks. You can construct your document's structure of the text but you have to leave the appearance of your document up to the computer and the browser displaying the document.

Graphics

You can use graphics to enhance the Web appearance. You can also use them to indicate where a link goes or what pages the link connects with. In most cases, text identification of the graphics should be used on each page.

Graphics should be used cautiously. For a children's section on a library site, using more graphics, flashing icons, bright colors, and animation is legitimate while using all of these in the adult section on the same site might annoy library users. You should always try not to use distracting graphics or backgrounds with no content. For a library online gallery, you may want to use "thumbnail pictures." If the reader clicks on the thumbnails, the full images are displayed. This will help the viewers to decide if the full images are worth seeing.

Consistency is also important. Graphics of the same type or in the same state (such as on and off in mouse-over) should be of the same size. Sometimes we see that the size of one button in the "off state" is far different from that of the button in the "on state." The result is that the mouse-over effect of that button is different from that of other buttons. As far as the placement of graphics is concerned, you should also be consistent with the location of repeated graphics.

Since graphics files are larger than text files, developers sometimes are compelled to make a choice between an attractive yet very slow graphical display and a much less attractive but faster text display. The only solution is to strike a balance and make use of graphics in a meaningful way and only when necessary.

Software Consideration

Keep in mind that some technologies require users to download new versions of browsers or plug-ins to view things such as Flash, Java, Shockwave, RealVideo, QuickTime, and so forth. This may be a challenge for some people. You need justification to use these technologies for sites meant to reach a wide audience that uses different kinds of hardware, software, and connection to the Web. Don't forget to explain the requirements for the use of the media on your Web site. The following is an example of requirements for watching library online video at *www.asu.edu/lib/tutorials/libonline/*.

Requirements for Viewing the Online Video:

32 MB of RAM
56.6 Kpbs modem
Internet Explorer 4, Netscape 4, or higher
Sound Card
Speakers, earphones or headphones
RealPlayer (free download: *www.real.com*)

Terminology

Pay attention to consistency of language across pages. Ambiguity and library jargon should be avoided. Try not to use words hard to understand for common people. Many library Web designers use "Finding Books" and "Finding Articles" to replace the technical terms "Catalog" and "Index" respectively because they are confusing to some people.

Keep Description of a Section Simple

Describe each section in your site as clearly and briefly as possible. Bear in mind that most people do not read word by word a long description of all the features of a section. It is better to cover everything else by using an "and more" link.

Make It Easy to Browse and Scan

Since the viewing area of a Web browser is smaller than a printed page, it is necessary to reformat your documents to fit this new environment, instead of dropping an existing document into your HTML editor. Most people like to browse or scan a Web page, picking out individual words or sentences, which appear to be important to them. Because of this, you'd better make it easy for people to browse or scan the page. One way to achieve this is to use columns similar to those of newspapers or magazines for your text. You can use tables to create columns for text layouts. HTML tags such as "DL" tag can be used for formatting text that requires indentation.

Put URL, Contact, and Update Information on Your Page

There are people who want to print out your page. Sometimes, the browser or printer won't be able to put the address of a file to a printed page. If there is a URL on your library page, users with the printed page can easily find your page online. A good Web page should also contain contact information as well as the date on which the page was last revised.

Content is the King

Remember that content is always the king. Presentation is always second to content. No matter how sophisticated the interface design is, it always serves the purpose of enhancing the content. No fancy design makes poorly composed content worth looking at.

File Naming Conventions

You should use lowercase in naming all files. Some servers are case sensitive. Using upper case will cause problems in uploading. Remember to keep a file name short (no more than 8 characters) and meaningful. There should be no spaces in file names. Underscores can be used as substitutes for spaces; for example, lib_tour.htm. You ought to save your homepage as index.html or index.htm. Last but not least, keep all your files in one folder. This will help in the linking process later on.

Navigation

Navigation is one of the most important parts of library Web site interface design. When we take a look at a Web page, we may not have many clues to where we will be led to, how much information is provided at the other end of the link, and if the linked pages are closely related to the current page. It is the responsibility of the designers to provide these functional and context clues to the visitors. The site must be intuitive. It must be easy to get around on.

It is essential to make it easy for the users to:

- Know how different elements in your site are connected.
- Understand the navigational information.
- Draw a simple map in their mind showing how the elements are linked and how to go to one place from another.
- Figure out everything they can see or do in your site.
- Figure out if they have seen everything.
- Determine if there is anything new and when the changes took place.

Generally speaking, there are five questions, which should be taken into consideration for designing the navigation set.

1. Where am I?
   Each page should provide clues where the users are. Like the street map indication: "You Are Here," the page should be labeled clearly as to the page content. You can take the advantage of font size, color, style, and effects to differentiate a Web page's title from the body text.

2. Where have I come from?
   You should make the users aware which options they took to come to the page they are in now. "Bread Crumbs" (recursive navigation), which mark the path the visitors used through the Web site hierarchy, do a good job showing where the users have come from.

3. How do I get back?
   "Bread Crumbs" navigation works fine to get people around. The popular site Yahoo! uses "Bread Crumbs" as part of a navigation set, which proves to be effective since it lets the visitors know where they are, where they used to be, and allows the visitors to one-click back to any of the previous tiers in the site including the homepage. Figure

Figure 1–4 "Bread Crumbs" Navigation

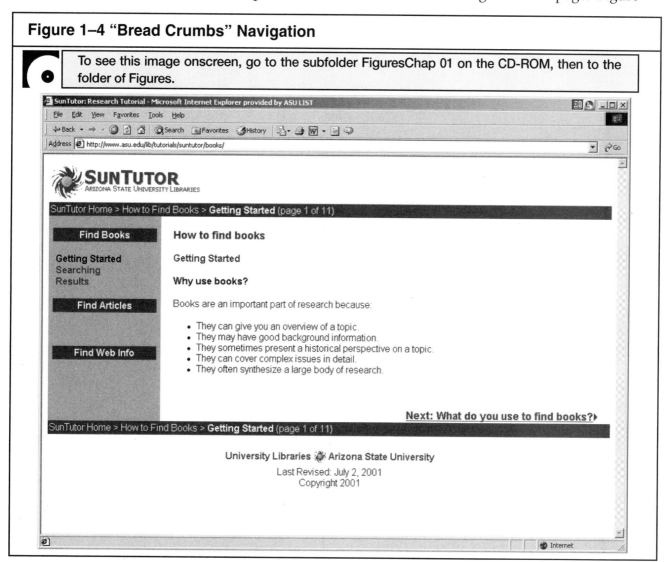

1–4 shows the "Bread Crumbs" navigation at the top bar in Arizona State University Libraries SunTutor site.

It is important that links should be provided for the users to go back to the homepage or to another major section of your library Web site. It is useful for people surfing your site to the main page, it is also useful for people getting to your site from other places. When users link to your pages, they may not always link to your homepage. It is necessary to provide useful information so that patrons who have traveled to your library Web site, not through a linear progression of page links but through an unstructured hop across the hierarchical structure or through a search engine, will know where they have ended up.

4. Where do I go from here?

The navigation should let the users see clearly the logic, order, and organization of the site. To reach this goal, horizontally, you should avoid putting too many links on one page, and vertically, you should avoid having too many levels or layers on your site. In other words, users should not be confused by too many options in one page. They should be allowed to click as few links as possible in different layers to get to the page with the information they need.

5. What do I do if I cannot find the information I need?

A Help Page providing some tips for site navigation and search hopefully will solve this problem. This page should contain information about getting started with research, how to find certain types of information, and technical assistance.

The best navigation scheme should be consistent, persistent, and predictable throughout the site. Not only does an effective navigation scheme answer the viewers' questions about getting information, it also answers them fast. The navigation should give clear visual clues that help users to reach their destinations with little effort. It must explain each option as it is offered so that the users can see easily which option they can take.

The main menu of a library Web site should be composed of five to eight high-level options for the major sections of the site. People usually view a page from top to bottom, left to right (one exception is that pages in Arabic are viewed from right to left and adjustments should be made accordingly). In most cases, the main menu is put at the left side of the page. To keep it consistent, the main menu should be put on each individual page at the same place in the site. All pages should point back to the homepage.

As far as the layout of the main page is concerned, the important information should be placed "above the fold." In other words, it should be possible to view that part of the screen without scrolling. The library's name and logo are important identifiers for a library Web site. They should be put on all the pages so that the viewers always know where they are.

Internal links and/or search tools are useful. Including a "Search the Library Site" feature in your site, such as keyword searching, will help users find what they need quickly if they know exactly what they are looking for. When developing keywords for a searchable library site database, you may need to create both the keywords and their synonyms so as to generate access points by which users can get information. For certain keywords, users may misspell. For example, some may type PsychInfo for the database: PsycINFO. In cases like this, it will help users if you put PsychInfo in your searchable meta fields for that database as well. Even though the users typed the wrong word, they still can get to that database.

Some users like to browse. It is better to include a site map or guide about the content of the Web site. A site map is an alphabetical list of items organized according to their nature. Sometimes it is easier to get information by browsing a site map than keyword searching if the users are not sure about what keywords they should use. It should be remembered that it is a good practice to annotate linked sources or online tools such as search engines. It will help users quickly get to know exactly what to expect. Generally, there are three major navigation tools, which will help you design your site.

1. Button Bars
   A set of button bars with links to your homepage and tables of contents is one of the primary navigation tools for Web users. It helps the users to understand the logic and organization of your site from the first glance. You can create a button bar using button graphics or text. They are usually placed vertically at the upper-left section of a page or horizontally at the top or bottom of the page.
2. Paging Buttons
   Hypertext links are a double-edged sword. On the one hand they provide flexibility for the users to go from one place to another; on the other hand, they make the users get lost easily. Unlike book pages, which have an ordered sequence, hyperlinks are bi-directional. Going "back" through the pages you have seen is different from paging "back" through the previous pages in a book. Sometimes the "Back" and "Forward" buttons in your Web browser only work for the most recent links you have visited. No doubt

they are not sufficient enough to let users follow an ordered sequence of Web pages. For documents in a sequential order such as papers or tutorials, you can incorporate "Next Page" and "Previous Page" buttons into them. You may also want to add clues such as "Page 1 of 19" in a page. Hopefully, these paging buttons will provide leads for users to follow the sequence of pages you have developed.

3. Anchors or Anchored Links

   Anchors provide a navigational scheme, especially, within a page. Typically, the links are created in a lengthy document, which will lead the users to go to the top or bottom of a page, or a specific section in that page. For more details about anchors, please see Chapter 2.

Web Accessibility

Web accessibility is now coming to the forefront of library Web site development. Due to the increasingly graphic nature of Web pages, it has become more difficult for the visually impaired to use the Web resources, because the reader software that "reads" the Web screen aloud has a hard time figuring out how to read frames, Java applets, Flash, PDF, and Imagemaps. It is the librarians' duty to provide accessible materials and electronic content to the disabled people. Libraries should create policies and guidelines that improve user access to Web-based information. The best way to provide an accessible site is to use the Web Accessibility Initiative (WAI) guidelines, HTML 4.0 tag enhancements, and cascading style sheets specification CSS2.

The World Wide Web Consortium's Web Accessibility Initiative

The WAI guidelines were developed by World Wide Web Consortium (W3C) to help solve problems for disabled people using the Internet (*www.w3.org/WAI*). Its guidelines are the most important source for standards in this area of Web design. They explain and provide recommendations on how Web sites can be made accessible to people with disabilities. The document includes information ranging from design principles, checkpoints, to techniques. Most items in the WAI are prioritized so that Web developers can address the most important accessibility issues first. W3C lists three priority levels of guidelines. There is an abbreviated list in the categories of "Required" and "Helpful But Not Required" guidelines. The following is a summary of the most important points we should be aware of.

Guidelines for Making a Library Web Site Accessible

- Provide alternative text for images, applets, Imagemaps, audio, video, animation, and other types of multimedia.
- For the moving objects or components on a Web page such as blinking, scrolling text, or auto-updating graphics, animations, and applets, it is necessary to provide a way to explain textually/aurally how the user can pause the movement of the objects.
- Offer transcripts for audio and video information.
- Offer auditory and textual descriptions of moving or visual information.
- Use features that enable activation of page elements via input devices other than a pointing device (such as a mouse). Some examples are keyboard or voice activation.
- Avoid using tables for layout, but if you use them at all, make sure they can be readjusted and interpreted by almost anyone.
- Provide different versions for different audiences. For example, provide a text-only site version for users with disabilities.

Helpful Tips for an Accessible Library Web Site

- Don't use structural elements to control style and presentation; control presentation with presentation elements and style sheets.
- Provide supplemental information needed to pronounce or interpret abbreviations, acronyms, or foreign text.
- Make sure that link phrases do not repeat on a page. Use one unique phrase to a resource. Make sure phrases are meaningful, when read out of context, and are both concise and brief.
- Navigation within the site should be logical and organized.
- Create a single downloadable file for documents that exist as a series of separate pages.

Evaluation Tools to Check Library Web Site Accessibility

- Bobby (*www.cast.org/bobby*)
  Bobby is a tool developed by the Center for Applied Special Technology (CAST). It is designed to test the Web site accessibility against the WAI priorities. If you put the URL of a Web page into Bobby's submission box, the site will quickly analyze the page for accessibility to the disabled

and give back a results page that tells you where problems are and where changes need to be made.

- Anybrowser (*www.anybrowser.com*)
  This site offers a few useful tools including HTML validation and link checking.
- Macromedia (*www.macromedia.com/macromedia/accessibility*)
  Macromedia developed an evaluation tool to check Web site accessibility. The tool lets developers know about accessibility problems and their location in source code, referring them to relevant W3C guidelines.
- Better Access to the WEB (*www.braillenet.jussieu.fr/accessibilite/livreblanc/english*)
  This site provides information on how individuals with visual impairments use the Web and how to make a site accessible. It also includes recommendations on how to use various HTML features and editors. There are links to resources such as the companies providing adaptive technology products and services that check Web sites for accessibility.

STRUCTURE

The structure of a library Web site is concerned with how many hierarchical layers the site has and how the different pages will be linked. For the front page, there should be only the most frequently used functions. It is very essential to place the important information in the part of a screen that can be viewed without scrolling. The less frequently used functions should be placed in other pages. You also need to put like things together on a page because it makes your site look logical, organized, concise, and cohesive. Since users are not so patient when reading online as they are when reading print-based materials, the Web developers should divide the site into logical units of information, which are shorter than their print-based counterparts.

Bear in mind that excessive structural hierarchy will hinder people from navigating effectively. So you should avoid creating a library site with multiple layers and a profusion of links. Try to simplify your site's hierarchical structure as much as possible. If it takes more than three clicks to get to an important section, that means you have too many levels of hierarchy in your site. The hierarchical relationship between the different units must be established, that is, which information will be presented first, and how pages will be linked. There are different approaches to create the structure for a site. To sum up, there are four major structural approaches:

- Sequence or linear approach (Pages follow a strict straight line approach. See Figure 1–5.)
- Hierarchical approach (Structure resembling a family tree or company flow chart. See Figure 1–6.)
- Grid approach (Structure looks like a grid. See Figure 1–7.)
- Web approach (Structure similar to a spider's web. See Figure 1–8.)

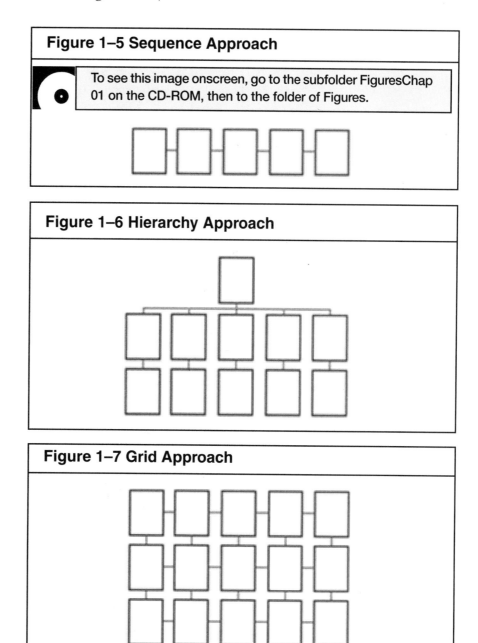

Figure 1–5 Sequence Approach

To see this image onscreen, go to the subfolder FiguresChap 01 on the CD-ROM, then to the folder of Figures.

Figure 1–6 Hierarchy Approach

Figure 1–7 Grid Approach

Figure 1–8 Web Approach

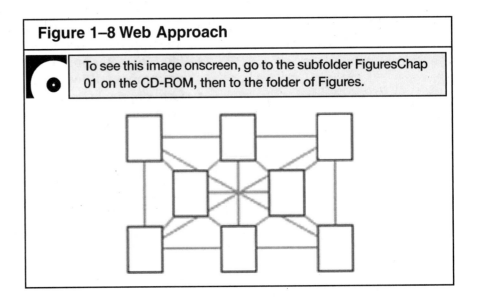

To see this image onscreen, go to the subfolder FiguresChap 01 on the CD-ROM, then to the folder of Figures.

The sequence approach presents a predictable structure. It is based on simple linear narrative. However, it is the least flexible among the four. Hierarchy and grid are somewhere in between. At the other side of the spectrum, the Web structure, typically nonlinear and hyperlinked, is the most flexible but may be complex and confusing for uneducated audiences. In reality, developers may want to use a combination of these approaches. The final goal is to create a hierarchy of menus and pages that are well organized and easy for users to navigate.

Before you start, you'd better develop a conceptual model—what the library site will look like—by drawing a flowchart or storyboard. Storyboarding a Web page keeps everything organized. It will give you a brief idea of the structure of the content for each page of a Web site, as well as the links to other pages or sites. Creating a flowchart or storyboard can save a lot of time in the long run because it helps developers to decide how the information will be presented. Without a storyboard, you can quickly become lost in the maze of separate files, links, graphics, and other elements that make up the Web presentation. The following are some steps to guide you through the storyboarding process and a template that you can use.

Storyboarding Processes

- Specify the purpose of your page.
- Identify the audience for this page (primary, secondary, and other).
- Determine what technologies you will use.
- Determine what interactive features you will apply.

- Select the main heading and subheading for the page.
- Define major categories of information to be put on your page.
- Plan how you will link information. Identify which links are relative and which are absolute.
- Determine what images you will use (JPG or GIF files).
- Decide how navigation will be provided (navigation types: buttons, bars, or text; positions: top of the page, bottom of the page, or side of the page).
- Create a simple diagram depicting how the pages or topics link to each other and how this page fits in the overall scheme of pages.

Figure 1–9 shows a simple storyboard for a site structure.

Figure 1–9 A Storyboard for Page Layout

To see this image onscreen, go to the subfolder FiguresChap 01 on the CD-ROM, then to the folder of Figures.

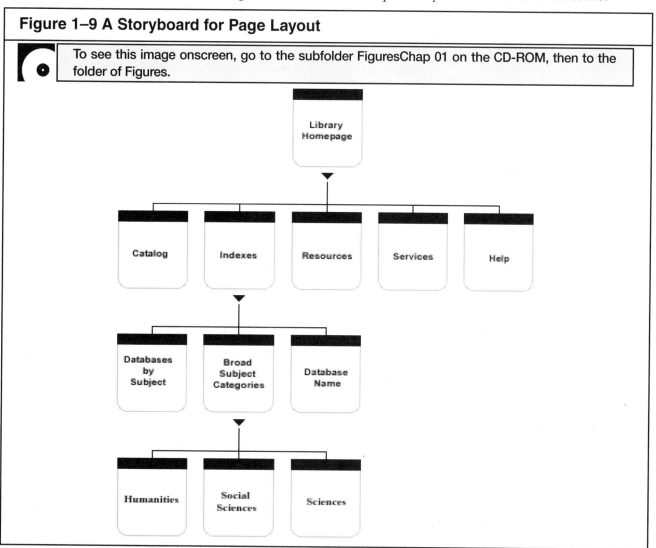

For a visual display of the second phase, take a look at Figure 1–10.

Figure 1–10 Phase 2: Site Structure Development

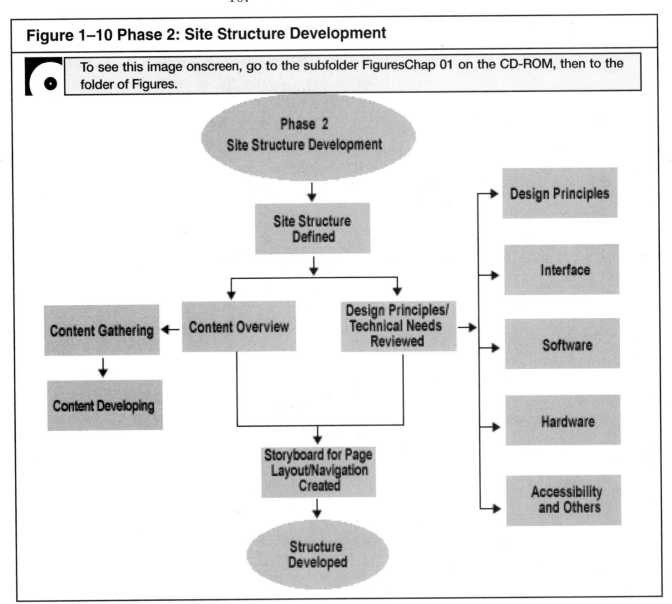

To see this image onscreen, go to the subfolder FiguresChap 01 on the CD-ROM, then to the folder of Figures.

PRODUCTION

After you make your plan and take all the issues above into consideration it is time to get down to business with detailed design and development. Based on the plan, flowchart, or storyboard you draw, the graphics designers will create the library's logo and other identity components such as the navigational buttons or bars. The HTML coders will create the page layout. The content providers and developers will prepare the contents. The programmers with other team members will work on databases, forms, multimedia, interactivity, and other advanced features for the library site. Most importantly, the team leader will coordinate all of the production activities. Finally, you will assemble all elements and make them ready to be uploaded. For a visual display of this phase, take a look at Figure 1–11.

Figure 1–11 Phase 3: Production

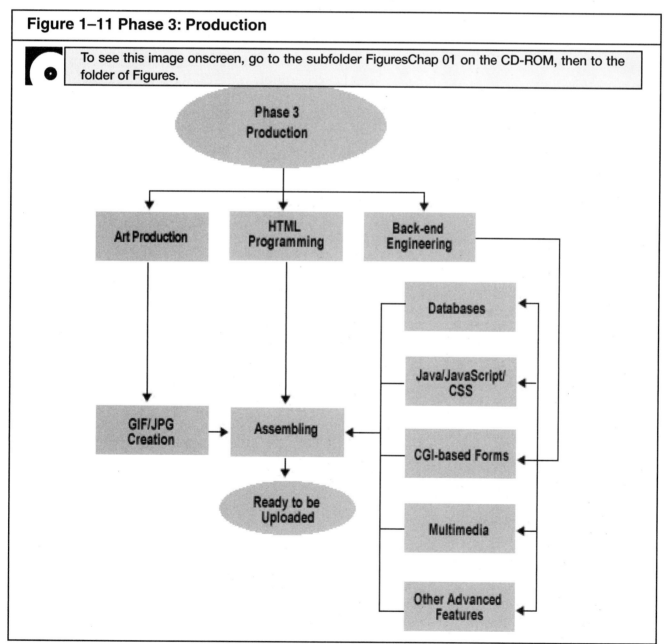

To see this image onscreen, go to the subfolder FiguresChap 01 on the CD-ROM, then to the folder of Figures.

PUBLISHING

Now you are ready to publish your site. You need to use an FTP program to upload your files to the Web server. Before you make your site available, always remember to check the appropriateness of contents, styles, and structures, and test the functionality of the whole site. You need to proofread. Typos and grammar mistakes due to sloppiness will affect the overall presentation and will reflect poorly upon the library. You should do browser testing to see how your Web site looks in different kinds and different versions of browsers. You also need to do platform testing. Link checking is very important. You have to make sure that all links are working. Last but not least, you need to check your site accessibility and the functions of other advanced components such as Java applets, multimedia, and so on.

Here is a checklist for your reference. The list is composed of two parts:

1. Content and organization
   - Is content jargon free?
   - Is content presented in correct sequence?
   - Are resources current?
   - Are structures of lists parallel?
   - Is contact information provided?
   - Are search tools available on the site?
   - Are site maps, indexes, or content lists available and in alphabetical order?
   - Are capitalization, spelling, grammar, and punctuation error free?
   - Are graphics, figures, and tables aligned appropriately?
   - Is white space used appropriately?
   - Is information presented in readable blocks?
   - Is it possible for users to ask questions and get help?
   - Are headings within a page labeled appropriately?
   - Do headings provide brief and accurate information?
   - Is there a link in every page leading to the homepage?
   - Are links to outside resources appropriate, authoritative, and reliable?
   - Can patrons accept the reading level?
   - Is there consistency of the use of terms?
   - Is the date of the last update indicated?
   - Is new information indicated?
2. Technical functionality
   - Is the HTML code correct?

- Is metadata used properly?
- Does your site work fine with Internet Explorer and Netscape?
- Does your site work on Windows, Mac, and Unix platforms?
- Do the pages display well on different sized screens?
- Does the homepage fit on one screen?
- Can the homepage be displayed within ten seconds with a 28.8 modem?
- Is each page size under 70k?
- Is there notice about the file size before downloading large files?
- Do advanced components such as Java applets, JavaScript, CSS, CGI-based forms, databases, search engines, multimedia, and others function well?
- Do all the links work?
- Are there redundant text links if Imagemaps are used?
- Does the page have a text equivalent for graphics, animations, applets, or other non-text elements?
- Is information accessible for people with disabilities such as blind or color-blind people?
- Is there navigation showing previous, next, up, down within a page?
- Is browsing or scanning possible?
- Do all the text and graphics print on A4 (8.5 by 11) paper?

For a visual display of this phase, take a look at Figure 1–12.

Figure 1–12 Phase 4: Publishing

To see this image onscreen, go to the subfolder FiguresChap 01 on the CD-ROM, then to the folder of Figures.

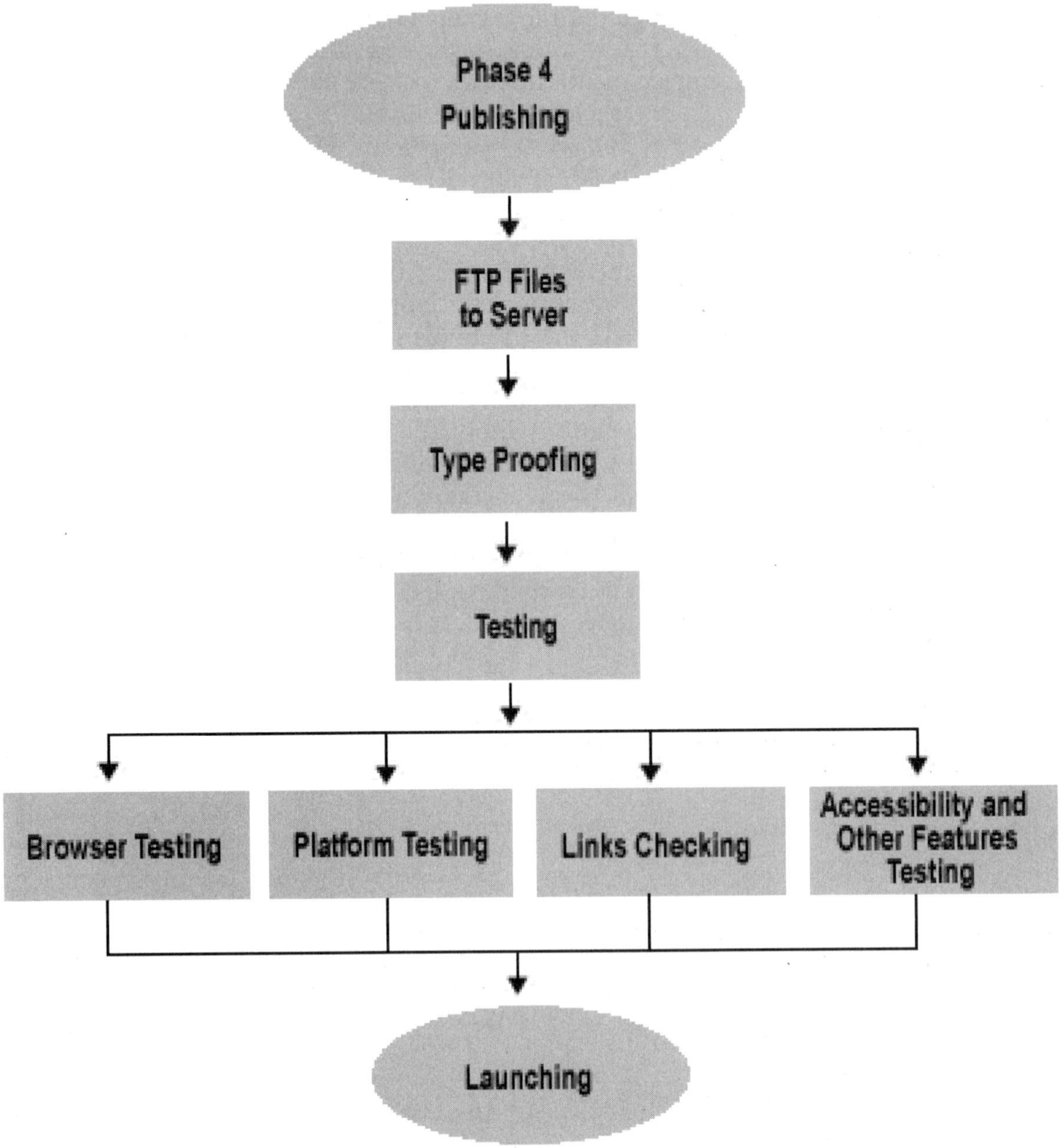

Phase 4 Publishing

FTP Files to Server

Type Proofing

Testing

Browser Testing | Platform Testing | Links Checking | Accessibility and Other Features Testing

Launching

MAINTAINING AND PROMOTING

MAINTAINING

Maintaining a library Web site involves updating information, checking hyperlinks, adding new Internet resources, deleting resources that are no longer active or useful, adding new features using new technologies, and so on. You may also get into reorganizing, redesigning the site, or changing the whole interface.

Centralized Maintenance Model vs. Decentralized Maintenance Model

Centralized approach means that one person or a team takes the responsibility for maintaining the whole library site, while the decentralized approach involves distribution of maintenance workload to individuals in different departments, each being responsible for only one section of the Web site.

There are advantages and disadvantages for both models. Centralized maintenance puts everything including content and style under tight control of one or a few individuals ("Web Nazis"). This approach will guarantee the consistency of site design, look and feel, and overall organization. It also means less expenditure in hardware, software, and training. Lack of a richer variety of creative ideas and broader visions, however, might be the downside of this model. Moreover, staff turnover may become an issue because only one or a few know how to maintain a library site technically. Generally, centralized approach is more suitable for small libraries. For those who adopt this model, it is necessary to actively consult other library staff and users for input, feedback, and advice.

In the situation of the decentralized model, sections of resources and services in a library Web site will be given to those who know the information in those sections best. The disadvantage of this model is a loss of control over content and appearance of the site. To solve this problem, a policy for maintenance should be created, and a package of a style sheet or template, and graphics should be provided. For example, Arizona State University Libraries established a Web creation and maintenance policy for page masters in each department. One section of the policy addresses the issue of continuity and it includes information about reusable templates:

> All Library Web pages must contain the standard header, navigation bar, footer, copyright statement, address, a link for comments, and information on the page cre-

ation. These items are contained in two standardized templates (http://www.asu.edu/lib/templates/template1.htm and http://www.asu.edu/lib/templates/template2.htm). They differ only in the size of the header and page designers may choose between them.

The policy also covers issues such as content, copyright, browsers, graphics, consistent look and feel, etc. For more details about the policy, please read the whole document (*www.asu.edu/lib/library/pagemaster/policy.htm*).

Creation of Maintenance Documentation and Guidelines

To maintain a library Web site, you need to create maintenance documentation and guidelines. They provide the rationale behind the development of the site and address user needs through an analysis of needs. The guidelines will outline what should be maintained and updated, how it should be maintained, and who has access rights. They will also cover issues such as page layout and design, navigation, organization of files, etc. These guidelines serve as a ready reference and a useful record for the current Web developers and managers as well as their successors. They keep you on track and let you know what information will be put on your library site and how for the time being and for the future. Besides allowing for continued maintenance of the Web site, the guidelines will help you to assign your resources. The following are five main components in the maintenance guidelines.

1. A List of Resources
   Your guidelines should list resources needed for the maintenance of the site, which include:

   - Personnel to maintain and manage the site.
   - Maintenance schedule for Web managers to continue to develop the site, check links, update links, consult with users, and update knowledge.
   - Money for salaries, for upgrades of equipment and software, and for training.
   - Training of staff in the use of new hardware and software, and training of users.

2. Documentation of Technical Decisions
   The guidelines should explain technical decisions. It is necessary to have a clear documentation of the design, layout, navigation, use of graphics, the size and style of the text, formats of files used on your site, etc.

3. Templates

   Templates serve as standards for your design. They are essential to let your site maintain a consistent look and feel. They will specify page headings, naming conventions, use of fonts, background, logos, navigation tools, and so on.

4. Backup

   You should keep more than one backup copy for all the work done in order to prevent loss and damage. Copies should be put in different places. They should be updated whenever there is a change.

5. An Archive

   You need to establish an archive of all the versions of previous site designs including the original design. On one hand it will provide a reference and documentation of what has been done before for future designers; on the other hand, it will help prevent reinventing the wheel.

Continuous Maintenance

It is important to make sure your links still go to sites you want your users to see. The ephemeral nature of Web sites decides that Web sites change constantly. You should get rid of sites that are gone. It is necessary to check the links on your library site at least once a month. You should update your site regularly by adding new links and new information such as "What's New" announcements, notices, changes of policies, schedules, and calendar of events. It should also include lists of new books, CD-ROMs, periodicals, databases, videos, subject guides, bibliographies, and so forth. It is friendly to inform others when a page has moved. This can be easily accomplished with a <META> tag:

```
<META> HTTP-EQUIV= "Refresh"
CONTENT="10;URL=http://www.domain.library/directory/">
```

There are several link checkers available on the Web, which will warn you if the URL of a hyperlink has changed or is no longer active. One free link checker is developed by W3C (*http://validator.w3.org/checklink*). It will go through the links on your pages, locating broken links, and create a summary. You can also use free link checkers from Xenu LinkSleuth (*http://home.snafu.de/tilman/xenulink.html*). The graphics below show the interface of the W3C's link checker and the report.

Figure 1–13 W3C's Link Checker Interface

 To see these images onscreen, go to the subfolder FiguresChap 01 on the CD-ROM, then to the folder of Figures.

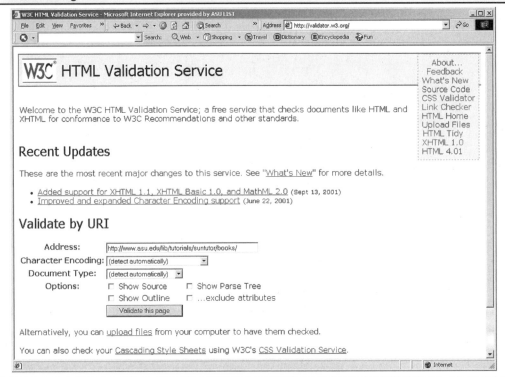

Figure 1–14 W3C's Link Checker Report

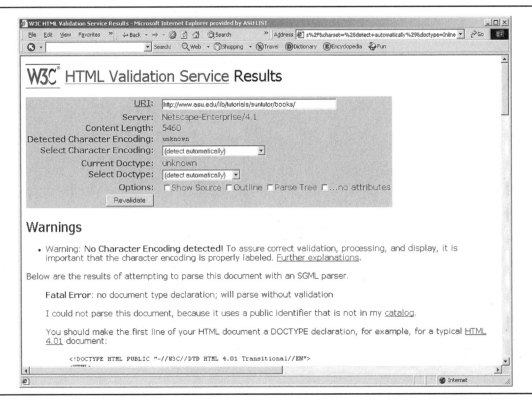

Reorganization

Reorganization of your library Web site involves changes to logical and physical organization of content. When you have a major change for your Web site, it is often easier to start a new site rather than trying to "tweak" the existing Web site. Remember that having existing site consistency (through the use of templates and styles) can help you ease the reorganization of the site.

Evaluation

Evaluation of the effectiveness of the Web sites can help you to improve your site. You can do it by analyzing the Web statistics and user feedback. One way is to check the number of accesses (the number of times people have visited the site). You can put a counter to your library Web site. You can also use Web log files on your server to collect data to quantify use. Bear in mind, the number of accesses to your site is not the sole indicator of your site's popularity. Another way for evaluation is to provide a feedback mechanism for users to evaluate sources and content. You may ask users to sign a guest book and fill in a feedback form or a suggestion form giving their views on the usefulness of your site. A more aggressive evaluation approach involves usability testing.

Usability Testing

As the judges of a product, the users will have the final say in deciding if the Web site is good or not. This ensures the good quality of the product and service for the real customers, who are the harshest critics of the product. Usability testing turns the user into the designer. Usability testing is the observation and analysis of users' behavior while they surf a Web site or a Web site prototype. Web designers should involve users of all types in the design process on a regular basis. Usability testing is very essential in Web development. First of all, it helps save time and money. Doing usability testing through the development of the project allows you to make user-centered changes as you go before you have so much time and money invested in the project that it makes it difficult to make changes.

Usability testing allows the developers to take an objective look at the site. It distances the developers from the product. Instead of focusing on what designers think or like, designers could focus on what the user thinks or likes. This makes the developers more open-minded and leads them to design the site for users rather than for themselves. Usability testing also helps the developers to settle their disputes over the merits and demerits of a site design. In addition, usability testing is good public relations. It lets people know that the library is concerned about what the user thinks and needs.

There are a number of ways to do usability testing, from Web-based forms to surveys, to formal user evaluations. Collecting statistics on site use is also an important form of feedback. The statistics will help you to know which of your Web pages are used the most, and by whom. Gathering this information is very useful for future library Web site design. Currently, there are some software packages available to analyze Web statistics.

Eight Steps for Usability Testing

1. Decide who your target audience is and what are the most important tasks they should be able to accomplish on your site.
2. Write questions that will require the users to perform the tasks.
3. Test the test.
4. Find subjects to be tested. (Subjects should be representative for the general user population.)
5. Conduct the test.
6. Record the test results.
7. Analyze the results and find out the design problems.
8. Make plans and redesign your library site based upon the analysis of the test results.

Conduct the Test

At least two people are needed for testing. One person asks the questions and a second person records what the subject does and says. When you conduct the test, try to explain to the participants that you are interested in discovering their opinion about the library site, both good and bad. Let them know that you are an objective observer who will not provide them with guidance throughout the site. Reassure them that this is not a quiz and there are no right or wrong answers. Ask them to "talk out loud" about what they see, think, and experience as they move through the site. In this way you can record what is in their minds. When they seem to go nowhere, you can let them do another task or ask them to explore another part of the site.

Analyze the Results

Concentrate on the majority's views. If the majority of your test takers have a difficult time finding something, it indicates that there must be something wrong with your information structure.

Sample Questions for Usability Testing

Here are some sample questions for usability testing for Arizona State University Libraries.

- How would you find library hours?
- How would you find information resources in a subject area when your teacher assigns a paper to you?
- How would you find a journal or newspaper article about gun control?
- How would you find a book about gun control?
- How would you find what your teacher has reserved for your class?
- How would you find if you have any overdue books or any library fine?
- What do you think of the library site in general?

Web Statistics and Analysis Tools

Besides user testing and evaluation, you can use Web statistics to generate Web traffic analysis reports. These reports will enable you to gain insight into individual behavior on your site and help you to increase the effectiveness of your library Web site. You can get the information from access files (log files) and run them through a Web statistics program. To get the log files, you have to set up your Web server to store the log files. Check with your systems administrator for more information. Here is a log file example (Combined Log Format):

```
128.965.23.4—[19/Jun/2002:00:49:41—0500] "GET /library/
service.htm HTTP/1.0" 200 1341 "http://www.domain.library.org"
"Mozilla/4.0 (compatible; MSIE 4.0; AOL 4.0; Windows95)"
```

From this log file, we can get the following information:

- 128.965.23.4
  This is the user's IP address or host name.
- [19/Jun/2002:00:49:41—0500]
  The date and time of request is displayed.
- "GET /library/service.htm HTTP/1.0"
  This shows the object requested. In this case the file library/service.htm is accessed.
- 200
  This number is the status code. It indicates a successful hit.
- 1341
  This is the number of bytes transferred for this request.

- "http://www.domain.library.org"
  This is the URL (referring URL) of the page, which includes the link chosen to access the current page.
- "Mozilla/4.0 (compatible; MSIE 4.0; AOL 4.0; Windows95)"
  This provides the browser information. It shows that Web browser Netscape 4.0 was used by the visitor.

There are some powerful commercial Web statistics analyzing products such as WebTrends' Log Analyzer. These programs create databases and work with servers that can write entries to a relational database as people visit the site. Generally, these tools provide the valuable Web analytics you need for your Web site. They produce essential reports on Web site visitor patterns, referring sites, visitor paths, demographics, and much more. They help you to learn which sites and keyword searches have referred the largest number of visitors to your site. These applications present data, detailed and in-depth, in an organized and concise tabular format sometimes with full-color graphs. They also track internal and external bandwidth trends with proxy server analysis to assist you in maintaining your library site.

In addition, they help you to optimize your site's performance by reporting on broken links, slowest loading pages, URL, and hyperlink syntax errors. They also offer alerting, monitoring, and recovery services. Usage data collected for your site may allow you to decide if the resources rarely used on your site should be highlighted or removed. The following is a list of typical reports found in many Web traffic analysis products. It may help you to decide what kind of products you need.

- Top requested pages.
- Top referring sites.
- Visits by day and time.
- File activity by day and time.
- Errors and abandonment.
- Most used browsers and versions.
- Most used platforms (operating systems).
- Average daily hits.
- Average number of pages displayed per visit.
- Average length of visit.
- Top entry pages of people coming to the site.
- Top exit pages of people leaving the site.

However powerful the programs are, they have limitations. For example, the average length of visit sometimes can be erroneous.

People may get onto your library Web site, then take a break for half an hour with the computer on. That certainly does not mean that they stay in your site for half an hour.

A Few Popular Web Traffic Analysis Products

- Sawmill (*www.sawmill.net*)
  It is a multi-platform tool featuring a hierarchical navigation of gathered statistics.
- Stat Trax Professional (*www.stattrax.com*)
  This is a powerful statistics program with many features mentioned above.
- Website Reporter (*www.websitereporter.com*)
  It provides a configurable Web site statistics package with a variety of report formats.
- WebTrends Log Analyzer (*www.webtrends.com*)
  This software features server log and firewall analysis, site monitoring, and management for Internet and Intranet sites.

Figure 1–15 shows the graphic interface of WebTrends Log Analyzer used at Arizona State University.

Figure 1–15 WebTrends Log Analyzer

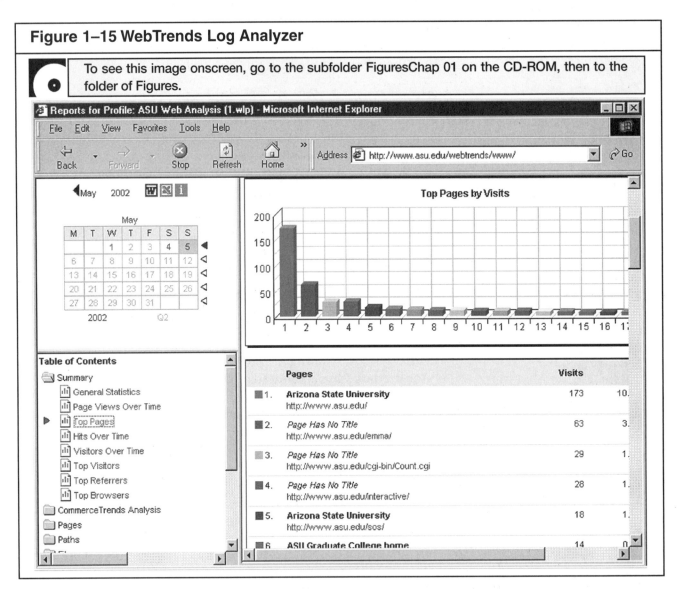

To see this image onscreen, go to the subfolder FiguresChap 01 on the CD-ROM, then to the folder of Figures.

Continuous User Evaluation and Future Developments

It is necessary to keep up with users' needs and ensure that this is reflected in the Web site. A user evaluation should be conducted regularly according to set time frame and evaluation format, for instance, having user interviews or questionnaires for every six months. The users' creative suggestions should be incorporated into the modified library site. As a Web developer, you may want to create a wish list to further enhance your Web site. For example, you may wish to create online interactive quizzes for library instruction or build a library portal for your patrons. Without this wish list your site might become static. It is very important for the Web developers to be aware of the recent Web development tools and technologies. The resources, which will help you to remain up-to-date with changes, include training courses, news groups, trade journals, professional conferences, etc.

PROMOTING

Promoting and publicizing your library Web site will enhance people's awareness about your resources and services. Here are some tips to do this. First you can use the traditional channels to publicize your site: local newspapers, library newsletters, posters, flyers, bookmarks, bibliographical instruction classes, student orientation sessions, library events, public fairs, so on and so forth. Having your site listed on the search engines will help visitors to locate your site. One way is to let your library Webmaster submit the site's URL to those search engines. The other way is to provide the URL to a service that will submit the address to many search engines. There are sites that help you to send your Web address to search engines, directories, and indexes for free.

You may want to join an online network or a Web ring. Web rings are sites that have joined together to form their sites into a linked circle. This free navigation service provides directory listings of sites that have registered into rings. A ring usually has at least five sites. The directory is searchable and in the system there is a comprehensive index of all rings. A library could use this kind of navigation by joining or organizing a ring of the Web sites in its local community. You may also want to organize a group of library sites sharing common interest into a ring. In Arizona, for example, Arizona State University, Northern Arizona University, and University of Arizona link their libraries into a ring. Users can easily get access to the three universities' library catalogs from each individual library's catalog page. As for a public library, it might join a ring with local school libraries, special libraries, and public institutions.

Other approaches include:

- Write an effective press release to promote your library Web site.
- Submit your sites for consideration for the various Internet awards.
- Use discussion lists and news groups to promote your site. If there is a particular subject content in your Web site, for example, a rarely known genealogical resource, or a newly digitized collection, you may send a message to an appropriate discussion list or news group providing the Web address and a brief description of the content.

With the development of information technology, people will come up with new ways of promoting libraries. So you should always keep yourself informed about the recent advancement in technology. For further information, you may also want to consult some Web sites such as Web4lib (*http://sunsite.berkeley.edu/Web4Lib*) and LibraryHQ (*www.libraryhq.com*). Also check How to Announce Your New Web site at: *http://ep.com/faq/webannounce.html*.

For a visual display of this phase, take a look at Figure 1–16.

Figure 1–16 Phase 5: Maintaining and Promoting

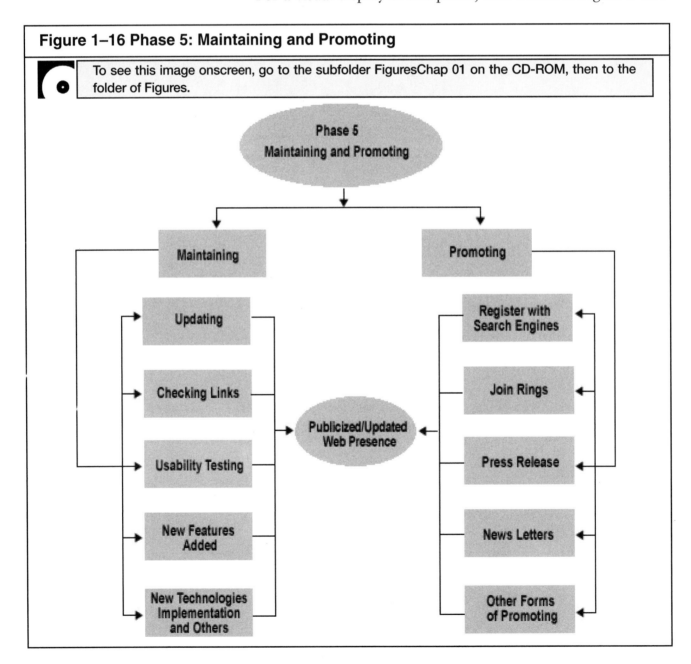

To see this image onscreen, go to the subfolder FiguresChap 01 on the CD-ROM, then to the folder of Figures.

COPYRIGHT

Copyright may be a concern in developing a library Web site, depending on the uses of the material, how widely access is granted, the age of the material, and its current availability in the marketplace. Easy access to and easy duplication of texts, graphics, codes, or other media files on the Web tempted people to copy. Library professionals have been noted for being good defenders of copyrights. Library Web developers should pay special attention to this issue. Every institution should have a good resource to review individual cases involving copyrights. Unless you get permission from the original creator or copyright holder, don't use copyrighted materials for your site. It is recommended that all inquiries regarding the reproduction of the online materials, especially graphics, should be directed to the copyright holder.

EXAMPLES OF GOOD LIBRARY WEB HOMEPAGES

To develop good library Web sites, developers should always try to stay abreast of all new developments, technologies, facilities, and happenings with regard to the Web. They should read literature in this field and check related sites such as other libraries and Web development sites, and engage in professional communication while taking note of the theory and practice of Web design. These sources will no doubt provide them with new ideas and inspiration for creating good library sites.

The Web is an interactive, dynamic, and rapidly changing new communications medium that your library Web site should reflect. Well-selected, well-organized, edited, and timely, original content presented in an appealing, interactive, and consistent format are some characteristics of good library Web sites. Good library Web sites have managed to combine attractive design with optimal user choices. The following are some well-designed library Web sites.

- The University of Chicago's Library Web Site (*www.lib.uchicago.edu*)
  The site is well designed. It provides a good example of synthesis in the content and presentation. Navigating the

Figure 1–17 University of Chicago Library Web Site

To see this image onscreen, go to the subfolder FiguresChap 01 on the CD-ROM, then to the folder of Figures.

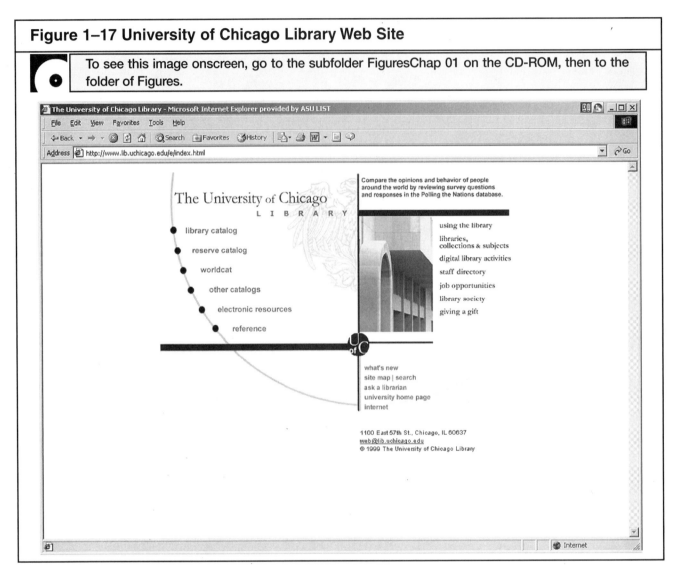

site is quite easy. The buttons tell users clearly what they can find at the site. There are eighteen different links on this page but the screen is not cluttered. It shows a very good use of links and structure. This page provides options that are easier to read and the elements have more space, which makes the page more visually appealing. The choice of color is brilliant—the simple colors of black and white exude class and elegance. The color scheme also matches that of the University of Chicago's homepage. With the graphical connection to the school's main page in mind, the designers specifically tried to create something that had a distinct look and feel, while still harmonized with the University's page. This is absolutely a very important design consideration. On the whole, the site has excellent readability.

- The Boston Public Library's Web Site (*www.bpl.org*)

Figure 1–18 Boston Public Library Web Site

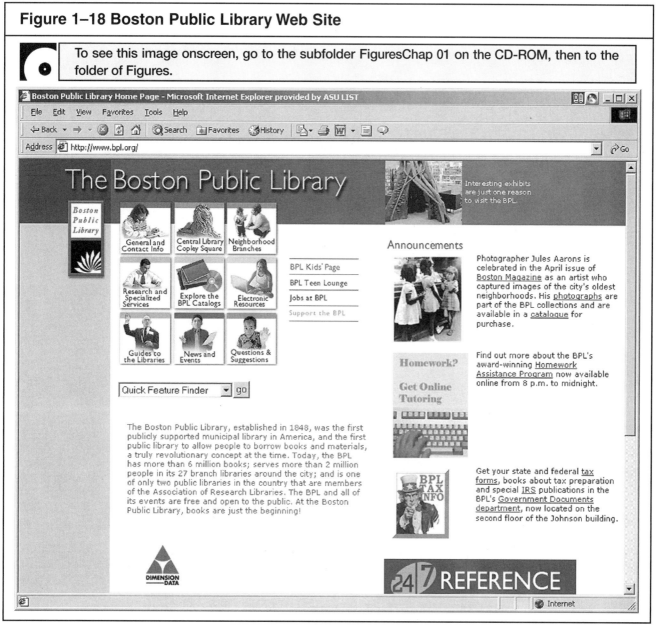

With an attractive, appealing public library Web site design, this site has solved a typical problem, information overload (presenting too much information on a page will cognitively overload your audience). For some sites, when you first look at the homepage, it takes you quite some time to figure out where to start.

• Southern Utah University Library Web Site (*www.li.suu.edu*)

Figure 1–19 Southern Utah University Library Web Site

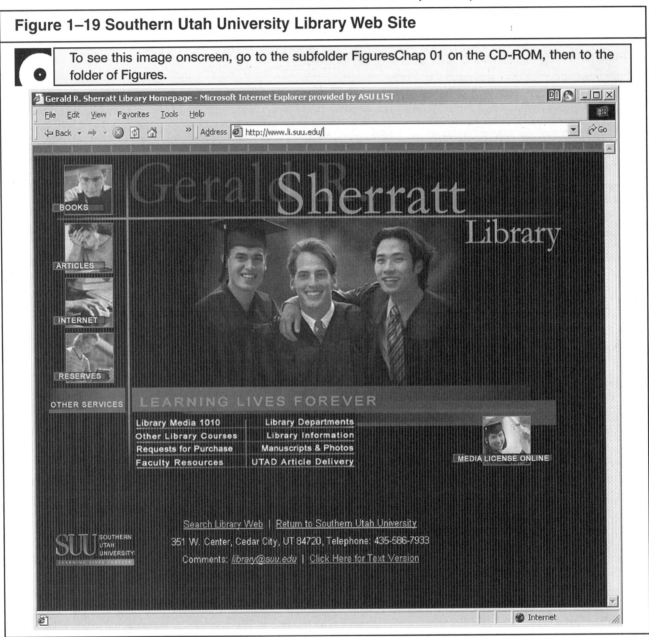

To see this image onscreen, go to the subfolder FiguresChap 01 on the CD-ROM, then to the folder of Figures.

This site is characterized by good design and easy navigation. It is clean, neat, and well chunked. The contrast, scale, communication hierarchy, visual language, and typography are all well done. The use of a dark background for a site is always a challenge to Web designers. The developers of this site did a good job matching the background color and that of the text.

- The Columbia University Library Web Site (*www.columbia. edu/cu/lweb*)

Figure 1–20 Columbia University Library Web Site

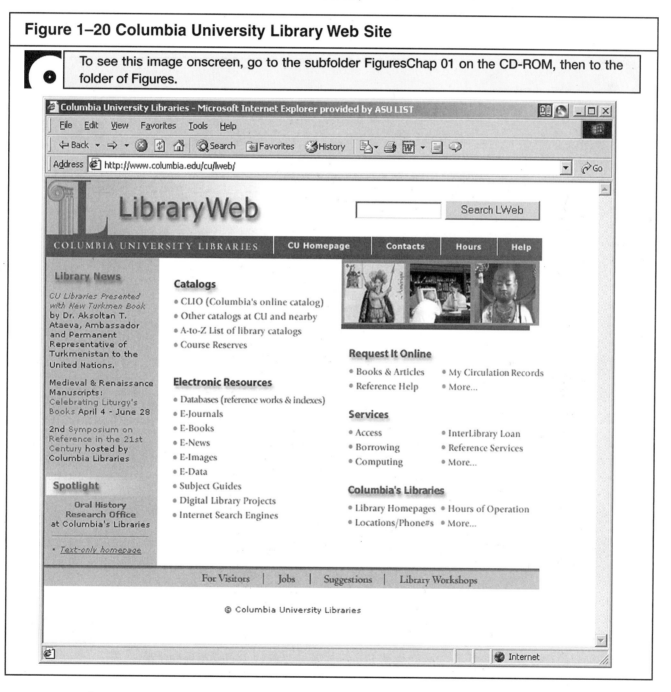

This site offers many options in a satisfying block design. Clean design is characterized by four columns with medium fonts.

- UCSC Net Trail (University of California at Santa Cruz's Online Literacy Courses: *http://nettrail.ucsc.edu/master/ index.htm*)

Figure 1–21 Net Trail: University of California at Santa Cruz

To see this image onscreen, go to the subfolder FiguresChap 01 on the CD-ROM, then to the folder of Figures.

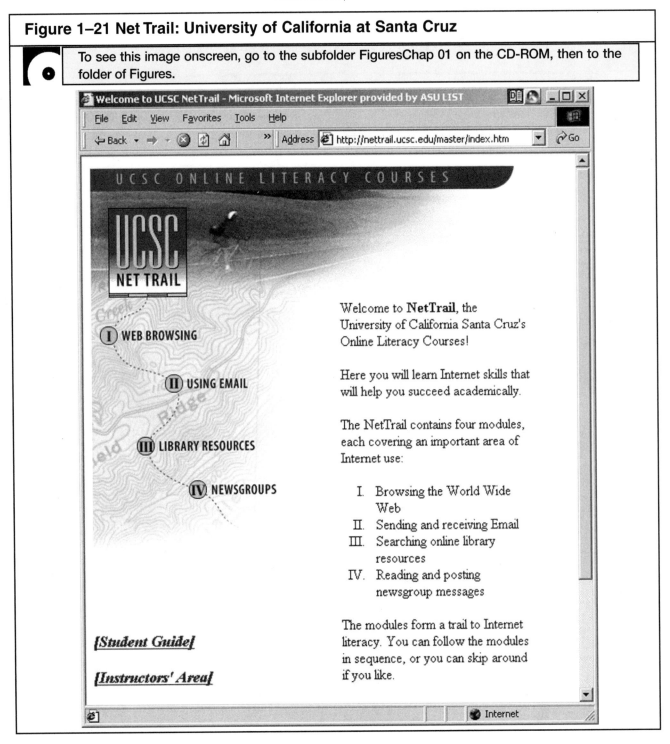

The metaphor of the trail for this site is well chosen. As part of the navigation set, the markers and graphics on the trail are easy to understand and they help users to know where they are.

- Augustana College Library Web Site (*www.augustana.edu/library/index.html*)

Figure 1–22 Augustana College Library Web Site

To see this image onscreen, go to the subfolder FiguresChap 01 on the CD-ROM, then to the folder of Figures.

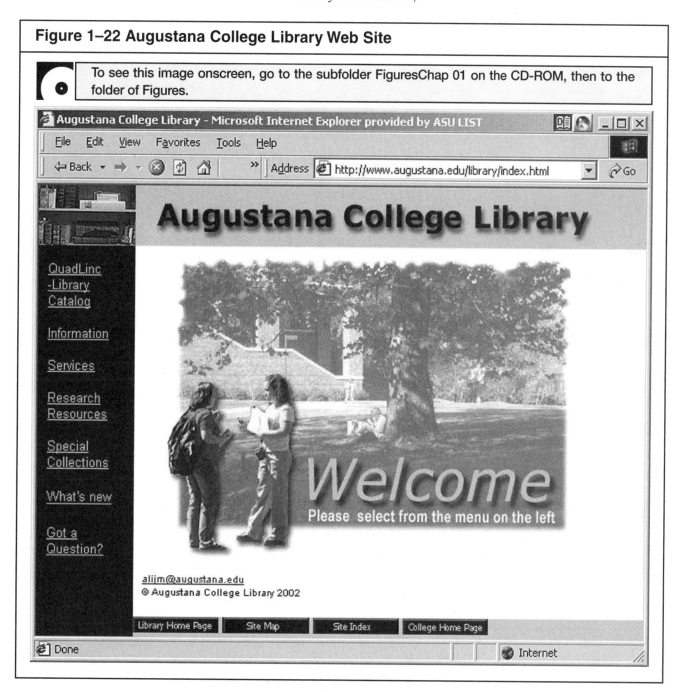

This is a small college library Web site. The design of the site is simple but not simplistic. From its clean and uncluttered interface, you can find most essential choices.

- Brooklyn Public Library Web Site (*www.brooklyn publiclibrary.org*)

Figure 1–23 Brooklyn Public Library Web Site

To see this image onscreen, go to the subfolder FiguresChap 01 on the CD-ROM, then to the folder of Figures.

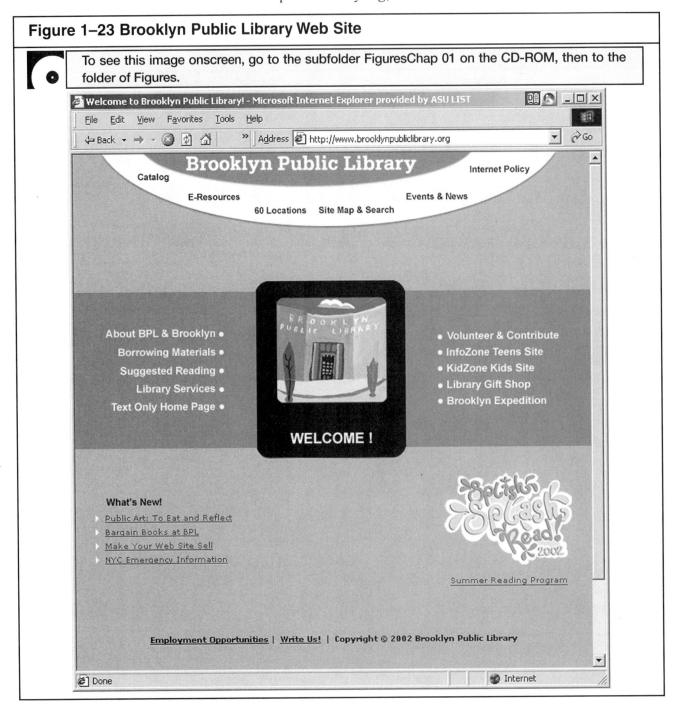

The page is scalable and extensible since everything is aligned at the center. It fits in the major browsers with normal screen sizes. It is a sophisticated and elegant design.

- Arizona State University Libraries SunTutor Web Site (*www.asu.edu/lib/tutorials/suntutor/*)

Figure 1–24 ASU SunTutor Web Site

To see the Web site, go to Chapter 1's SunTutor folder on the CD-ROM and click on SunTutor.htm.

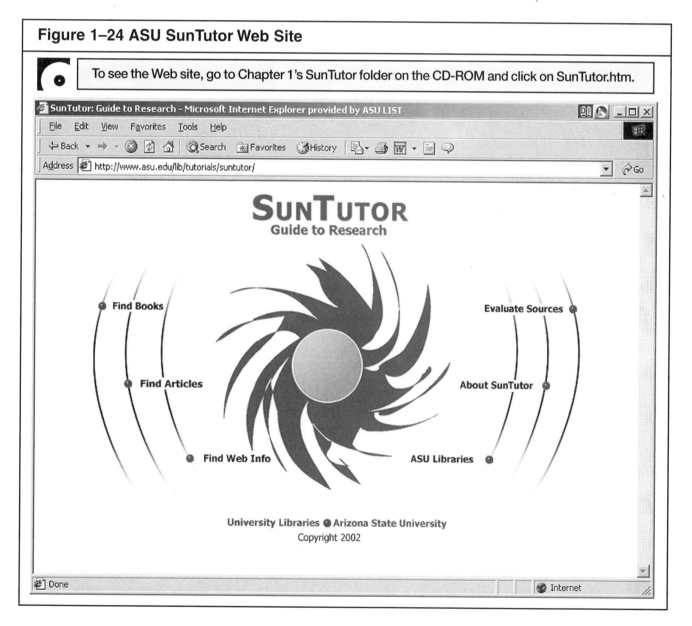

The site is unique and eye-catching. The metaphor is well chosen. The design is balanced.

- Arizona State University Libraries Library Services for Distance Learners Web Site (*www.asu.edu/lib/distance/* — under construction)

Figure 1–25 ASU Library Services for Distance Learners Web Site

To see the Web site, go to Chapter 1's Lib_Distance_Service folder on the CD-ROM and click on Lib_Distance_Service.html

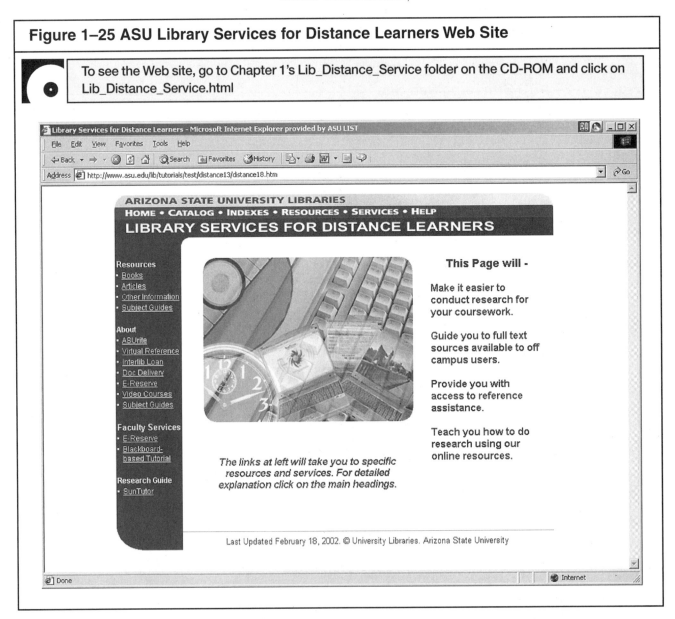

This site is a good example of clear communication and simple interface. It compels users to click and go deeper within the site. The designer's target audience is distance learners.

- Arizona State University Libraries Library Staff Training Web Site (*www.asu.edu/lib/library/training/*)

Figure 1–26 ASU Library Staff Training Web Site

To see the Web site, go to Chapter 1's Staff_Training folder on the CD-ROM and click on Staff_Training.htm.

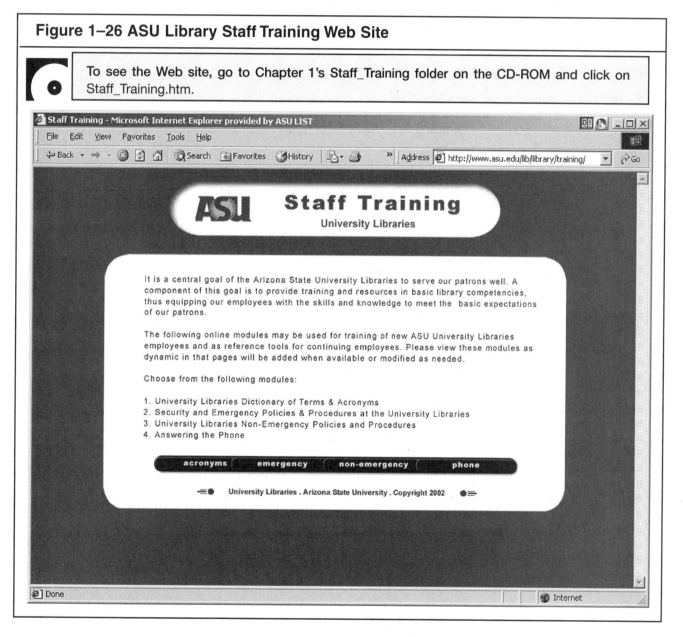

The site is designed for an internal audience. Clean and simple, it presents most essential choices for an Intranet library site.

2 LEARNING AND MASTERING HTML BASICS

This chapter describes the basics of HTML (Hypertext Markup Language). For the librarians who are new to this technology, there are simple definitions and visual examples of Web sites and HTML documents. For the librarians who have some knowledge of HTML, they will find useful advice for adding advanced service-based features such as forms, tables, and frames.

WHAT IS HTML?

HTML is the language for publishing hypertext on the Web. It is a nonproprietary format based upon SGML (Standard General Mark-up Language). HTML programs are written as plain, ASCII text files. It can be created and processed by a wide range of tools, from simple plain text editors such as Notepad or SimpleText to sophisticated WYSIWYG (What You See Is What You Get) authoring tools such as Macromedia Dreamweaver or Microsoft FrontPage. HTML is designed to be platform independent, not bound to a particular hardware or software environment. It features hypertext links where you click on a string of highlighted text (or graphics with hyperlinks) and access a new document at that site or any other sites in the world. The new document is located with its URL (Universal Resource Locator). It can be another HTML document, videos, animation, pictures, sound files, and so on. HTML uses tags such as <H1> and </H1> to structure text into headings, paragraphs, lists, and hypertext links. HTML is designed to be "white space insensitive." It doesn't read tabs, line breaks, paragraph breaks, or even extra spaces. You have to use elements to produce these effects. HTML is not case sensitive. In other words, HtmL will be read by the computer the same as HTML.

As mentioned, HTML files are simple plain ASCII text files that can be created with any text editor such as Notepad. You can use your word processor program of choice; just make sure the filename ends with the extension .htm or .html. It is important to know that new or specialized HTML features may not be compatible with certain browsers or certain versions of HTML. It usually takes a long time before the users have downloaded a browser that supports these features. So do not use browser-specific HTML features. You should also remember that HTML is not a page description language or page formatting language. It is designed for displaying information and for interacting with the user.

WHY SHOULD ONE LEARN HTML?

Why should we learn HTML when there are WYSIWYG authoring tools that will create the HTML codes for us? The answer is that there is no tool that covers all possible extensions and updates of HTML codes due to the ever-changing nature of the HTML standard. Many editors provide only limited control over certain elements of a page. It is frustrating when your most sophisticated authoring tool won't be able to create the layout, features, or effects you want. There are smart applications of HTML such as the transparent single pixel gif, advanced uses of tables, and other tricks that cannot be created with HTML editors. Not all editors can handle well some Web site components or features like JavaScript, Java applets, DHTML, style sheets, multimedia, database-driven pages, and so forth. To add these components or features to your site, you need to code by hand. Doing some "tweaking" of the HTML codes can help you to get the desirable look or effect. Another problem with editors is that some of them create a lot of junk codes in an HTML document.

There are a few ways to learn HTML. You can create a simple page by typing the raw HTML codes in an editor such as Notepad, save the file as an HTML document, then open it in a browser to see the results. In this way, you can learn some of HTML's basic elements and their functions. Or you can create a simple Web page with an HTML authoring tool and then study the codes it created in the HTML source window. Another way is to download a page you like from the Web using File>Save command from your browser. You then open the file in a plain text editor and take a look at the HTML source of the page. You can also load the page into an HTML authoring program, make some changes with the tool, and study the effect.

The quickest way to create a Web site is to first create your document with an HTML authoring tool. Then go through the document, editing and refining the HTML codes using all the little tricks and extensions you know. If you have a good understanding of the nuts and bolts of HTML and the structure it creates, you can add features and make changes in your pages at will.

BASIC HTML

WHAT ARE TAGS AND ATTRIBUTES?

An HTML document is made up of different kinds of elements. A typical element looks like: <H1> Heading 1 Element </H1>. The brackets at the beginning and end of the element, <H1> and </H1>, are called tags and they enclose some text. The text within the < > defines what kind of element you want. The <H1> marks the start of the element, the </H1> with the forward slash indicates the end. Some elements can be without ending tags. Elements like this are called empty or open elements. For example, <BR>, which breaks the text line, does not have an ending tag. HTML tags serve two distinct functions: They "tell" the text how to behave (bold, italic, underlined, and so on), and make the text act as a command to insert a link, picture, video, or sound to your page.

One important HTML component is the attribute. An attribute is a variable that has a value such as a filename, a number, etc. Some elements contain attributes within the tag. The following element IMG has the attribute SRC in it: <IMG SRC = "library_photo.gif">. Here, SRC indicates the source of the image. The library_photo.gif is the name of a graphic file. The IMG tag will order the Web browser to display this particular graphic (library_photo.gif) in a Web page.

THE BASIC STRUCTURE HTML CREATES

Here is an example of the overall structure of a simple HTML document:

```
<HTML>
<HEAD>
<TITLE>Title</TITLE>
</HEAD>
<BODY>
<P> Content displayed in browser. </P>
</BODY>
</HTML>
```

If you want to try this out, type the above into a text editor such as Notepad and save the file as "my_test.html," then view the file in a Web browser. If the file extension is ".html" or ".htm" then the browser will recognize it as HTML and display it as such.

An HTML document has a logical structure. Elements are nested within each other without overlapping. <HTML> indicates that this is an HTML document. This HTML document is itself one big HTML element. It starts with a <HTML> tag and ends with a </HTML> tag. <HEAD> is the first distinct part of your document. It is used for descriptive information about the document such as the TITLE; it is not used for displaying information. You can put other descriptive information such as JavaScript and style sheets in this section. <TITLE> defines the title of your HTML document. It will be displayed on the blue bar at the top by a browser when someone matches the keywords that are applicable to your site. <BODY> contains all information displayed in a browser. It also contains other tags, such as those that will link to other Web sites, and those that will jazz up your pages with images, videos, and sounds. It is within the <BODY> section that you display all your information. <P> denotes the start of a new paragraph. Each paragraph you write should start with a <P> tag. The </P> is optional, unlike the end tags for elements like headings.

The Head and Body elements can have a few other attributes:

- Meta: provides author name, keyword information, content description, etc.
- Base: defines the absolute URL.
- Background: uses a repeating background image.
- Bgcolor: uses an assigned color of background.
- Text, Link, Vlink, Alink: color of normal or hyperlinked text.

COMMON ELEMENTS
Headers

<H1>Heading 1</H1> provides a heading element. (There are actually six levels of headings, starting from the biggest and boldest <H1> heading and finishing with the smallest and weakest <H6> heading.) In other words, H1 is the most important, H2 is slightly less important, and so on down to H6, the least important. Here is the code:

```
<H1> Heading 1</H1> (Most prominent header)
<H2> Heading 2</H2>
```

```
<H3> Heading 3</H3>
<H4> Heading 4</H4>
<H5> Heading 5</H5>
<H6> Heading 6</H6> (Least prominent header)
```

Text

To highlight text in HTML documents, you need to enclose the highlighted text within the following commonly used tags:

- Bold <B>...</B> Used to bold type.
- Italic <I>...</I> Used to *italic type*.
- Underline <U>...</U> Underlines text.
- Typewriter Text <TT>...</TT> Displays a single-spaced font, usually used for variable names or HTML code.
- Strike-Through <STRIKE>...</STRIKE> Strikes through text as if you're ~~crossing it out~~.
- Subscript _{...} Puts text in $_{subscript\ style}$.
- Superscript ^{...} Puts text in $^{superscript\ style}$.
- Preformatted <PRE>...</PRE> Puts text as is, in preformatted format.
- Center <CENTER>...</CENTER> Centers the text in the middle.
- Blink <BLINK>...</BLINK> A tag that makes the text blink.
- Block Quote <BLOCKQUOTE>...</BLOCKQUOTE> is used for: Quotes, displayed as indented, and often create a line break before and after. Text needs air around it to breathe. In the printing world, most documents have margins. For a Web page you can solve the breathing space problems by using the "Blockquote" tag, which gives a margin on both sides of the page. You can nest Blockquotes to change the width as necessary. Keep in mind running text the full width of the screen will create long lines of text that are hard to read.
- Align <ALIGN> Specifies a relationship to surrounding text. The argument for align can be one of top, middle, or bottom.
- Line Break
 Forces a line break immediately and retains the same style.
- Horizontal Rule <HR> Places a horizontal rule between sections of text.

Font Tag

The font tags: <FONT>...</FONT> in an HTML file define the font types. Here is an example:

```
<FONT SIZE=2 FACE=TIMES COLOR="#000000"> text </FONT>
```

The Font element can have a few attributes:

- Size
  You can specify the size of the font from 1 to 7. The default size is 3. Keep in mind the font may look different in other people's browsers since the users can set up the display of font size in their browsers. Here you do not have complete control over the appearance of an HTML document.

- Color
  You can define the color of your font by giving the attribute COLOR a hexadecimal number placed within quotes and with a # before the number.

- Face
  You can define the typefaces by assigning the attribute FACE a font name. The most popular typefaces are TIMES and ARIAL.

Special Characters

When you want to put certain characters such as brackets <> in your page, you need to use special characters in order to display these characters. The browsers won't be able to read them if you put <> in your HTML document because "<>" as components of HTML codes are assigned unique meanings as opening tag and closing tag. The following is a list of special characters for certain characters.

<	&lt;
>	&gt;
&	&amp;
"	&quot;
®	&reg;
©	&copy;
Non-Breaking Space	

Images

To have your pictures displayed on a Web page, you should use certain HTML tags to "point to" the picture files (like your HTML files) on a server. The <IMG> element is used to display images. The <IMG> element takes the form:

```
<IMG SRC="picture.gif">
```

The SRC attribute in the IMG tag denotes the source of your

graphic. SRC is short for the SouRCe. The picture.gif is the URL of your graphic. If our graphic file and your HTML file are in the same folder or directory, then you only need to put in the filename. If the graphic is in a different folder, which is in the same site, you should put the folder's name as well. For example, <IMG SRC="/images/picture.gif">. This is called a partial URL or relative path for providing information about the location of the graphic file. But if the graphic file is in a different site from your HTML document, you need to use the complete URL of the graphic file:

<IMG SRC="http://www.domain/library/graphics/picture.gif".

This is called absolute URL or path. The use of relative path and absolute path also applies to other file formats.

Image Attributes

The Image element can have a number of other attributes:

- Align: aligns the graphic to surrounding text.
- Alt (Alternate): allows a text string to be displayed in the place of the image in clients' machines that cannot display images.
- Dimensions: specifies the size of the graphic.
- Border: defines border if the graphic is a hyperlink.
- Runaround Space: defines space around the graphic.

Links

The Link element <A HREF> </A> is designed to link one document to other documents. The text enclosed by <A HREF></A> tags becomes a hypertext link. By clicking on the link, you will be led to the linked document or page. The browser usually displays the link underlined or in a different color than the regular text. The Link element takes the form:

<A HREF="my_page.html"> My Page</A>

HREF stands for Hypertext Reference. It is the attribute and is assigned the URL of the destination file. Like the graphics file mentioned above, if the linked file and your main HTML file are in the same folder or directory, then you only need to put in the filename. But if the linked file is in a different directory or folder, or a different place from your HTML document, you may need to use the complete URL of the file (A HREF = "http://www.library/filename.html"). You can also use a partial URL or relative path to provide information about the location of the linked file.

Graphics can be used as hypertext links. You need to put the <IMG> element within the link tags. For example:

```
<A HREF="http://library.lib.asu.edu"><IMG SRC="/lib/images/
catalog.gif"></A>
```

Anchors

The Anchor element is designed to link one section of a document to another section in the same document. To mark the destination on the page, move your cursor to the text of the destination and enter a <A> tag that uses the NAME attribute:

```
<A NAME= "members">Book Club Members</A>
```

To put the link, type a <A> tag with an HREF attribute at the location where you want to place the link with a # sign.

```
<A HREF="#members">list of book club members</A>
```

When users click the "list of book club members" link, they jump to the Book Club Members section in that page. An anchor name can be added to go to another anchor in any Web age, for example:

```
<A HREF= "http://www.domain.library/clubs.html#members">list
of book club members</A>
```

Mailto

For a mail link on your site, you make it in a way similar to creating a site link. Use the MAILTO command as the following example does:

```
<A HREF="MAILTO:yuwu.song@asu.edu">yuwu.song@asu.edu
</A>
```

In this case, when you click on yuwu.song@asu.edu, the mail screen with that e-mail address pops up if an e-mail program is set up in your computer.

Lists

Numbered (Ordered) and Unnumbered Lists

Lists are used for simple listing of items. You can use HTML codes to present text lists as numbered or unnumbered lists. You surround the list itself with an opening and a closing tag. You don't have to use paragraph separators to separate the list items because each item starts with a tag that separates it from the other items. Numbered or ordered lists number each item sequentially while unnumbered or unordered lists bullet them. An unnumbered or unordered list is structured as follows:

```
<UL>
<LI>The first thing in the list
<LI>The second thing in the list
<LI>The third thing in the list
</UL>
```

In a browser it will look like this:

- The first thing in the list
- The second thing in the list
- The third thing in the list

An ordered or numbered list is structured like this:

```
<OL>
<LI>The first thing of the list
<LI>The second thing of the list
<LI>The third thing of the list
</OL>
```

In a browser it will look like this:

1. The first thing of the list
2. The second thing of the list
3. The third thing of the list

Lists can be nested, one within another. For instance:

```
<OL>
<LI>The first list item</LI>
<LI>
The second list item
<UL>
<LI>The first nested item</LI>
<LI>The second nested item</LI>
</UL>
</LI>
<LI>The third list item</LI>
</OL>
```

You may also have other list elements: menu lists <MENU> and directory lists <DIR>. Menus and directories don't use any bullet to the left of each item.

Definition Lists (Glossary Lists)

HTML can also create the definition list. It lets you list terms and their definitions or a descriptive text. This kind of list begins with a <DL> tag and ends with </DL>. Each term begins with a <DT> tag and each definition starts with a <DD>. The end tags DT and DD are optional and can be left off. Here is an example:

```
<DL>
<DT>Web Abbreviations
<DT>CGI
<DD>Common Gateway Interface.
<DT>ASP
<DD>Active Server Page.
</DL>
```

This example definition list will be displayed in the browser like this:

```
    Web Abbreviations
CGI
    Common Gateway Interface.
ASP
    Active Server Page.
```

Meta Tags

The major meta tags include description, keyword, author, and so on. When search engines index Web sites, they look for keyword meta tags to store in their database. If you created a site for a library, the meta tag description keywords could include the name of the library, the city that the library is located in, and anything that is associated with the specific library. The description meta tag is the sentence that comes up when the browser displays the search results. The meta tag from eSCENE (www.escene.org) is a good example that uses both description and keywords to aid the search engines in finding the site for readers that are interested in short stories.

```
<HTML>
<HEAD>
<TITLE>eSCENE 1997</TITLE>
<META name="description" content="eSCENE is the world's only
yearly electronic anthology dedicated to providing one-click ac-
cess to the Internet's best short fiction and authors.">
```

```
<META name="keywords" content="fiction, ezine, short stories,
world's best fiction, best american short stories, story, stories,
best short stories, best fiction, anthology, writing, fiction writing,
story writing, internet fiction, web fiction, internet stories, web
stories, jeff carlson, robert olen butler, diana gabaldon, frederick
barthelme">
</HEAD>
```

AN EXAMPLE OF HTML DOCUMENT

The following file: basic_html.htm contains the basic tags of
HTML. The graphic accompanying this file shows what the code
looks like in a Web browser.

```
<HTML>
<HEAD>
<TITLE>HTML</TITLE>
</HEAD>
<BODY BGCOLOR="#FFFFFF">
<P>This is regular text.</P>
<P><B>This is bolded text.</B></P>
<P><I>This is italicized text.</I></P>
<UL>
<LI>This is bulleted text.</LI>
<LI>This is bulleted text.</LI>
</UL>
<OL>
<LI>This is numbered text.</LI>
<LI>This is numbered text.
<BLOCKQUOTE>
<P>This is indented text.</P>
</BLOCKQUOTE>
</LI>
</OL>
<P><FONT size="3" color="#0000FF" face="Arial">This text font
is Arial, color is blue (#0000FF).</FONT></P>
<P><FONT size="7">This text size is 7.</FONT></P>
<P><FONT size="6">This text size is 6.</FONT></P>
<P><FONT size="5">This text size is 5.</FONT></P>
<P><FONT size="4">This text size is 4.</FONT></P>
<P><FONT size="3">This text size is 3.</FONT></P>
<P><FONT size="2">This text size is 2.</FONT></P>
<P><FONT size="1">This text size is 1.</FONT></P>
<H1>This is Heading 1 text.</H1>
<H2>This is Heading 2 text.</H2>
<H3>This is Heading 3 text.</H3>
<H4>This is Heading 4 text.</H4>
<H5>This is Heading 5 text.</H5>
<H6>This is Heading 6 text.</H6>
```

```
<PRE>
This is preformatted text.
</PRE>
<P>This text is aligned left.</P>
<P align="center">This text is aligned center.</P>
<P align="right">This text is aligned right.</P>
<P><A HREF="http://www.yahoo.com">This is text with a
hyperlink: Yahoo.</A></P>
<P><A HREF="mailto:yuwu.song@asu.edu">This is an e-mail link:
yuwu.song@asu.edu</A></P>
<P>This horizontal rule below is 100% of the screen:</P>
<HR>
<P>This horizontal rule below is 50% of the screen:</P>
<HR width="50%">
<P>This horizontal rule below is 25% of the screen:</P>
<HR width="25%">
<P align="left">Below is a picture of ASU Hayden library in-
serted:</P>
<P align="left"><IMG SRC="hayden.gif" width="365"
height="273"></P>
</BODY>
</HTML>
```

Figure 2–1 Basic HTML

To see the basic HTML example, go to Chapter 2's HTML folder on the CD-ROM and click on HTML.htm.

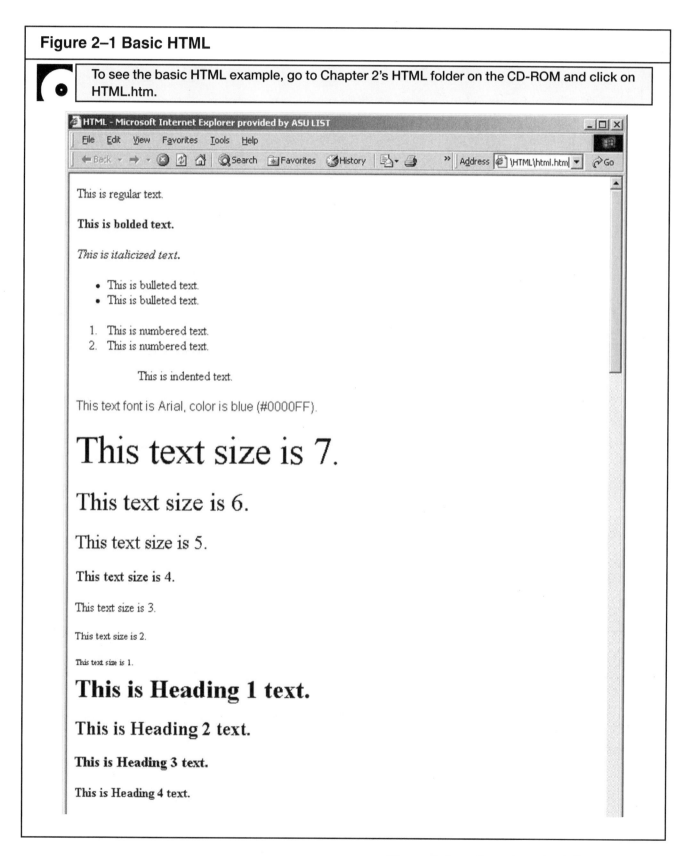

Figure 2.1 continued on the following page

Figure 2–1 Basic HTML *(Continued)*

This is Heading 5 text.

This is Heading 6 text.

```
This is preformatted text.
```

This text is aligned left.

This text is aligned center.

This text is aligned right.

This is text with a hyperlink: Yahoo.

This is an e-mail link: yuwu.song@asu.edu

This horizontal rule below is 100% of the screen:

This horizontal rule below is 50% of the screen:

This horizontal rule below is 25% of the screen:

Below is a picture of ASU Hayden library inserted:

FORMS

The interface of HTML forms allows document creators to define HTML documents containing forms to be filled out by users. The FORM element is a useful tool of HTML. It enables users to actively interact with your Web site. A form is a section in an HTML document containing normal content, markup, or special elements called *controls* such as checkboxes, radio buttons, drop-down lists, menus, and text areas. Users enter text, select menu items in the forms before submitting the form to a Web server, or to a mail server for processing. The server will usually prepare an HTML document using the information supplied by the user and return it to the client for display. In most cases, you need a CGI program on the server to process the data if you wish to use forms in your site.

HTML uses <FORM>...</FORM> to define a form within a document. A document may contain multiple <FORM> elements, but <FORM> elements may not be nested. There are two important form attributes, which are the core of a form. The first one is: action="URL." It tells the location of the program that will process the form. The second one is: method=post. It is the method chosen to exchange data between the client and the program for processing the form. In some cases, "get" is used instead of "post." However, post is preferred for most applications. For the difference between "get" and "post," look at Chapter 3.

The form attributes in the real world looks like this:

```
<FORM action="http://www.domain/cgi-bin/form.cgi" method=
post>
...
</FORM>
```

INPUT FIELD ELEMENTS

The tag <INPUT> specifies an input field where the user may make selections. Each input field has a value to a variable, which has a specified name and a specified data type. The "type" attribute defines the data type for the variable.

The most commonly used input items include the following:

- Text
  This element creates a single line input control or field. The size of the field is defined by SIZE (in pixel) attribute. You can use MAXLENGTH attribute to limit the input

data size: the text will scroll if the user exceeds the field size. Here is a text input example:

```
<INPUT type="text" id="email" SIZE=60>
```

- Password
  This provides a single line of text but the text typed is displayed as asterisks. The size of the password is set by the attribute SIZE.

```
<INPUT TYPE="password" NAME="password" VALUE="..."
SIZE=8>
```

- Checkbox
  Checkboxes are on/off switches that may be toggled by the user. A switch is "on" when the control element's checked attribute is set. A user clicks on or off and returns a value of "on" or "off."

```
<INPUT TYPE="checkbox" NAME="button" VALUE="on">
```

- Radio Buttons
  Radio buttons are like checkboxes except that when several share the same control name, they are mutually exclusive: when one is switched "on," all others with the same name are turned "off." Here is an example:

```
<INPUT type=RADIO NAME=rating VALUE="excellent">Excellent
<BR>
<INPUT type=RADIO NAME=rating VALUE="very good">Very
Good <BR>
<INPUT type=RADIO NAME=rating VALUE="good">Good <BR>
<INPUT type=RADIO NAME=rating VALUE="boring">Boring
```

- Select
  This offers users options from which to choose. The SELECT element creates a drop-down menu, in combination with the OPTION elements. The option selected is the value sent when the form is submitted. More than one option can be selected.

```
<SELECT NAME="books_I_like" SIZE=20>
<OPTION> Option 1
<OPTION> Option 2
<OPTION> Option 3
</SELECT>
```

- Text Area Element
  This element permits users to put a message in a text box. Form tags <TEXTAREA>...text by default... </TEXTAREA> specify a field where the user can enter text. It is optional to put "text by default" in between <TEXTAREA> tags. In other words, if you put a message within the element, it will be shown as an initial value. The "default text" will show up in the rectangular field. Without it the field will be empty. Text area attribute name="textstring" identifies the <TEXTAREA> variable. Attributes "rows" and "cols" define values, which specify the lines and number of characters per line in the <textarea>. Here is an example:

```
<TEXTAREA COLS=70 ROWS=9 NAME="message"></
TEXTAREA>
```

- Submit
  Submit displays a Send Message button. Clicking this will send all the form data to the server.

```
<INPUT TYPE="submit" VALUE="Send Message">
```

- Reset
  This resets all the fields in the form to their original status.

```
<INPUT TYPE="reset" NAME="Reset" VALUE="Reset">
```

A FORM EXAMPLE

The following is the HTML codes for a typical form:

```
<FORM ACTION=
"http://www.domain/library/form/cgi-bin/form.pl"
METHOD="POST" >
<UL>
<LI>
<FONT face="verdana, arial"> Your name:
<INPUT type=TEXT name=who size=30 maxlength=30>
</FONT>
<P>
<LI>
<FONT face="verdana, arial">Your email:
<INPUT type=TEXT name=email size=30 maxlength=30>
</FONT>
<P>
```

```
<LI>
<FONT face="verdana, arial">How would you rate this site?
<INPUT type=RADIO NAME=rating VALUE="excellent">Excellent
<INPUT type=RADIO NAME=rating VALUE="very good">Very
Good
<INPUT type=RADIO NAME=rating VALUE="good">Good
<INPUT type=RADIO NAME=rating VALUE="boring">Boring
</FONT>
<P>
<LI>
<FONT face="verdana, arial">What would you like us to add?
<INPUT type=CHECKBOX NAME=news VALUE="news">News
<INPUT type=CHECKBOX NAME=weather VALUE="weather">
Weather Updates
<INPUT type=CHECKBOX NAME=photos VALUE="photos">
Photos of our Staff
<INPUT type=CHECKBOX NAME=calendar VALUE="calendar">
Calendar
</FONT>
<P>
<LI><FONT face="verdana, arial">How did you find this site?
<SELECT name="how">
<OPTION value="friend">A friend recommended it
<OPTION value="browsed">Surfed in from another site
<OPTION value="search">Via a search engine
<OPTION value="other">Other
</SELECT>
</FONT>
<P>
<LI><FONT face="verdana, arial">Comments:
<TEXTAREA name=comments cols=40 rows=5 wrap=virtual>
</TEXTAREA>
</FONT>
</UL>
<FONT face="verdana, arial">
<INPUT type="submit" value="Submit!">
<INPUT type="reset" name="Reset" value="Reset">
</FONT>
</FORM>
```

In a browser, the form is displayed like this:

Figure 2–2 Form

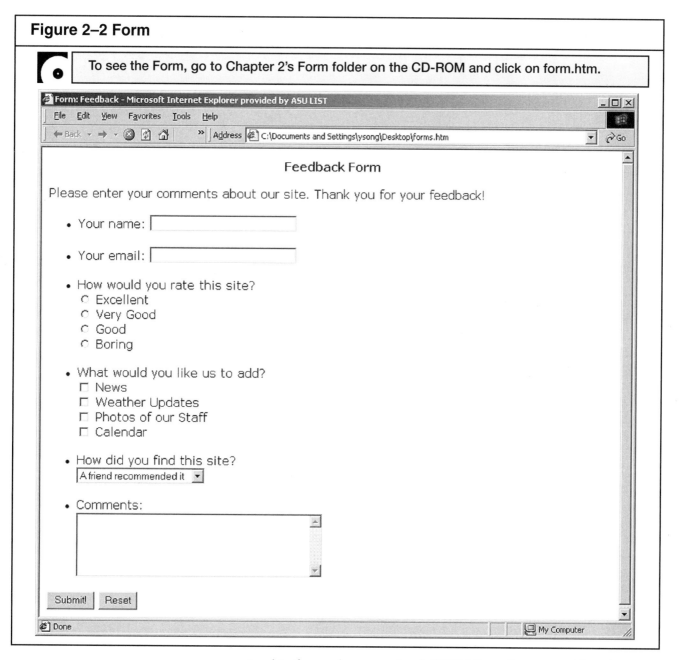

To see the Form, go to Chapter 2's Form folder on the CD-ROM and click on form.htm.

In this form element, the ACTION attribute specifies the URL where the form content is to be sent. In most cases this is a CGI program on the Web server that processes the data. The METHOD attribute gives the method for sending information to the specified URL. The type of input element depends on the attribute TYPE. Within the FORM element there are several input items. Each item contains a variable name: NAME and the actual data: VALUE sent by the users to the CGI program.

USEFUL ONLINE LIBRARY FORMS
The following is a list of Useful Online Library Forms:

Public Services
University of Pennsylvania Library Book Renewal (*www.library. upenn.edu/forms/renew.html*)

Reference
University of Pennsylvania Library Appointment Request (*www.library.upenn.edu/forms/appointment.html*)

Library Instruction
University of Pennsylvania Library Instructional Request (*www. library.upenn.edu/forms/bi.html*)

Interlibrary Loan
University Libraries of University of Texas at Tyler (*www.uttyler. edu/library/ILLForm.htm*)

Billing
Welch Medical Library (*www.welch.jhu.edu/forms/billing.cfm*)

Course Reserve
Arizona State University Libraries (*www.asu.edu/lib/access/submit/haysub.html*)

Suggest a Book
Wake Forest University Baptist Medical Center Library (*www.bgsm.edu/library/purform.html*)

TABLES

The HTML tables allow Web authors to arrange data such as text, preformatted text, images, links, forms, form fields, and other tables into tabular forms including rows and columns of cells. Tables also allow designers to have a tight control over the look of the pages. With tables you can break your page into precise segments and control the placement of graphics, text, or forms. To achieve this, you create columns and grids to contain these elements. Tables can be used within tables as subunits. To obtain the effects of contrast to other sections of a page, you can fill table columns or rows with a different color. Tables provide some navigational functionality of frames without the restraints of frames.

TABLE ELEMENTS

The TABLE element usually has four subelements:

- Caption
  Each table may have an associated caption element that provides a short description of the table's purpose. This element shows the caption or title at the top of the table.
- TH
  Table Header: this element encloses the headings for a row or column. Any table heading text is bold and centered.
- TD
  Table Data: this element encloses the data contents for a table cell.
- TR
  Table Row: this element indicates the start of a new row.

AN EXAMPLE OF TABLE

Let us take a look at an example of a table:

```
<TABLE BORDER=3>
<TR>
<CAPTION>Weekend Library Hours</CAPTION>
<TH>Saturday</TH>
<TH>Sunday</TH>
<TR>
<TD>9:00 am to 5:00 pm </TD>
<TD>1:00 pm to 5:00 pm</TD>
</TABLE>
```

The browser will show the example like this:

Figure 2–3 Table

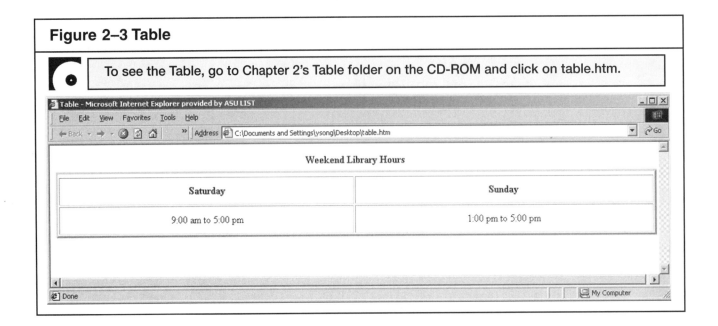

To see the Table, go to Chapter 2's Table folder on the CD-ROM and click on table.htm.

ATTRIBUTES WITHIN THE TABLE ELEMENT

- Width
  Width specifies the width of the table. You can specify the table's width by assigning it a number in pixels, or a percentage of the document width. For example, <TABLE WIDTH=500> defines a table of width 500 pixels.
- Border
  Border specifies the width of the border. You can define the width of the table's border in pixels, giving it a numerical value: 1, 2, 3,...To create a table without border, set BORDER=0. For example, <TABLE BORDER=0>.
- Cellspacing
  Cellspacing defines spacing between table cells in pixels.
- Cellpadding
  Cellpadding defines the amount of margin space within each table cell, in pixels. CELLPADDING=4 means there is a 4 pixel margin between the cell edge and the text or graphics in the cell.
- Align
  Align denotes the alignment of the table. Attributes include LEFT, CENTER, or RIGHT. For example, <TABLE ALIGN=RIGHT> makes the table appear on the right side of the page.

ATTRIBUTES WITHIN THE TD, TH ELEMENTS

- Align
  It horizontally aligns the text to either LEFT, CENTER, or RIGHT.
- Valign
  This attribute vertically aligns the text to TOP, CENTER, or BOTTOM. Center vertically centers the baseline of the text to the center of the table cell.
- Rowspan
  Rowspan sets the number of rows spanned by a cell. The default is 1.
- Colspan
  Colspan sets the number of columns spanned by a cell. The default is 1.

TABLES FOR EXACT PLACEMENT

Tables are good tools for layout design. They can be used for exact placement of Web components such as forms. The following example shows how to make a form appear in a place you want by using a simple two-column format. The table header is set up as right aligned. You use a standard table tag for the input sections of the form. The two table data cells at the right side of the bottom contain the centered Submit and Clear buttons. The first table data cell is empty. The input boxes and Submit and Clear buttons are aligned in a neat, centered row. Tables can be created within tables that place more complex form elements like radio buttons, drop-down menus, and checkboxes in desirable positions.

```
<FORM ACTION=POST>
<CENTER>
<TABLE>
<TR>
<TH ALIGN=RIGHT>Name:
<TD>
<INPUT TYPE=TEXT SIZE=30>
<TR>
<TH ALIGN=RIGHT>Email:
<TD>
<INPUT TYPE=TEXT SIZE=30>
<TR>
<TD>
<TD ALIGN=CENTER>
<INPUT TYPE="SUBMIT" VALUE="SUBMIT">
<INPUT TYPE="RESET" VALUE="CLEAR">
</TABLE>
</CENTER>
</FORM>
```

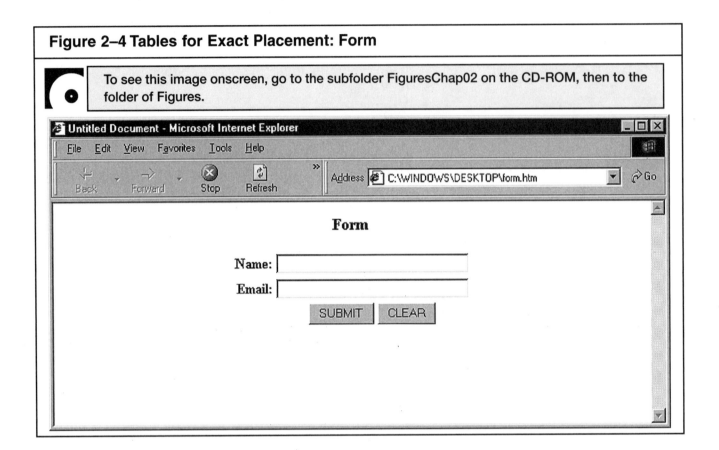

Figure 2–4 Tables for Exact Placement: Form

To see this image onscreen, go to the subfolder FiguresChap02 on the CD-ROM, then to the folder of Figures.

EXAMPLES OF LIBRARY WEB SITES USING TABLES

However useful the tables might be, there are some challenges and drawbacks in using tables. For instance, it takes more time to load pages with tables than pages without tables. Due to the complexity of tables, you need to decide if you should have the width of a table fixed (fixed width in pixels guarantees the final appearance) or make the width variable. A variable width is specified as a percentage of the browser width. If the table width is a variable one, the horizontal dimensions of the table make readjustments based on the current browser width. The variable width offers more flexibility: the table will always fit into the screen no matter what size the screen is. To strike a balance, you may want to have a combination of fixed and variable width for the different sections of the table. When you are done, you should try your table-based pages in computers of different sizes to find the best results. The following are some examples of library Web sites using tables.

Net Trail Web Site

Tables can be used for left alignment for the whole site layout. Take a look at the graphic (the dotted lines show the layout of the tables) below:

Figure 2–5 Tables for Exact Placement: Net Trail Web Site

To see this image onscreen, go to the subfolder FiguresChap02 on the CD-ROM, then to the folder of Figures.

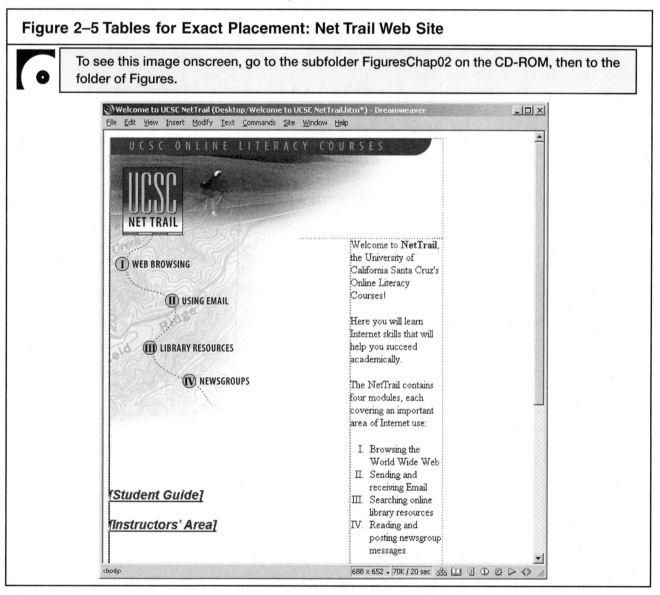

From the image you can see that the top bar and the side bar are well designed and they are fixed on the left side. But there is a problem with this kind of placement. It is perfect for a 13-inch computer with 640 x 480 resolution; however, people using computers with larger monitor screens or higher resolutions will see a lot of white space on the right. The graphics below show the difference.

Figure 2–6 Net Trail Web Site (in a 640 x 480 monitor)

To see this image onscreen, go to the subfolder FiguresChap02 on the CD-ROM, then to the folder of Figures.

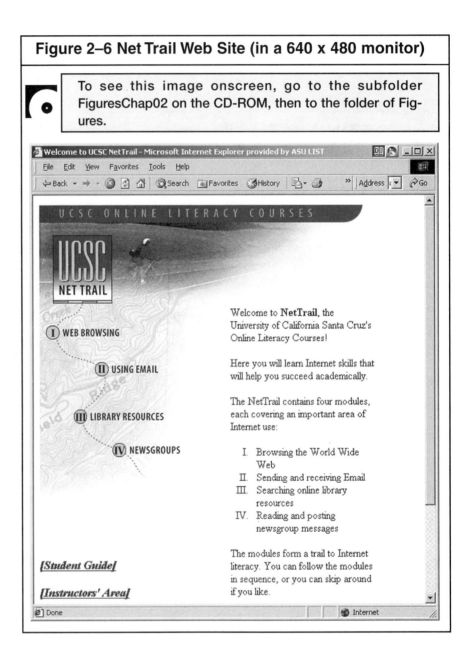

Figure 2–7 Net Trail Web Site (in a 1024 x 768 monitor)

 To see these images onscreen, goto the subfolder FiguresChap02 on the CD-ROM, then to the folder of Figures.

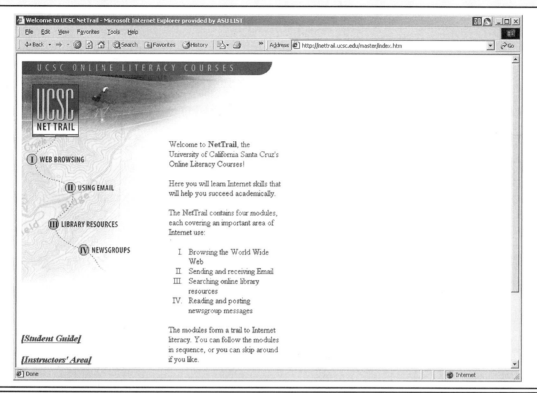

Figure 2–8 Net Trail Web Site (in a 1280 x 1024 monitor)

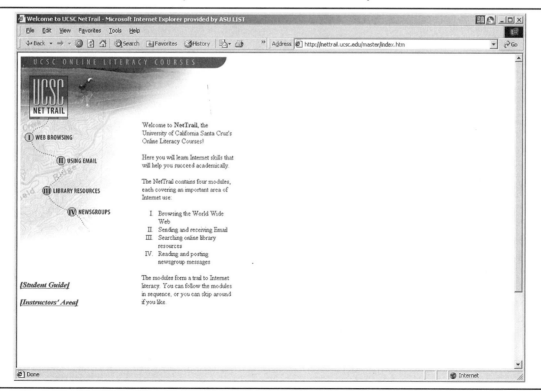

Brooklyn Public Library

To solve the problem of fixed left alignment, you may want to use tables to create centered alignment. With centered alignment, no matter how large the screen is, everything is always at the center of the page. Although there is unused space, the layout on the whole looks balanced. Here is an example from Brooklyn Public Library.

Figure 2–9 Tables for Exact Placement: Brooklyn Public Library

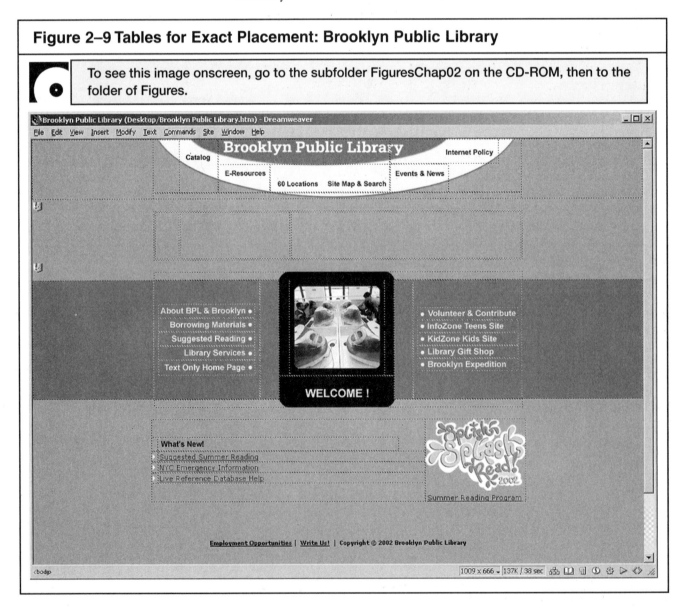

The graphics below show the difference of the site in different monitors.

Figure 2–10 Brooklyn Public Library Web Site (in a 640 x 480 monitor)

To see this image onscreen, go to the subfolder FiguresChap02 on the CD-ROM, then to the folder of Figures.

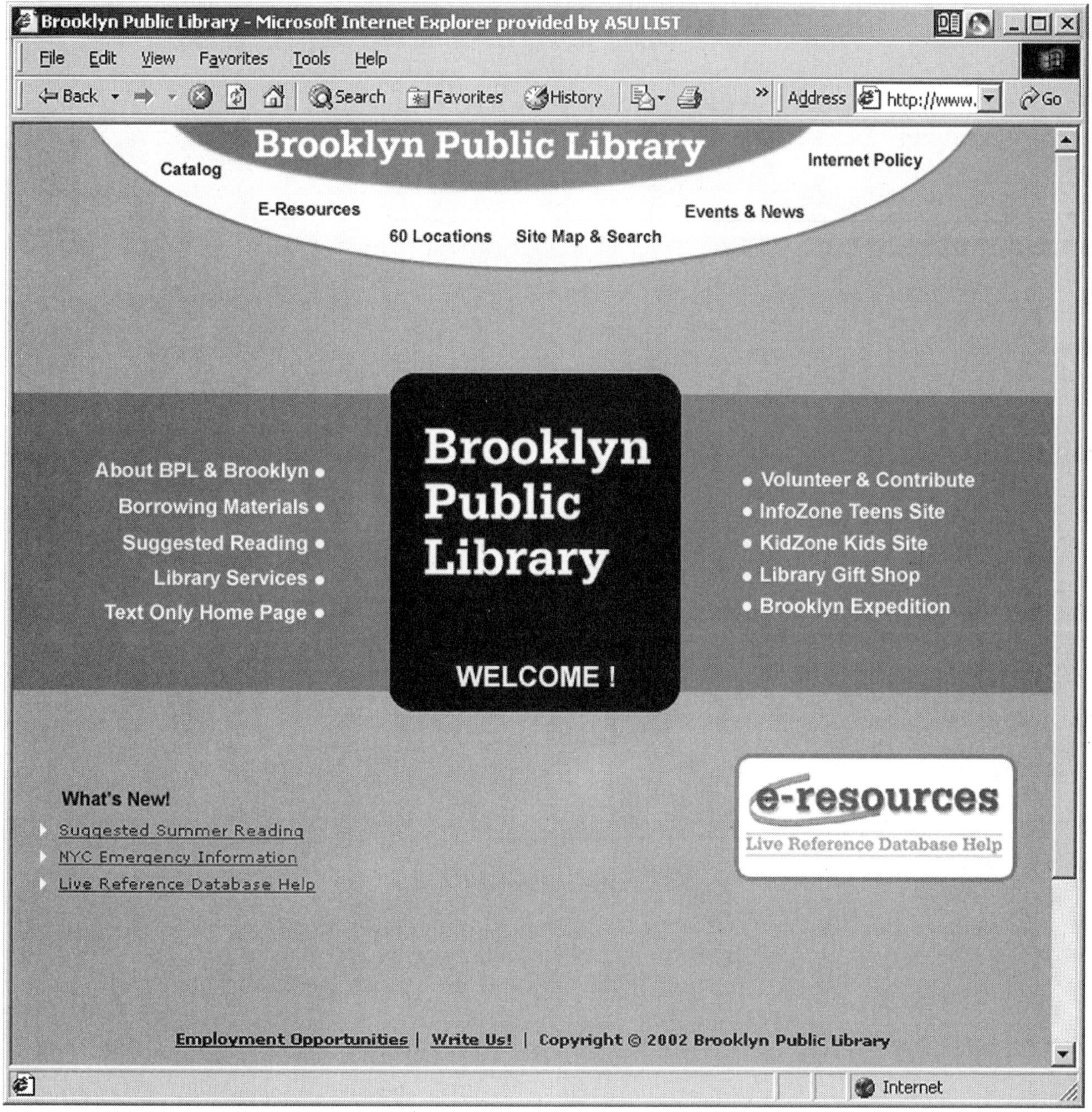

Figure 2–11 Brooklyn Public Library Web Site (in a 1024 x 768 monitor)

To see this image onscreen, go to the subfolder FiguresChap02 on the CD-ROM, then to the folder of Figures.

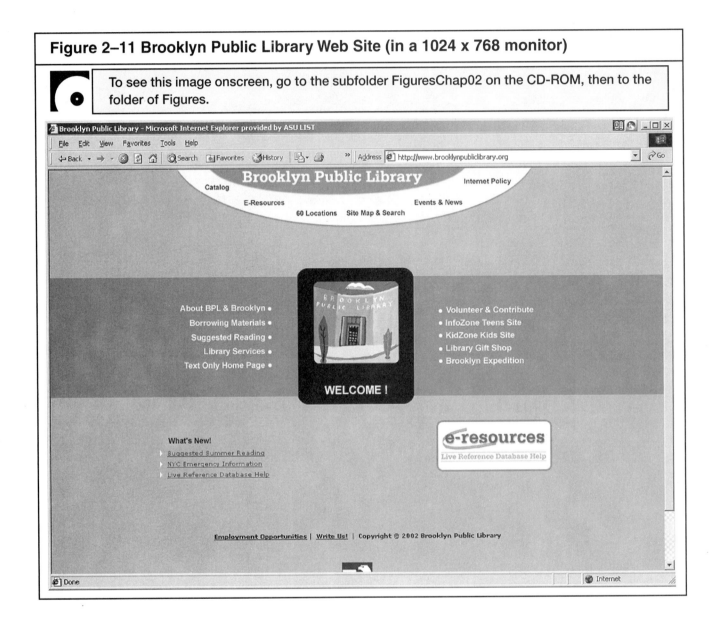

Boston Public Library

You can also create complex tables so that all is extensible: the texts or images will fill out the whole page regardless of the monitor size. Boston Public Library's site presents a very good example.

Figure 2–12 Tables for Exact Placement: Boston Public Library

To see this image onscreen, go to the subfolder FiguresChap02 on the CD-ROM, then to the folder of Figures.

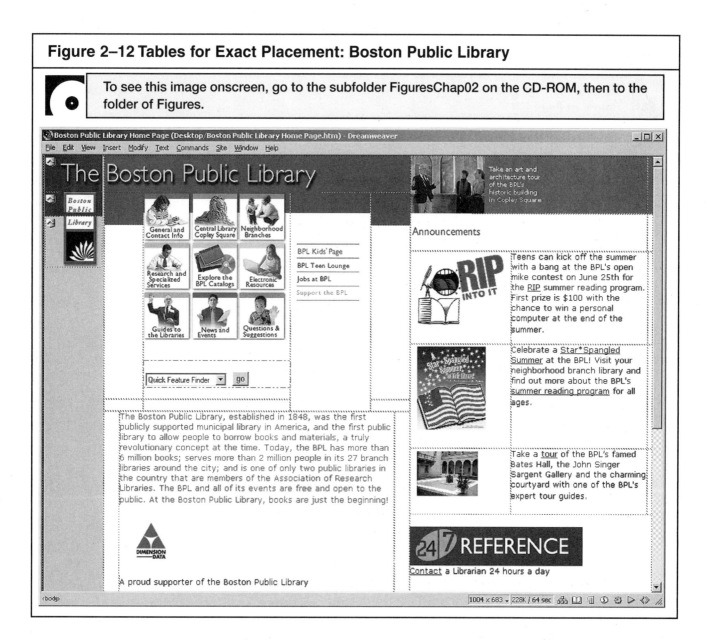

The graphics below show the difference of the site in different monitors.

Figure 2–13 Boston Public Library Web Site (in a 640 x 480 monitor)

To see this image onscreen, go to the subfolder FiguresChap02 on the CD-ROM, then to the folder of Figures.

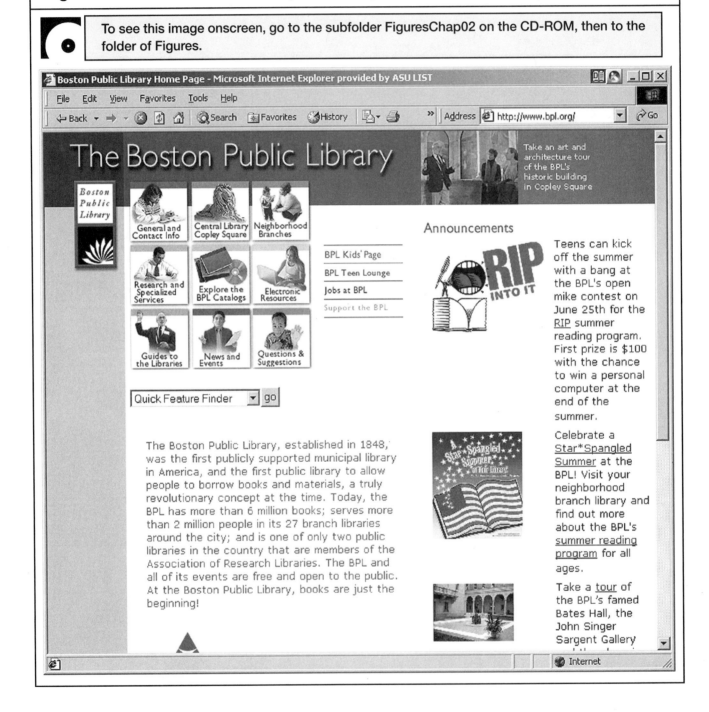

Figure 2–14 Boston Public Library Web Site (in a 1024 x 768 monitor)

To see this image onscreen, go to the subfolder FiguresChap02 on the CD-ROM, then to the folder of Figures.

FRAMES

HTML frames enable Web developers to present documents in multiple views, which may be independent windows or subwindows. Multiple views give developers a way to keep certain information visible, while other views are scrolled or replaced by linked pages. For example, within the same window, one frame might display a static banner, a second a navigation menu, and a third the main document that can be scrolled through or replaced by linked documents when you are navigating in the second frame. The separate, scrollable areas on a page make it easier to organize information and navigate in a Web site. Netscape 3.0 and Internet Explorer 3.0 above support borderless frames, which allow designers to incorporate one or more frames inside the page while having it look like a single page with no frames.

A FRAME-BASED PAGE EXAMPLE

Here is a frame-based HTML document:

```
<HTML>
<HEAD>
<TITLE>A simple frameset document</TITLE>
</HEAD>
<FRAMESET cols="20%, 80%">
<FRAMESET rows="100, 200">
<FRAME src="contents_of_frame1.html">
<FRAME src="contents_of_frame2.html">
</FRAMESET>
<FRAME src="contents_of_frame3.html">
```

Figure 2–15 Frame Chart

To see this image onscreen, go to the subfolder FiguresChap02 on the CD-ROM, then to the folder of Figures.

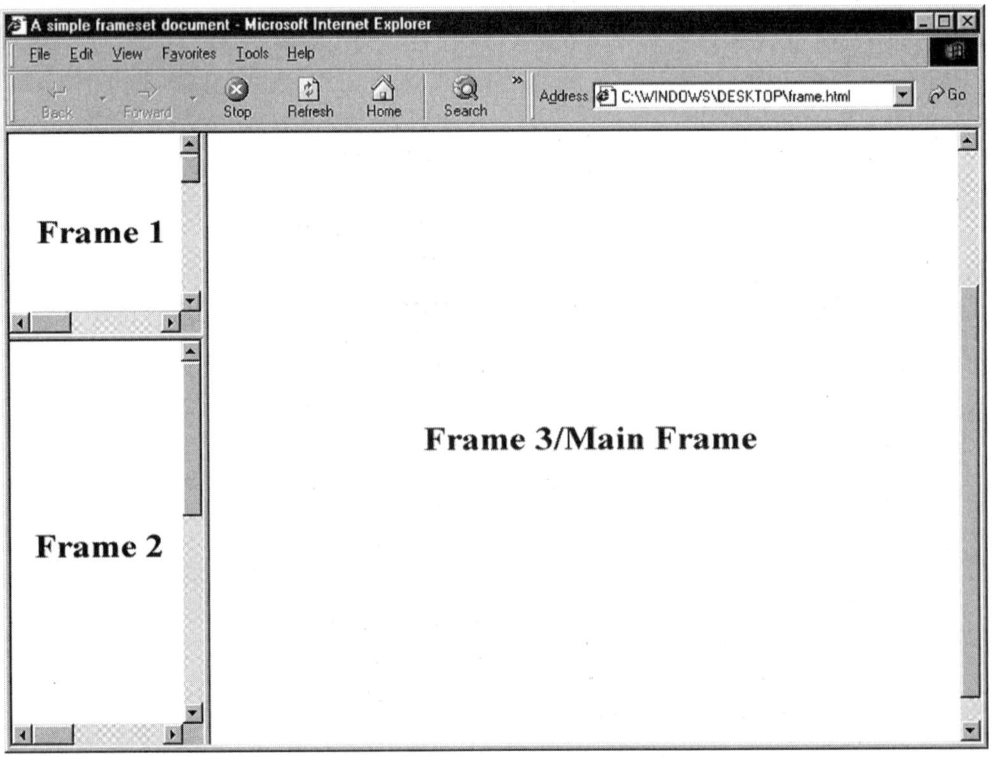

```
</FRAMESET>
</HTML>
```

FRAME-BASED SITE EXAMPLES

A frame-based site offers more flexibility. For instance, a site can be designed to have a file for navigation/instruction, and another file for content. Here is an example of the use of frames: (*www.asu.edu/lib/tutorials/suntutor/tryit/articles.htm*). This is a Web-based live exercise for online searching. The designers created a frame: one part of the screen for the viewer that never changes, which contains detailed instruction for the users to do a live searching in the right side of the screen. The only alternative is two separate windows, one for instruction while the other for searching. But for those who do not know how to deal with two windows such as resizing the windows to make them fit on the screen, it might create a problem. So a frame-based site is a better choice.

```
<HTML>
<HEAD>
<TITLE>Articles</TITLE>
</HEAD>
<FRAMESET  rows="102,546*"  cols="*"  border="0"
framespacing="0">
<FRAME   name="cornerFrame"   src="articles1.htm"
scrolling="NO"
frameborder="NO">
<FRAMESET  cols="186,822*"  rows="*"  border="0"
framespacing="0"
frameborder="NO">
<FRAME  name="leftFrame"  scrolling="YES"  noresize
src="articles2.htm">
<FRAME name="mainFrame" src=
"http://www.asu.edu/lib/resources/db/ebscohst.htm"
frameborder="NO">
</FRAMESET>
<NOFRAMES>
</NOFRAMES>
</FRAMESET>
</HTML>
```

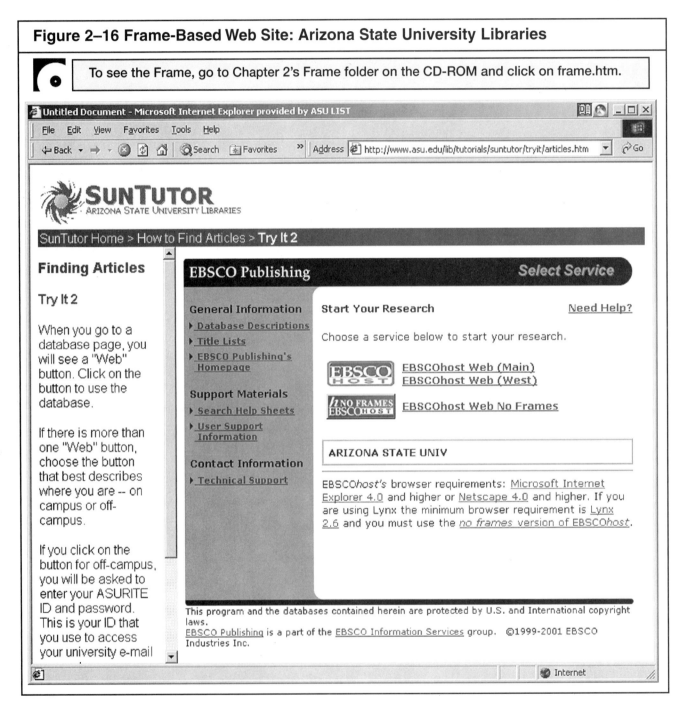

Figure 2–16 Frame-Based Web Site: Arizona State University Libraries

To see the Frame, go to Chapter 2's Frame folder on the CD-ROM and click on frame.htm.

Another example for a frame-based Web site is "Milton Reading Room" (*www.dartmouth.edu/research/milton/reading_room/pl/note/index.html*). This site is a collection of John Milton's books of *Paradise Lost*. Thomas Luxon and Sarah Horton, the designers, created a part of the screen for the viewers that is fixed and contains a menu that will take them to other pages within the site. Frames helped them to lock the row (footer frame) or column (navigation) so they don't scroll off the screen. The left-most frame provides the links: Book 1, Book 2,…etc. The main frame on the right displays the content of the books. The texts with annotations in the main frame are linked to a footer frame, and clicking on the text reference causes the corresponding note to show up in the footer frame. This frame-based structure makes the site not only highly interactive but also a coherent whole.

Figure 2–17 Frame-Based Web Site: Dartmouth College

To see this image onscreen, go to the subfolder FiguresChap02 on the CD-ROM, then to the folder of Figures.

THE DISADVANTAGES OF A FRAME-BASED SITE

Although a frame-based structure provides a good deal of flexibility, there are some disadvantages:

- Splitting your screen to separate windows will reduce the usable real estate to a smaller fraction of the screen.
- Because of the complicated structure, the browser's "Back" button may create unexpected results: you are thrown completely out of the framed site. In other words, the frames are broken.
- Users can no longer use the URL bar to see where they are.
- It is hard to print framed pages even with the newest versions of browsers such as Netscape 6.
- Since only the URL of the main page is displayed, it is impossible to bookmark one of the pages within your site. In a frame-based site, what you get is the URL of your main page. And if there is a problem in your pages, it will be difficult to report.
- Linked pages in your framed site to other sites will be displayed within your frame, making the navigation even harder.
- A search engine may not be able to index some of your pages due to the complicated structure.

To overcome these difficulties, you may want to create a nonframed version. A nonframed version of a site in conjunction with the framed version lets the users decide what they like. For example, for those who want to print a certain page properly and bookmark the page directly, the nonframed version will allow them to do this easily. To create a nonframed version, insert <NOFRAMES></NOFRAMES> tags under the </FRAMESET> tag.

WEB AUTHORING TOOLS

One of the most intriguing things about the Web is that it makes it possible for anyone to become a content publisher. Spending a little bit of time and effort, one can create pages with text, graphics, and multimedia. A simple page with text-based content and some inline graphics are easy to create. But to develop a more polished and sophisticated library Web page generally requires some special tools and more than a little patience. Those who have tried to create a table or an image map, or to build frames, and create mouse-over effects know the true meaning of frustration.

With the development of Web authoring tools, the good days of hand-coded Web sites using Notepad, WordPad, SimpleText, vi, pico, or other plain text editors are over. Now the WYSIWYG Web authoring tools take care of the annoying details and free you to work at a higher level. Web editors, serving many levels of expertise, from simple pages to multi-layered sites, can do more and do it better. Moreover, these tools automatically do housekeeping for you, for instance, defining the height and width of all the graphics so that your Web page loads faster.

The features of these tools have reduced repetitive tasks to a simple click. These tools help you create sites with sophisticated navigation features that are hard to update by hand. Previous developers know the pain when they insert pages in a developed site or move pages around in a hierarchical structure. Most of the authoring software can do the work with ease. When you have finished your hand-coded work, it is possible that the color scheme needs to be changed. For a hand-coded site, you have to make changes sometimes page by page. With a Web development tool, you just click an option and the changes are made immediately.

For those who want to have interactive features such as buttons or graphics changing color on mouse-over, and animations triggered by clicks, you need to understand JavaScript coding. But with the tools, you can accomplish these things without playing with JavaScript. Another advantage of the tools is that they allow you to flip back and forth between code views and page views so that you can check and make sure everything looks all right.

There are a few shortcomings for the Web editors. Some of the WYSIWYG tools are in reality WYSINQWYG (What You See Is Not Quite What You Get). They create more HTML codes than necessary. Although the extra text will not affect the page loading very much, the complicated codes will present a problem when you want to tune up your page by hand coding. In addition, these tools are not flexible enough for you to add newly developed Web elements or features such as multimedia components to your page.

In general, these tools automate much of the otherwise tedious and time-consuming aspects of creating Web pages. Although Web authoring tools do a wonderful job for you, there will always be reasons to know something about the code so that you can fix problems generated by the tools. We should always remember that Web editors and converters are no substitute for a good working knowledge of HTML.

There are a few user-friendly Web authoring programs that allow users to create professional looking documents, images, and Web pages. They include Macromedia Dreamweaver, Adobe GoLive, Microsoft FrontPage, HoTMetal PRO, and NetObjects Fusion. Librarians, who have little experience in designing a Web site, are now able to enliven their Web sites and complete these daunting tasks with ease. Among these tools, Dreamweaver is the most popular with Web developers because of its good user interface design, sophisticated features, and ease of use. For more information about Dreamweaver, please take a look at Appendix 4, Dreamweaver Tutorial, which is a brief introduction to Dreamweaver basics. Here we provide a brief introduction to the top three Web authoring tools.

MACROMEDIA DREAMWEAVER

The Macromedia Dreamweaver combines an intuitive visual design environment with programming capabilities. It features new versions of Macromedia Dreamweaver 4, Dreamweaver UltraDev 4 and Fireworks 4. The new upgrade provides Web developers with an integrated Web developing platform that increases individual and team productivity in creating Web sites, especially database-driven Web sites. Dreamweaver 4 and Fireworks 4 integrate code authoring, layout, and graphics creation.

Dreamweaver UltraDev 4 allows fast Web application development using industry standard application servers. The UltraDev 4 and Fireworks 4 studios offer Web developers powerful graphics capabilities. Roundtrip Graphic Editing enhances team work by allowing a smooth interchange of graphics and code within the applications and between team members. The software includes XML-based design notes, which further improve team workflow, support for content management standards, and integration with version control solutions.

The three new applications feature the Macromedia User Interface, which makes learning much easier. Both Dreamweaver 4 and Dreamweaver UltraDev 4 include integrated online code reference from O'Reilly and Associates, the most popular publisher on Web development. This enables beginners to learn the basics, and provides the experienced designers with an easy way to check code examples and standards.

ADOBE GOLIVE

Adobe GoLive 5.0 is integrated with other Adobe products such as Photoshop, Illustrator and Live Motion. The native support of

.psd, .ai and .liv files enhances workflow of Web development. The software provides site layout and management functionality. The use of the Adobe Photoshop imaging engine within GoLive makes it easy to develop images for the Web.

MICROSOFT FRONTPAGE

Microsoft FrontPage enables designers to create and manage all types of Web sites. The newest version is FrontPage 10, which provides powerful new site-creation capabilities and control and management innovations. The software includes graphic and content tools that allow users to import and display photos and other information in a professional looking format.

TOOLS FOR CLEANING UP HTML

When you develop your Web site using HTML, you may create some wrong codes. There are tools to help you clean up your HTML by finding the nonstandard codes for you. One of the popular tools is Doctor HTML at: *www.imagiware.com/RxHTML/*. Another powerful utility is Tidy Online at: *http://valet.htmlhelp.com/tidy/*. Using this tool, you can do more than just clean up the HTML, you can indent element content; convert HTML to XHTML, a hybrid of XML and HTML; omit optional end tags; force tags to uppercase; replace font and center tags by CSS; output numeric rather than named entities, and so on.

FTP PROGRAMS

After you finish your Web site design, you need to use an FTP program to put everything on the Web. FTP is the acronym for "File Transfer Protocol." It is a process by which most files (Web pages, graphics, video, etc.) are transferred to and from a server and your computer. One of the most popular FTP programs is WS_FTP. However, this program has become an easy target for hikers since there is no security encoding and decoding mechanism set up. Applications such as Dreamweaver and FrontPage have FTP programs built in. Again there are some concerns about using them because safety of file transmission cannot be guaranteed. For your file transfer security, it is better to use secure FTP applications. Check with your systems administrator about the most reliable FTP program. Right now SSH Secure File Transfer is considered to be a secure FTP program. The figure below shows the interface of this program.

Figure 2–18 SSH Secure File Transfer

To see this image onscreen, go to the subfolder FiguresChap02 on the CD-ROM, then to the folder of Figures.

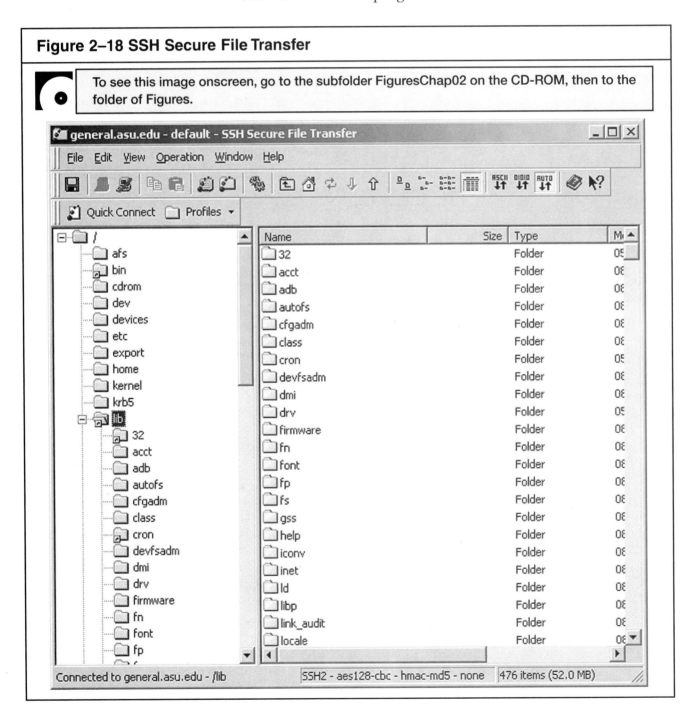

3 MOVING BEYOND HTML

With HTML, we can present data such as text and graphics in a browser in different kinds of shapes, sizes, and colors. Moreover, we can provide interactive features such as hyperlinks. But the power of HTML is quite limited. Other programming languages and technologies are needed to supplement HTML and make your library Web site more interactive, for example, JavaScript, CSS, and CGI.

As a powerful tool, JavaScript can help improve the appearance and functionality of library Web sites. For example, JavaScript can be used to create rollovers, which enhance the interactivity of the site. It can also be used for form validation, random display of messages and images, mouse-over pop-up windows, online slideshow, display of time and date, interactive quizzes, and so on.

CGI scripts are widely used in library Web sites for executing library forms such as renew, recall, interlibrary loan, suggestion, search, survey, fine payment forms, and so on. CGI can also be used to create a counter, which will automatically count how many people have visited your library site. With CGI, you can create a library guest book, which allows users to sign in and leave their name, contact information, and comments. It can also redirect users to a different page after signing, log entries and e-mail upon new entries. In addition, you can use CGI to develop a threaded discussion forum that allows library users to post new messages, follow up on existing messages, and more. A very simple CGI logging script will provide you with some statistical information about library usage by telling you where your users come from and what browser they used. Another useful application of CGI is link checking for your library Web site. When you run the program, it will check all the links on your site and let you know if there are any broken links.

CSS (Cascading Style Sheet) gives library Web developers more control over the layout of a page. CSS makes it possible for library Web site designers to create a consistent look and feel for the pages, while keeping the Web style separate from the Web content. You can use a style sheet for a single Web page or have it linked to all pages. The main advantage of linked CSS is that you can make flexible changes for your library site. If you plan to change the appearance of pages, you just change the CSS, and all the pages that link to that style are immediately changed. Style sheets bring more flexibility in offering the presentation effects. Besides font types, developers can apply properties such as background, margin, border, and so on, to all elements. They can use a style for all level-one headings, or all italic text, or all paragraphs. Using CSS, you can create margins rather than putting the whole page in a table.

JAVASCRIPT

Developed by Netscape, JavaScript is a powerful but easy-to-use client site scripting language that can be embedded in the header of the Web pages. With JavaScript you can easily create interactive Web pages. JavaScript comprises a set of procedures that can be used within HTML documents to produce various special effects. As a dynamic language, JavaScript can be used to perform calculations, check forms, validate forms, create interactive games, produce pop-up windows, and present slide shows. Moreover, it can add special effects such as button rollovers.

JavaScript scripting techniques can also be used to lead viewers to the appropriate pages. Because some of the HTML tags had been brought into the HTML 4.0 DTD, and others had not, the result of using these tags is that your pages will never look the same in all browsers. The only solutions that an HTML writer has are: not use those tags or use those tags and state that the page is meant for one browser or another. With JavaScript, you can write multiple pages and use scripting techniques to direct readers to the appropriate pages. What is most unique about JavaScript is that no compiling, no client-server interaction, and no plug-ins are required. This makes writing and running JavaScript much easier. To run JavaScript, you need Netscape Navigator Version 2.0 or above or the Microsoft Internet Explorer Version 3.0 or above. The two browsers are widely spread so many people can run scripts written in JavaScript.

Although sophisticated tools have been developed to create JavaScript effects or applications, such as mouse-overs, automatically without you messing around with the arcane code, it is still necessary to know the basics of this scripting language and its functionality because the tools have their limitations and they cannot be used to develop or customize more advanced features or applications.

To understand JavaScript, we need to understand a few concepts: Objects, Methods, Properties, and Events.

OBJECTS

An object is a container that stores some information. It provides a way for you to read that information and a way for you to write to, or change, that information.

METHODS

You can access certain information in the object directly. However, other information may require you to use a method to access it. Different objects can do different things, just as a window can open and close. You can open a new document with the method: document.open(). You can write "This is a new doc" into a document by typing document.write("This is a new doc"). The object: document has two methods—open() and write().

PROPERTIES

The information you directly access in the object is its properties. With properties, you see what you are doing to the object; while with methods, you only see the effects of what you are doing. A Web page is an object. A table, form, button, image, or link on your page can also be called an object. Each object has its own properties (information about the object). Color may be a property for an object. For example, the background color of your page can be written as: document.bgcolor. You can give the page a specific color by providing a value "red": document.bgcolor="red."

EVENTS

JavaScript makes an element respond to an action. The process is called an event. JavaScript deals with event handlers that call up the action. A hyperlink is activated when you click on it. It is an onClick event. A link may change its color when the cursor passes over it, and this is detected by an onMouseOver event. Another event is the onLoad event, which is connected to the body element. When the body element has completely loaded, the action such as calling a function occurs. Take a radio button for example: when a radio button is clicked, the computer automatically selects it. Each radio button calls a corresponding function that shows the change of selection in the text box.

Another example is a button that might create a pop-up window when clicked. In other words, the window should pop up as a reaction to an onClick event. The event definition includes: onClick="trigger_my_function()." The onClick event or event handler (the name is self-explanatory) will start the function when the user clicks on the button. This means the event handler orders the computer what to do if this event occurs. If the mouse moves across a link an onMouseOver event occurs. Other examples of events include: onMouseOut, onFocus, onBlur, onLoad, and onUnload. There are around 50 predefined events. You should refer to a JavaScript reference if you want to know what kind of events or event handlers are available.

EMBEDDING JAVASCRIPT

To have JavaScript work for you, you need to embed it in the <HEAD> area with tags <SCRIPT LANGUAGE="JavaScript"> and </SCRIPT>:

```
<HTML>
<HEAD>
<SCRIPT LANGUAGE="JavaScript">
Your JavaScript
</SCRIPT>
</HEAD>
```

Everything between the <SCRIPT> and the </SCRIPT> tag is interpreted as JavaScript code.

JAVASCRIPT EXAMPLES

The following code is an example of a simple event handler onClick embedded in an HTML document:

```
<HTML>
<HEAD>
<SCRIPT LANGUAGE ="JavaScript">
</SCRIPT>
<TITLE>JavaScript</TITLE>
</HEAD>
<BODY>
<FORM><INPUT type="button" value="Click" onclick=
"alert('Hello world!')"></FORM>
</BODY>
</HTML>
```

Above we created a form with a button. We put onClick="alert ('Hello world!')" inside the <INPUT> tag. This defines what happens when the button is clicked even though there is nothing in between <SCRIPT LANGUAGE ="JavaScript"> and </SCRIPT> tags. If an onClick event takes place the computer will execute alert('Hello world!'). Here, alert() creates pop-up windows. Inside the brackets you specify a string—'Hello world!.' This is the text to be displayed in the pop-up window when the user clicks on the button.

Another example involves calculation:

```
<SCRIPT LANGUAGE ="JavaScript">
function calculation() {
 var x= 2;
 var y= 5;
 var result= x * y;
 alert(result);
}
</SCRIPT>
<FORM>
<INPUT type="button" value="Calculate" onclick="calculation()">
</FORM>
```

In this script we define a function. This is done through the lines:

```
function calculation() {
 var x= 2;
 var y= 5;
 var result= x * y;
 alert(result);
}
```

The commands inside the {} belong to the function calculation(). This means that the function of calculation can be executed through a function call. The button calls the function calculation(). The function does certain calculations. Here a variable is defined with the keyword var. We use the variables x, y, and result. Variables are used to store different values such as numbers, text strings, and other things. The line var result= x * y; orders the browser to create a variable result and store in it the result of x * y (that is 2 * 5). The calculation of the variable result is 10. The command alert(result) is the same as alert(10). So we will see a pop-up window with the number 10 in it.

JAVASCRIPT ROLLOVERS

Rollovers bring about interactive effects with the use of the mouse. That is, if you mouse over an image, a new image will show up replacing the original image; if you move the mouse away from the new image, the old image will reappear giving the impression that the image is turned on and off. This feature is widely used in enhancing navigation tools such as buttons, bars, arrows, and so on.

The following is the code:

```
<HTML>
<HEAD>
<TITLE>Basic JavaScript Rollover</TITLE>
```

```
<SCRIPT LANGUAGE="JavaScript">
Rollimage = new Array()
Rollimage[0]= new Image(12,15)
Rollimage[0].src = "image_on.gif"
Rollimage[1] = new Image(12,15)
Rollimage[1].src = "image_off.gif"
function ChangeOut(){
document.Rollover.src = Rollimage[1].src;
return true;
}
function ChangeBack(){
document.Rollover.src = Rollimage[0].src;
return true;
}
</SCRIPT>
</HEAD>
<BODY>
<P align="left"> The button below is a JavaScript rollover. If you
mouse over the button or the link, you will see the button changes
color.
<P align="left"><A HREF="http://www.yahoo.com/"
onmouseover="ChangeOut()"
onmouseout="ChangeBack()"><IMG SRC="image_on.gif"
NAME="Rollover" WIDTH=10 HEIGHT=12 BORDER=0>The link
will lead to Yahoo! Web site.</A>
</P>
</BODY>
</HTML>
```

Let's see what is going on in this set of code:
First, this block of code below preloads the images for the rollover.

```
Rollimage = new Array()
Rollimage[0]= new Image(10,12)
Rollimage[0].src = "image_on.gif"
Rollimage[1] = new Image(10,12)
Rollimage[1].src = "image_off.gif"
```

The first line initializes the array, and following is a set of numbered arrays for each image. The first line of each set declares the image's size and the second assigns its address. Then the two functions called ChangeOut and ChangeBack will start to work. They work to replace the "off" images with the "on" images. In the code wrapped by the HTML body tag, the link's attributes are specified. In the following code, the link includes onMouseOver and onMouseOut attributes that indicate the function, which should be called when those events are started.

```
<A HREF=http://www.yahoo.com/ onMouseOver="ChangeOut()"
```

```
onMouseOut="ChangeBack()">
<IMG SRC="image_on.gif" NAME="Rollover" WIDTH=10
HEIGHT=12 BORDER=0>
```

On the whole, the code is self-explanatory. It shows how the script works to create the effects.

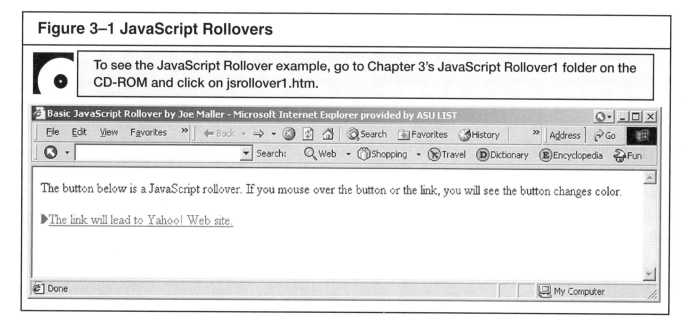

Figure 3–1 JavaScript Rollovers

To see the JavaScript Rollover example, go to Chapter 3's JavaScript Rollover1 folder on the CD-ROM and click on jsrollover1.htm.

A JavaScript rollover image can be displayed in a different location than the current one. The example JavaScript Rollover2 in the CD-ROM shows how it works.

To see the JavaScript rollover image displayed in a different location, go to Chapter 3's JavaScript Rollover2 folder on the CD-ROM and click on jsrollover2.htm.

FORM VALIDATION

Another popular use of JavaScript for library Web sites is form validation. It is frustrating for people to fill in a form and submit it only to find that they forgot to put certain information and have to refill every item in the form. JavaScript can help to check the form items such as name, user ID, password, e-mail, text field, radio buttons, and so on. If you clicked the Submit button when something is still missing, a window with a warning will show up letting you know that you need to put in the missing information before you can go on.

Here is the JavaScript code:

```
<SCRIPT LANGUAGE="JavaScript">
function checkform( thisform ) {
if (thisform.theName.value == null || thisform.theName.value ==
"" ) {
alert ("Please enter your name") ;
thisform.theName.focus() ;
thisform.theName.select() ;
return false ;
}
</SCRIPT>
```

As you can see, if you forget to enter certain data into the form it will alert you and cancel the submission. If you do enter all the correct information, it will send the form. For future reference, you should know that the form is named thisform, and its input is named thename. The first and most important code in form validation is an event handler in the form tag. This event handler, onSubmit, must return true for the form to be submitted. When the submit button is pressed, the event handler is triggered; it in turn runs function checkform(), which makes sure there are no errors in the form. The checkform() function determines if the name input is empty. If it is, it alerts the user and returns false. It won't allow the form to be submitted unless it has been filled out to a reasonable extent.

The following is the JavaScript embedded in an HTML file:

```
<HTML>
<HEAD>
<TITLE>Form Validation With JavaScript</TITLE>
<SCRIPT LANGUAGE="JavaScript">
function checkform( thisform ) {
if (thisform.theName.value == null || thisform.theName.value ==
"" ) {
alert ("Please enter your name") ;
thisform.theName.focus() ;
thisform.theName.select() ;
return false ;
}
}
</SCRIPT>
</HEAD>
<BODY>
<H1>The Library Survey</H1>
<P>Welcome to the Library Survey Page. Please fill out the fol-
lowing form.
<P>Use <B>Submit</B> to submit your results.
<HR>
```

```
<FORM METHOD="POST" ACTION="http://www.domain/library/
cgi-bin/post-query"
onSubmit="return checkform( this )" >
<P><B>Name: </B>
<INPUT TYPE="TEXT" NAME="theName">
<P><B>The Library Online Services You Like: </B>
<INPUT TYPE="CHECKBOX" NAME="loan">Interlibrary Loan
…
<INPUT TYPE="CHECKBOX" NAME="check">Check My Library
Records
<INPUT TYPE="SUBMIT" VALUE="Submit" >
<INPUT TYPE="RESET" VALUE="Clear Form" ></P>
</FORM>
<HR>
</BODY>
</HTML>
```

Figure 3–2 JavaScript Form Validation

To see the Form Validation example, go to Chapter 3's Form Validation folder on the CD-ROM and click on validform.htm.

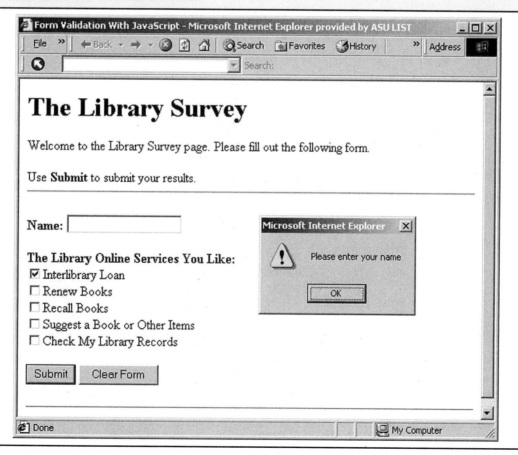

RANDOM DISPLAY OF QUOTES OR IMAGES

JavaScript can be used for random display of quotes or images, which can make a library Web site look more dynamic. The random() function of JavaScript enables you to generate random numbers that can be used in a variety of ways. You can randomly select an image to load when the Web page loads or randomly change the content to add variety to the Web page. So each time a user gets to your library Web site, he or she will see a new picture or a new quotation.

Take quotes for example. You first create a new array (holder) using the Array keyword. Add several quotes to the array. Then create a random number variable using the Math.random () function and multiply it by the length of the array. The script will write the quote to the browser with the document.write () function. When you open the HTML file in the browser, a quote will show up. Next time you open the page, a different quote will appear. You can test this by clicking the Refresh or Reload button. You will see that the page is reloaded and another quote is displayed. The following is the code:

```
<SCRIPT LANGUAGE="JavaScript">
QuoteArray = new Array(
"Never confuse motion with action.",
...
"The smaller the mind the greater the conceit.");
RandomNo = Math.floor(QuoteArray.length * Math.random());
document.write("<b>" + QuoteArray[RandomNo] + "</b>");
</SCRIPT>
```

To see the Random Quotation Display example, go to Chapter 3's Random Quotation Display folder on the CD-ROM and click on randomquot.htm.

The following is an example for random display of pictures. When you open the HTML file in the browser, a picture will show up. Click the Refresh or Reload button, the page is reloaded and another picture is displayed. The code is shown below:

```
<SCRIPT LANGUAGE ="JavaScript">
if (top.frames.length!=0) top.location=self.document.location;
</SCRIPT>
<SCRIPT LANGUAGE ="JavaScript">
var i;
function MakeArray()
{
this.length=MakeArray.arguments.length
```

```
for (var i=0;i<this.length;i++)
this[i+1]=MakeArray.arguments[i]
}
function LoadFrontPageImage()
{
// Enter the filenames for the photographs of asu
// in this array.
var photoarray = new MakeArray(
"asu_01.jpg",
...
"asu_11.jpg");
i=Math.floor((Math.random()*11+1));
document ["Photo"].src=photoarray[i];
}
</SCRIPT>
<SCRIPT LANGUAGE="JavaScript">
function GetRandom(start,end)
{
var range = end—start + 1;
var result = start + Math.floor(Math.random()*range);
return result;
}
</SCRIPT>
```

To see the Random Picture Display example, go to Chapter 3's Random Picture Display folder on the CD-ROM and click on randompic.htm.

JAVASCRIPT-BASED ONLINE SLIDESHOW

JavaScript can be used to create online slide shows, which may serve the purpose of a virtual library tour. The script controls the timing of the display of pictures and the duration of the cross fade effect. The code is shown below. By changing the variables and specifying the image files, you can customize the slide show to fit your own needs.

```
<HTML>
<HEAD>
<TITLE>Slideshow</TITLE>
<SCRIPT LANGUAGE = "JavaScript">
var slideShowSpeed = 5000;
var crossFadeDuration = 3;
var Pic = new Array();
Pic[0] = 'hayden1.gif'
Pic[1] = 'noble1.gif'
...
```

```
Pic[5] = 'hayden1.gif'
var t;
var j = 0;
var p = Pic.length;
var preLoad = new Array();
for (i = 0; i < p; i++) {
preLoad[i] = new Image();
preLoad[i].src = Pic[i];
}
function runSlideShow() {
if (document.all) {
document.images.SlideShow.style.filter="blendTrans(duration=2)";
document.images.SlideShow.style.filter="blendTrans(duration=
crossFadeDuration)";
document.images.SlideShow.filters.blendTrans.Apply();
}
document.images.SlideShow.src = preLoad[j].src;
if (document.all) {
document.images.SlideShow.filters.blendTrans.Play();
}
j = j + 1;
if (j > (p—1)) j = 0;
t = setTimeout('runSlideShow()', slideShowSpeed);
}
</SCRIPT >
</HEAD>
<BODY onload="runSlideShow(), MM_preloadImages('')">
<P>Virtual Library Tour: an Online Slideshow of ASU Libraries
<TABLE CELLSPACING=0 BORDER=0 WIDTH=226>
<TR>
<TD VALIGN="MIDDLE" COLSPAN=4>
<TBODY><IMG SRC="white.gif" WIDTH=366 HEIGHT=401>
</TBODY>
</TD>
</TR>
</TABLE>
</BODY>
</HTML>
```

In the code above, the line: var slideShowSpeed =5000; sets the slide show speed (milliseconds). The var crossFadeDuration = 3; sets the duration of cross fade (seconds). The var Pic = new Array(); specifies the image files. You can put images by adding to the array: Pic[4] = 'arch1.gif'. The code <IMG SRC="white.gif" WIDTH=366 HEIGHT=401> defines the size of the slide show and the starting image. The command: onload="runSlideShow(), MM_preloadImages('')" begins to load the image files and run the slide show when the Web page is open.

Figure 3–3 JavaScript-Based Online Slide Show

To see the JavaScript Slideshow example, go to Chapter 3's JavaScript Slideshow folder on the CD-ROM and click on slideshow.htm.

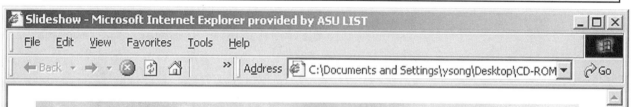

INTERACTIVE QUIZZES

JavaScript can be used to create other kinds of interactive applications. Take online quizzes for instance, you can create an HTML document with the quiz forms and customize the JavaScript and embed it in the HTML document. These quiz applications are very useful for Web-based library instructions and staff training.

Matching

Here is a matching practice. When you do the matching, JavaScript can trigger automatically a pop-up window to show you if you match correctly or not. In this script, you set up variables first, and then you decide the conditions and specify the correct answer: B, in this case. A mini window with an alert will pop up when you make a correct choice, showing you that the answer is right. If you choose the wrong answer, the message will say that it is incorrect and ask you to try again.

```
if (question =="q1" && alphabet == "B" ||
if (question =="q1")
document.test.B.click()
...
alert (question + " " + alphabet + " is correct.")
...
else {
alert (alphabet + " is incorrect for " + question + ". Please try
again.")
```

The following is the code:

```
<HTML>
<HEAD>
<TITLE>Matching</TITLE>
<BODY>
<SCRIPT LANGUAGE = "JavaScript">
function checkQuestion(selection) {
var alphabet, tempIndex, number
tempIndex=selection.selectedIndex
alphabet=selection.options[tempIndex].text
question=selection.name
if (question =="q1" && alphabet == "B" ||
question =="q2" && alphabet == "C" ||
question =="q3" && alphabet == "A" ||
question =="q4" && alphabet == "D" ||)
{
alert (question + " " + alphabet + " is correct.")
if (question =="q1")
```

```
document.test.B.click()
if (question =="q2")
document.test.C.click()
if (question =="q3")
document.test.A.click()
if (question =="q4")
document.test.D.click()
}
else {
alert (alphabet + " is incorrect for " + question + ". Please try
again.")
if (question =="q1" && document.test.B.checked)
document.test.B.click()
if (question =="q2" && document.test.C.checked)
document.test.C.click()
if (question =="q3" && document.test.A.checked)
document.test.A.click()
if (question =="q4" && document.test.D.checked)
document.test.D.click()
}
}
</SCRIPT>
<FORM action="" method=post name=test>
<TABLE cellPadding=0 cellSpacing=0>
<TBODY>
<TR>
<TD>
<SELECT name=q1 onchange="checkQuestion(this); blur()"
value="">
<OPTION selected>
<OPTION>A
<OPTION>B
<OPTION>C
<OPTION>D
</OPTION>
</SELECT>
1. Lexis-Nexis </P>
</TD>
<TD>
<INPUT name=A type=checkbox value=" ">
A. Identify books, journal titles, etc.
</TD>
</TR>
...
</TBODY>
</TABLE>
<INPUT name=resetButton type=reset value=Reset height="10"
width="10">
```

```
</FORM>
</BODY>
</HTML>
```

Figure 3–4 Matching

To see the Matching example, go to Chapter 3's Matching folder on the CD-ROM and click on matching.htm.

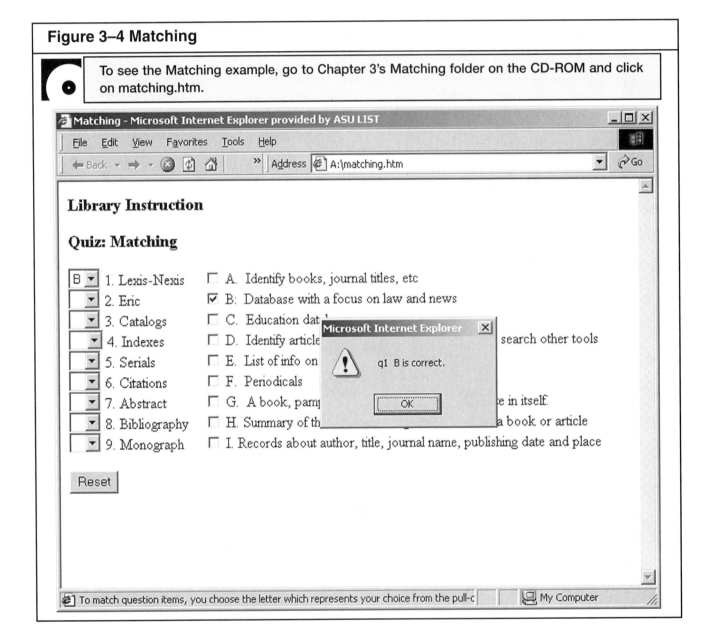

Fill-in-Blanks

For this interactive application, you fill in the blanks (in standard HTML form formats) then click to see the results. JavaScript can trigger automatically a pop-up window to show you if you choose the correct or incorrect words to fill in. The condition is set up as follows:

If you fill in the blank with the correct answer, Boolean, under:

```
if (question =="q1" && alphabet == "Boolean"||
if (question =="q1")
document.C2.A.value="C"
```

then the line of command: alert (question + " " + alphabet + " is correct.") will trigger the pop-up window showing that the answer "Boolean" is right.

Otherwise, the command—the alert (alphabet + " is incorrect for " + question + ". Please try again.")—will be called up and the pop-up window will show up saying that your choice is incorrect: Please try again.

The code is shown as follows:

```
<HTML>
<HEAD>
<TITLE>Fill in Blanks</TITLE>
<SCRIPT LANGUAGE="JavaScript">
function resetForm() {
 document.C2.submit()
 document.C2.reset()
}
function checkQuestion(selection) {
 var alphabet, tempIndex, number
 question=selection.name
 alphabet=selection.value
 if (question =="q1" && alphabet == "Boolean"||
 ...
 question =="q6" && alphabet == "index")
 {
 if (question =="q1")
 document.C2.A.value="C"
 ...
 if (question =="q6")
 document.C2.F.value="C"
 alert (question + " " + alphabet + " is correct.")
 }
 ...
 else {
 alert (alphabet + " is incorrect for " + question + ". Please try
again.")
 }
 }
</SCRIPT>
</HEAD>
```

```
<BODY>
<FORM ACTION="" METHOD=POST name=C2>
<TABLE CELLSPACING=0 CELLPADDING=0 >
`<TR>
<TD WIDTH="1%"><INPUT TYPE="checkbox" NAME="A"
VALUE="">
</TD>
<TD>1.This operator helps you narrow down your search
<INPUT     type="text"     Name="q1"     size="20"
onChange="checkQuestion(this); blur()">
</TD>
</TR>

...
<TR>
<TD><INPUT TYPE="checkbox" NAME="F" VALUE=" ">
</TD>
<TD>6.The tool that finds listings to specific articles in different
publications is
<INPUT type="text" NAME="q6" size="20" VALUE=""
onChange="checkQuestion(this);blur()">
</TD>
</TR>
</TABLE>
<INPUT TYPE="reset" VALUE="Reset" >
</FORM>
</BODY>
</HTML>
```

Figure 3–5 Fill-in-Blanks

To see the Fill-in-Blanks example, go to Chapter 3's Fill-in-Blanks folder on the CD-ROM and click on fillinblanks.htm.

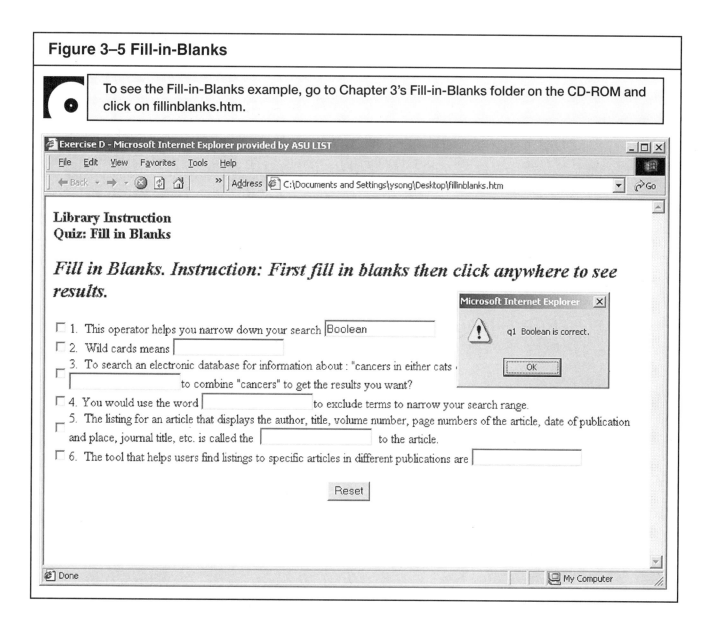

Multiple Choices

For this application, JavaScript can automatically calculate the score and add ten points for each correct answer:

```
function totalAdd(obj) {
total=0
if( (document.test.q1[0].checked)){
total+=10
document.test.Score.value= total
document.test.Question1.value="correct"
}
```

The code is self-explanatory: if option 0 in question 1 is checked, add 10 points to the total. Here 0 inside the brackets means Choice A in Question 1. Remember that JavaScript always starts with 0 instead of 1 when numbers are involved.

If you put a CGI program on your server, and have it called up when a user does the exercise, you can have the results e-mailed to you. It is possible for people to see the correct answers by viewing your JavaScript in your HTML source code. To avoid this, you can hide the script on your server by saving your JavaScript file as XXX.js and putting it in the same folder of your HTML. Then you can delete the JavaScript code in the HTML file and write in your HTML file: <SCRIPT LANGUAGE="JavaScript" SRC="XXX.js">…</SCRIPT> to refer to the JavaScript source file on the server.

The code is shown below:

```
<HTML>
<HEAD>
<TITLE>Multiple Choices </TITLE>
<SCRIPT LANGUAGE="JavaScript">
function totalAdd(obj) {
 total=0
 if( (document.test.q1[0].checked)){
 total+=10
 document.test.Score.value= total
 document.test.Question1.value="correct"
}
 …
}
</SCRIPT>
</HEAD>
<BODY>
<FORM ACTION="http://www.domain/library/cgi-bin/XXX.cgi"
METHOD=POST NAME=test>
<INPUT TYPE=hidden NAME=subject VALUE="Quiz Name">
<INPUT TYPE=hidden NAME=recipient VALUE="XXXX@XXXX.
edu">
<FONT SIZE="3"><B>Question 1</B>
<INPUT TYPE=hidden NAME=Question1 VALUE=wrong>
Which word or symbol would you use right in front of your search
term to produce the indicated result: Each Web page displayed
must include this term. </FONT>
<INPUT TYPE=radio NAME=q1 VALUE=a onclick=" ">
A. +
<INPUT TYPE=radio NAME=q1 VALUE=b onclick=" ">
B.-
<INPUT TYPE=radio NAME=q1 VALUE=c onclick=" ">
```

```
C. AND
<INPUT TYPE=radio NAME=q1 VALUE=d onclick=" ">
D. OR
…
<FONT="3">Score</FONT>
<INPUT TYPE=text NAME=Score VALUE="0" SIZE=4>
<INPUT TYPE=reset VALUE="Reset" name=resetButton>
<INPUT TYPE=submit NAME=Submit VALUE="Submit"
onclick="totalAdd(this.form.Score)">
</FORM>
</BODY>
</HTML>
```

Figure 3–6 Multiple Choices

To see the Multiple Choices example, go to Chapter 3's Multiple Choices folder on the CD-ROM and click on multiplechoice.htm.

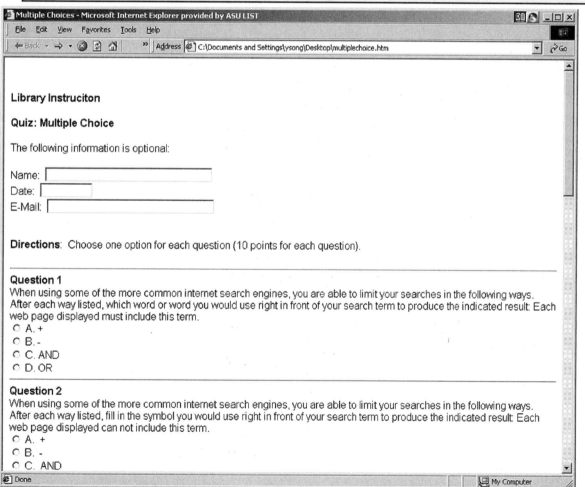

MOUSE-OVER POP-UP WINDOWS

JavaScript can also be used to create mouse-over pop-up windows. The window will pop up wherever you move your mouse. The following graphic is an example. If you mouse over the pictures of popular magazines or scholarly journals, pop-up windows with descriptions will show up.

Figure 3–7 Mouse-Over Pop-Up Window

To see the Mouse-Over Pop-Up Window example, go to Chapter 3's JavaScript Rollover3 folder on the CD-ROM and click on mouseover.htm.

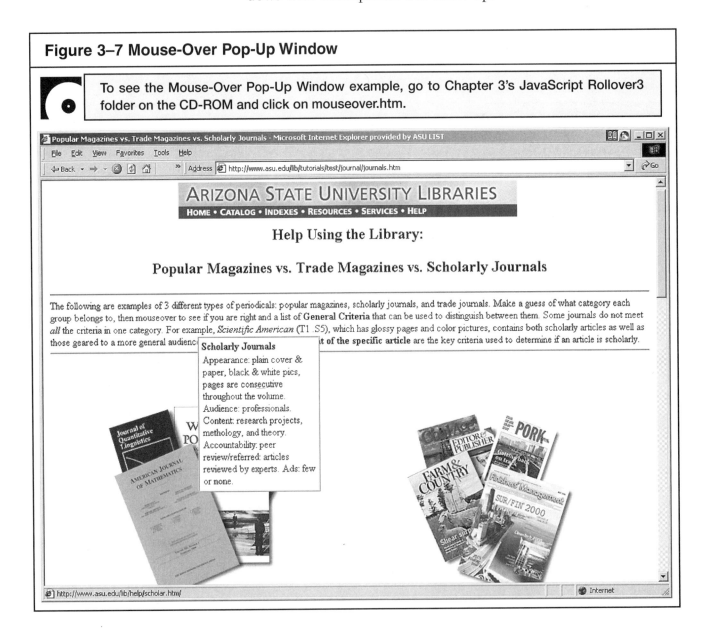

DYNAMIC DATE DISPLAY

JavaScript can create dynamic date display, which is a nice feature for a library homepage. Whenever the patrons enter your homepage, they will see the current date displayed. The following graphic is an example:

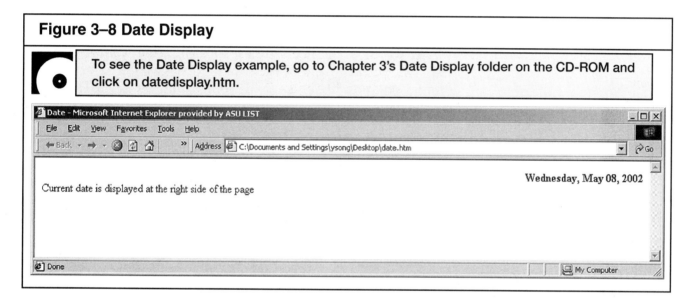

Figure 3–8 Date Display

To see the Date Display example, go to Chapter 3's Date Display folder on the CD-ROM and click on datedisplay.htm.

The JavaScript used is as follows:

```
<SCRIPT LANGUAGE ="Javascript">
// Array of day names
var dayNames = new
Array("Sunday","Monday","Tuesday","Wednesday","Thursday",
"Friday","Saturday");
// Array of month Names
var monthNames = new Array(
"January","February","March","April","May","June","July","August",
"September",
"October","November","December");
var now = new Date();
</SCRIPT>
```

In this set of code, "Array" is a holder of day names or month names. The browsers execute the command: var now = new Date(); and display the new date, which is represented by the time variables (date and month) right now.

CSS

WHAT IS CSS?

CSS (Cascading Style Sheets) is a flexible, cross-platform, standards-based language used to suggest stylistic or presentational features applied throughout entire Web sites. CSS are designed for setting up a "standard" that can be repeatedly used on a site. In other words, style sheets are used for sites that want to feature their style on each page of the site. In most cases, CSS are specified in a separate file and called from within the HTML header area when documents load into the CSS-enabled browser.

THE ADVANTAGES OF CSS

CSS provides a few advantages for Web developers:

- Better controls over typography and page layout
  CSS (Cascading Style Sheets) are designed for controlling style and layout of a Web page. With CSS, you can define traditional typography attributes such as font size, color, line spacing, letter spacing, indents, margins, element positioning, etc.
- Separation of style from structure
  Like a template, CSS makes it possible for designers to create a consistent look and feel for Web pages, while keeping the style separate from the content.
- Smaller file size
  Placing specifications once at the beginning of the HTML document instead of using tags such as <FONT> description for every individual element greatly reduced the number of characters in the document, thus cutting down the file size and reducing download time when one file has all the information on style.
- Easier site maintenance
  You can link multiple pages to a single style sheet, which means not only can you make one change that affects every instance of a particular element on the page, you can make style changes to hundreds of pages by editing a single CSS file. This makes a large library Web site more manageable.

CSS SYNTAX
Selector, Property, and Value

A style sheet is composed of style rules that provide information for a browser to present a file. Every rule has a selector—an HTML element such as BODY, or H1—and the style to be applied to the selector. Many properties can be defined for an element. Every property has a value, which along with the property, tells the browser how the selector should be presented. The CSS syntax is made up of three parts: a selector, a property, and a value:

```
selector {property: value}
```

The selector is normally the element/tag you want to specify, the property is the attribute you hope to change, and each property can take a value. The property and value are separated by a colon and surrounded by curly braces:

```
H1 {color: red}
```

The code above defines the color of the header element (H1) as red. With this definition, all the H1 headers in the HTML document will be in red. If you have more than one style declaration for a single selector, you can separate them by a semicolon:

```
selector {property1: value1; property2: value2; property3: value3}
```

Here is an example that shows how to define a center-aligned paragraph, with an Arial font and a black text color:

```
p {text-align: center; color: black; font-family: Arial}
```

Another example shows that you can define font size, weight, color, and background:

```
{font-size:110%; font-weight: bold; color:#0000ff; background-color: transparent}
```

Grouping

Selectors can be grouped. Separate each selector with a comma. In the following example we have grouped all the header elements in the document. Each header element will be red:

```
H1, H2, H3, H4, H5, H6 {color: red}
```

The Class Attribute

The class attribute helps you define different styles for the same element. Suppose you would like to have two types of paragraphs in your document: one right-aligned paragraph, and one left-aligned paragraph. With styles, you can easily do this:

```
P.right {text-align: right}
P.center {text-align: left}
```

You should use the class attribute in your HTML document:

```
<P class="right">
This paragraph will be right-aligned.
</P>
<P class="left">
This paragraph will be left-aligned.
</P>
```

For more details about CSS, check W3C's Web site at *www.w3c.org/style/CSS*. At this site you can find the CSS Specification, which defines all properties, attributes, and values.

HOW TO INSERT A STYLE SHEET

To let a style sheet work, you need to insert the style sheet in an HTML document. When a browser reads a style sheet, it will format the document according to it. There are three ways of inserting a style sheet.

External Style Sheet

An external style sheet is used when the style is applied to many pages. With an external style sheet, you can easily alter the feel and look of an entire Web site by changing one file. The HTML Version 4 defines that CSS can be put in the HEAD section of an HTML document or used as an external file. For an external file, you simply save the Style Sheet in a file with extension .css. You need to link each page to the style sheet using the <LINK> tag. The file is invoked from the header using that relative link in the same way as external JavaScript files:

```
<HEAD>
<LINK REL="stylesheet" type="text/css" HREF="stylesheet.css">
</HEAD>
```

The Web browser will read the style specifications from the file stylesheet.css, and format and display the document according to it.

Internal Style Sheet

An internal style sheet is used when a single document has a unique style. Internal styles are specified and inserted in the head section by using the <STYLE> tag, like this:

```
<HEAD>
<STYLE type="text/css">
HR {color: teal}
P {margin-left: 20px}
BODY {background-image: url("images/background.gif")}
</STYLE>
</HEAD>
```

Inline Styles

To use inline styles you use the style attribute in the relevant tag. The style attribute can contain any CSS property. The example shows how the style sheet changes the color and the left margin of a paragraph:

```
<P style="color: teal; margin-left: 20px"> This is a paragraph </P>
```

Another example is:

```
<H2 style="color:green"> This text is green</H2>
```

It is important to know that styles specified within a pair of tags can override any style in the header or an external style sheet.

MORE CSS EXAMPLES

There are many other things CSS can do. For instance, hyperlinks can be created without underline. To achieve this, you can use "text-decoration" property:

```
A:link {background: teal; color: yellow; text-decoration: none;}
```

You can create special effects to change the color of texts when moused over. One line of code does the trick:

```
<H2 onMouseOver="this.style.color='red'" onMouseOut="this.style.color='orange'">
```

You can highlight important text on your page or words you want to stand out, easily:

```
<SPAN STYLE="background-color:yellow">highlighted text</SPAN>
```

You can embed a background image that doesn't repeat:

```
<STYLE type="text/css">BODY {background: #ffffff url(bg.gif) no-
repeat}</STYLE>
```

You can also specify the location of the image, for example, center the background image. However, it will be centered as the background of the entire document, not centered on the screenful:

```
<STYLE type="text/css">BODY {background: #ffffff url(bg.gif) no-
repeat center}</STYLE>
```

Many library Web sites now use CSS. Here is an example of CSS in action. In the SunTutor site at Arizona State University Libraries, an external style sheet is used. Every page in this site links to tutorial.css file, which is referred to in the header section of the HTML page:

```
<HEAD>
<TITLE>SunTutor: Research Tutorial</TITLE>
<LINK REL="stylesheet" type="text/css" HREF="/lib/tutorials/
suntutor/tutorial.css">
</HEAD>
```

The CSS file: tutorial.css developed by Arizona State University Librarian Jenny Duvanay looks as follows:

```
BODY {background-color: #ffffff; font-family: Arial, Helvetica,
sans-serif}
Div.example{color: #336666; font-weight: bold}
A{color: #990033}
A:visited{color: #990066}
A:visited.nav{color: #ffffff}
A:visited.sidenav{color: #990033}
A:visited.bottomnav{color: #990033}
A:visited.foot{color: #990033}
A.test{color: #ffffff}
A.nav{color: #FFFFff; text-decoration: none}
A.sidenav{color: #990033; font-weight: bold; text-decoration:
none}
A.bottomnav{color: #990033; font-size: medium; font-weight:
bold}
A.foot{font-weight: bold; text-decoration: none}
H1, h2, h3, h4{color: #990033; font-family: Arial, Helvetica, sans-
serif}
P{font-family: Arial, Helvetica, sans-serif}
P.body{font-family: Arial, Helvetica, sans-serif}
P.nav{background-color: #cccccc}
P.sidenav{padding-left: 10px}
P.foot{font-size: small}
```

```
P.hint{background-color: #99ffcc;}
TD{font-family: Arial, Helvetica, sans-serif}
TD.left{background-color: #CC9999}
TD.sidenav{background-color: #990033; color: #FFffff; font-family:
Arial, Helvetica, sans-serif; font-size: x-small}
TD.nav{background-color: #990033; color: #ffffff; font-family: Arial,
Helvetica, sans-serif; font-size: small}
UL.sidenav{font-family: Arial, Helvetica, sans-serif; font-size:
small; margin-left: −15%}
UL{font-family: Arial, Helvetica, sans-serif}
Blockquote.example{color: #336666; font-weight: bold}
```

This set of code defines the appearance of the whole site by specifying page elements such as the font types and background colors for the side navigation, the bottom navigation, and the footer.
The pages on this site controlled by this style sheet look identical
and the appearance can be changed easily by altering the attributes
and values.

The graphic below is the SunTutor site.

Figure 3–9 CSS-Based Page: SunTutor of Arizona State University Libraries

 To see the CSS-Based Page example, go to Chapter 3's CSS-Based Page folder on the CD-
ROM and click on CSS_Based_ Page.htm.

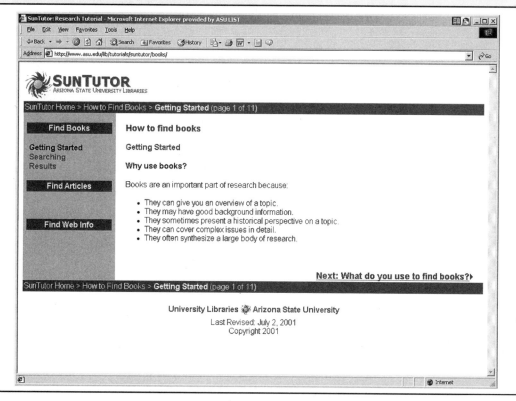

Another example for a CSS-based library Web site is "Milton Reading Room" at: *www.dartmouth.edu/research/milton/ reading_room/pl/note/index.html*. In this site, developers used CSS to help to add new values to the content: modern spelling has been coded in for every word that requires it. Passing the cursor over these words will produce a tiny window containing the modern spelling of the word.

The following is the regular code in the HTML file, which define the attributes and values for span class and title:

```
<P>
A fault <SPAN class="varspell" title="avoided">avoyded</SPAN>
by the learned Ancients both in Poetry and all good Oratory.
</P>
```

The CSS code hidden behind the scene specifies the function for recording modern spelling in title=" ":

```
.varspell {background-color: white;}
.title {text-align: center;}
```

It creates the window with the modern spelling "avoided" when you mouse over the old English word "avoyded."

Figure 3–10 CSS-Based Page: Milton Reading Room at Dartmouth College

To see this image onscreen, go to the subfolder FiguresChap 03 on the CD-ROM, then to the folder of Figures.

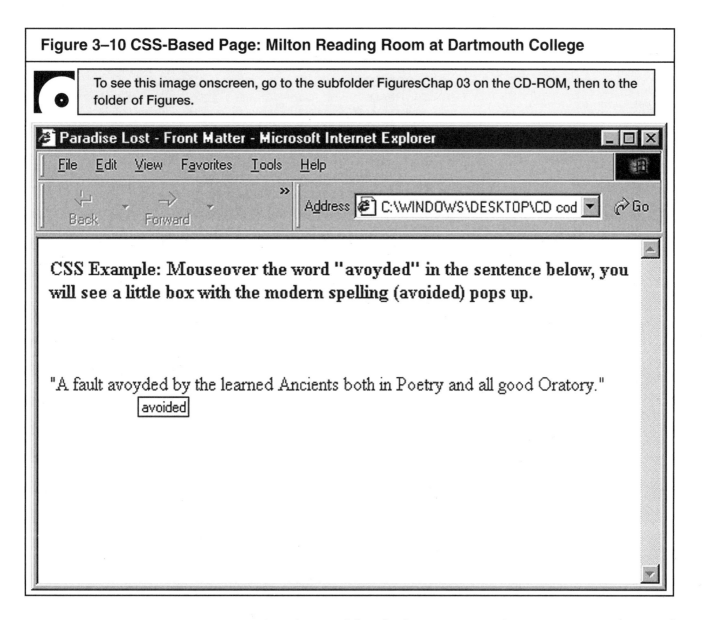

Another useful style sheet property that you can use to control how the background image scrolls on the Web page is the background-attachment property. This property has two settings: the scroll setting caused the background image to scroll along with the browser window. The fixed setting causes the background image to remain in its position when the browser window is scrolled. The code for a page with fixed background is as follows:

```
<HTML>
<HEAD>
<STYLE type="text/css">
BODY {background-image: url(asu.gif);
background-repeat: no-repeat; background-attachment: fixed}
```

```
</STYLE>
</HEAD>
<BODY>
<TABLE width="100%" border="0" cellpadding="1">
<TR>
<TD width="14%"></TD>
<TD width="52%">
<P>The fixed background attachment.</P>
<P>The fixed background attachment.</P>
</TD>
<TD width="34%"></TD>
</TR>
</TABLE>
</BODY>
</HTML>
```

 To see the Fixed Background Attachment example, go to Chapter 3's Background Attachment folder on the CD-ROM and click on background.htm.

The best way to learn CSS is to create a simple style sheet, change the variables in the sheet, and look at the results in the page. Then you will see how each CSS element functions. Generally speaking, style sheets offer great flexibility for Web designers. With the separation of content and presentation between HTML and style sheets, the Web developers have gained much control over the look and feel of Web pages. Although CSS is a very powerful tool, only Netscape 4 (or above) and Internet Explorer 4 (or above) support it. Older versions of Netscape or Internet Explorer display plain, unformatted text. If the text is wrapped up with a pair of regular HTML tags, the normal effects of the tags are what can be seen in the browser. Keep in mind some CSS can be used by either Internet Explorer or Netscape but not by both. So it is a good idea to use only standard CSS specified by World Wide Web Consortium.

DHTML

DHTML (Dynamic HTML) is a combination of a scripting language such as JavaScript, CSS (Cascading Style Sheets), and HTML. DHTML allows a Web page to change after it has been loaded in the browser, typically by relying on a combination of style sheets and scripts. In other words, we can change the HTML page while it is being displayed, and provide animated content to the viewer. It was the Microsoft Internet Explorer development team that developed DHTML first. Netscape was trying to catch up with its Netscape Version 4.

To understand DHTML, you should know something about Document Object Model (DOM). DOM is a structure containing objects displayed by a browser, such as forms, images, layers, etc. You can use this framework to access and manipulate what appears on your page. The DOM is nested inside the BOM (Browser Object Model: a holder of information about the user's system).

Our goal is to use DHTML to manipulate HTML elements such as paragraphs, tables, and hyperlinks. We need to employ a mechanism to refer to them. Being a container, the DOM stores information about each element in the currently loaded document. The BOM serves as a holder of information about the user's browser type, the location of the current document, the screen resolution, the history of the browser, the frame hierarchy, and so forth. As a component of DHTML, JavaScript is used to access and change the DOM during run-time. The following sections provide some examples of what DHTML can do.

SCROLLING TEXT

Scrolling text is produced with the change of the position of the text inside a DIV element. With DHTML and Dynamic Styles, you can change the values of these styles to move an element such as a chunk of text around in a cleanly cut container in your page.

```
<HTML>
<HEAD>
<TITLE>Scrolling Text</TITLE>
<SCRIPT>
sp=100;
function scroll() {
if (sp<-350) sp=100;
sp--;
scrolling_text.style.top=sp;
setTimeout('scroll()',50);
}
</SCRIPT>
</HEAD>
<BODY onload="scroll();">
<DIV
STYLE="position:absolute;overflow:hidden;top:100;left:100;width:100;
height:100;background-color:yellow">
```

```
<SPAN ID="scrolling_text"
STYLE="position:relative;top:100;left:0;width:100;height:100">

Now you can see a chunk of text scrolling in a container on the
screen. It is created with DHTML, namely, the merging of
JavaScript, Style Sheet, and regular HTML.

</SPAN>
</DIV>
</BODY>
</HTML>
```

There are two styles contained in the DIV element that define the
position of an element. They specify the position, the boundaries,
the background color, and the action of the element when its contents overflow the element boundaries. These two styles keep the
distance of the element from the top of the browser screen as
well as from the left of the browser screen.

The SPAN element, identified as scrolling_text, is positioned
relative to its DIV element. The coordinate system places (0,0) as
the top-left of the DIV element. The scrolling text is positioned
in the SPAN element. The scroll function decrements the scroll
position (sp), and then adjusts the relative position of the SPAN
element accordingly. This creates the movement, and the display
is within the defined container since any text overflows outside
the DIV element will not show up. The setTimeout function sets
time out for animation, and the scroll is repeated by detecting sp,
which is at the end of the text (sp=−350), and resetting it to the
beginning position of the text (sp=100).

Figure 3–11 Scrolling Text

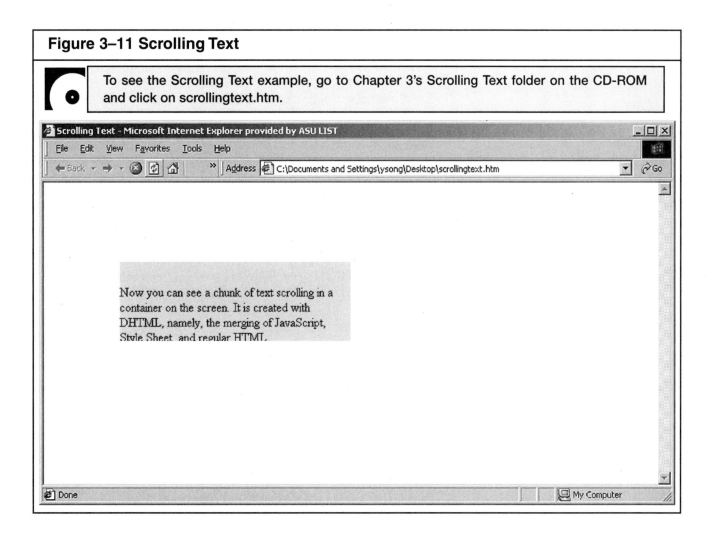

To see the Scrolling Text example, go to Chapter 3's Scrolling Text folder on the CD-ROM and click on scrollingtext.htm.

SELECT BOXES

You can use select boxes to alter their contents by making a choice. This example presents a radio box to decide the user's sex, and then asks for the TV channels they like most.

```
<HTML>
<HEAD>
<TITLE>TV Channels</TITLE>
<SCRIPT>
function change(s) {
switch (s) {
case 'm' : {
mySelect.options[0].value="TBS";
mySelect.options[1].value="ESPN";
mySelect.options[2].value="TNN";
mySelect.options[3].value="Golf";
```

```
break;
}
case 'f' : {
mySelect.options[0].value="Life Time";
mySelect.options[1].value="HGTV";
mySelect.options[2].value="AMC";
mySelect.options[3].value="Food";
break;
}
}
optiontext();
}
function optiontext() {
mySelect.options[0].innerText=mySelect.options[0].value;
mySelect.options[1].innerText=mySelect.options[1].value;
mySelect.options[2].innerText=mySelect.options[2].value;
mySelect.options[3].innerText=mySelect.options[3].value;
}
</SCRIPT>
</HEAD>
<BODY onload="optiontext();">
<INPUT TYPE="radio" NAME="sex" VALUE="m" CHECKED
onclick="change('m');">Male
<BR>
<INPUT    TYPE="radio"    NAME="sex"    VALUE="f"
onclick="change('f');">Female
<BR>
<SELECT SIZE="4" NAME="mySelect">
<OPTION VALUE="TBS" SELECTED>value</OPTION>
<OPTION VALUE="ESPN"></OPTION>
<OPTION VALUE="TNN"></OPTION>
<OPTION VALUE="Golf"></OPTION>
</SELECT>
</BODY>
</HTML>
```

In this set of code, the switch statement is used to differentiate between male or female. The radio buttons' onclick event handlers call a respective change() function. After the body is loaded, the optiontext() function is called, which uses innerText to fill the options box texts. Individual options of a select box is referred by using selectobject.options[index]. Here the selectobject is mySelect, while the mySelect.options[n].value refers to the value property of each chosen option.

Figure 3–12 Select Boxes 1

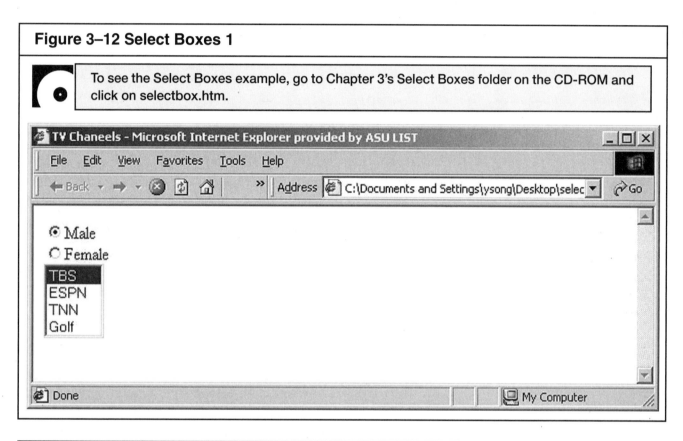

To see the Select Boxes example, go to Chapter 3's Select Boxes folder on the CD-ROM and click on selectbox.htm.

Figure 3–13 Select Boxes 2

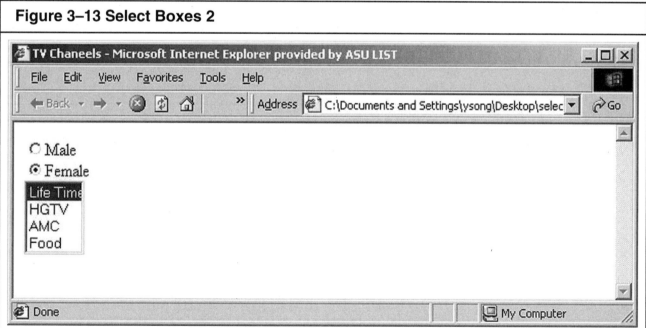

CHANGING FONT COLOR

You can use DHTML to change the color of the fonts.

```
<HTML>
<HEAD>
<TITLE>Font Color Change</TITLE>
<STYLE>
P {color:black}
</STYLE>
</HEAD>
<BODY>
<P onmouseover="style.color='red';" onmouseout="style.color=
'black';">Mouse over to change the color to red.</P>
<P onmouseover="style.color='blue';" onmouseout="style.color=
'black';"> Mouse over to change the color to blue.</P>
<P onmouseover="style.color='green';" onmouseout="style.
color='black';"> Mouse over to change the color to green.</P>
</BODY>
</HTML>
```

Move the mouse over the first line, you change its color to red, and when you leave the line, you will change the color to black. We refer to styles by referring to the style object of the element. Here style.color reads the color property of the style object of the P element.

To see the Changing Color example, go to Chapter 3's Changing Color folder on the CD-ROM and click on changecolor.htm.

CGI

WHAT IS CGI?

The Web has been dynamic from its inception. All of the queries to a search engine, a database, or a form submission use technologies behind the scenes for serving up dynamic content. CGI scripting provides supports for those features. CGI stands for Common Gateway Interface, which is designed for enhancing the interactivity on the Web. CGI provides an interactive interface between a user or an application and a Web server.

CGI is often used in forms. A user puts entries into text fields for either sending information or searching a database, then submits this information via his or her browser back to a host server. The host server calls up a CGI program, oftentimes located in a directory called "cgi-bin" on the Web server to process the information. The output of this program is then sent back to the client's browser. CGI usually executes one round trip from the user's browser to the host server and back again.

CGI scripts can be written in any programming language such as Perl, C, C++, Python, Tcl, and Visual Basic. But Perl has become a popular choice for CGI programming because it is available for all platforms. Perl has many useful tools that are ideal for the Web. Nearly all Web servers support Perl. Moreover, it is the easiest language to find examples. Comparatively speaking, Perl is easy to learn to modify. CGI is powerful, yet it has some drawbacks. Because it spawns a new program for each user request, it can be slow. Meanwhile, many requests sent at the same time can crush the server.

The majority of CGI scripts are written for specific purposes, but there are also CGI scripts for free public downloading on the Web. Many library Web developers download and modify those scripts to provide dynamic content on their sites (typically support for forms). However, for more advanced use of CGI, programming expertise is needed.

Many Web servers have standard CGI scripts already installed. All you have to do is to point to the CGI from your page. You can also upload to the server the scripts you customized or created to fulfill more complicated tasks.

There are quite a few Web sites offering free CGI scripts. They include detailed documentation that would help even the beginners to customize, configure, and install the scripts on the Web server. These Web sites are:

- Matt's Script Archive (*www.worldwidemart.com/scripts*)
- MU Perl and Perl CGI Materials (*www.cclabs.missouri.edu/things/instruction/perl*)
- Freescripts.com (*www.freescripts.com*)
- Selena Sol's Public Domain CGI Script Archive (*www.extropia.com/Scripts*)
- The CGI Resources Index (*www.cgi-resources.com*)

Before you run a CGI program, you need to check with your systems administrator about a few things:

- Are there CGI scripts on your server that meet your needs such as sending information via e-mail?
  (If you have them already on the server, you don't need to reinvent the wheel.)
- Does the server support the CGI of your choice?

- Do you have access to the cgi-bin directory?
  (For the access issue, you need the systems administrator to set up an account for you so that you can upload your script and make your CGI readable and executable by others. Most of the Web librarians may not be familiar with the servers and systems. It is important to cooperate with the systems administrator who is able to compile Web server software, configure, customize, install additional server components, and change file permissions.)
- What is the pathname of the script after it is installed?
  (You need to use this in the Action setting in a Web form to reference the CGI script.)
- What method, POST or GET, is used for transmitting form information?
  (GET and POST are two different methods defined in HTTP that do very different things, but both happen to be able to send form submissions to the server. POST has some advantages: you're unlimited in the data you can submit, and you can count on your script being called every time the form is submitted. One advantage of GET is that your entire form submission can be encapsulated in one URL, like for a hyperlink or bookmark. POST is more general-purpose, but GET is fine for small forms.)

HOW TO USE AVAILABLE CGI SCRIPTS

After you download CGI scripts, you need customization before installing and letting them run on your server. Upon downloading, you are given the script and also a detailed documentation that outlines step by step the process for using the script. You should read the documentation carefully before you configure and upload the script to your server. You need to create a Web page with a component to be executed by a CGI such as a form. You should define the "action" attribute as the URL of the CGI script on your server.

Now let's look at how to take advantage of the power of CGI by using one that is already made. In our example below, we are going to customize a Perl program and the form it executes. This Perl application below (form.pl) is a freeware developed by Steven E. Brenner (S.E.Brenner@bioc.cam.ac.uk). The program receives comment fields and e-mails them to a receiver. It has two parts. The first part will create a thank-you page in the form of an HTML page. The second part will e-mail information to the receiver.

To customize this program, you only need to change a few variables (highlighted in bold type in this example):

1. The pathname of the CGI on your server (in the first line of the script): **#!/usr/local/bin/perl**.
2. The user name: **$username="Yuwu Song."**
3. The pathname of your server's e-mail program: **"| /usr/lib/ sendmail-n-t."** It defines the location of your "sendmail" program on your server, which sends out the e-mail message.
4. The name of the e-mail receiver: **$username\@emailaddress\n**. You may change it into something like: **$yuwu.song\ @asu.edu\n**.
5. Variable names:
   From: $in{**'who'**}
   Email: $in{**'email'**}
   Rating: $in{**'rating'**}
   Found us: $in{**'how'**}
   We should add: $in{**'news'**}-$in{**'weather'**}-$in{**'photos'**}-$in{**'calendar'**}
   Comments: $in{**'comments'**}

When you change the variable names, you should also change the corresponding names in your HTML form.

Here is the CGI code. In this example, the words following the # sign is a brief description of what the line(s) of the code is (are) doing:

```
#!/usr/local/bin/perl
#Use the Perl interpreter in /usr/local/bin
$username="Yuwu Song";
&saythanks;        # Part I below
&mailstuff; # Part II below
#————————————————————-Part I
#Creates a thank you page in the form of an HTMLI page.
sub saythanks {
#Parses the incoming string of fields arguments end up in the
array $in{}
&ReadParse;
#Prints header to standard output ("screen"), this tells the browser
the file is of type html
print "Content-type: text/html", "\n\n";
#Prints out the html coding for the output page
#You may change the HTML coding between the "print" and the
"EOD" lines to whatever you like.
print <<EOD;
<HTML>
```

```
<HEAD>
<TITLE>Feedback Form</TITLE>
</HEAD>
<BODY bgcolor="#FFFFFF">
<FONT face="verdana, arial">Thank you for your feedback!<BR>
Your comments have been sent to us!<BR>
</FONT>
<HR>
<FONT face="verdana, arial">Back to our <A HREF=
"http://www.domain.library.org">Homepage</A></FONT>
</BODY>
</HTML>
EOD
}
#————————————————————————————-Part II
#E-mails info to the receiver
sub mailstuff {
open (MAIL, "| /usr/lib/sendmail-n-t");
#Sends out the email message.
print MAIL "From: $in{'email'}\n";
print MAIL "To: $username\@emailaddress\n";
#Change the lines between the "print" and "EOD" lines to reflect
the information you wish retrieved from the form and emailed to
you.
print MAIL<<EOD;
Subject: Comments on Library Services
From: $in{'who'}
Email: $in{'email'}
Rating: $in{'rating'}
Found us: $in{'how'}
We should add: $in{'news'}-$in{'weather'}-$in{'photos'}-
$in{'calendar'}
Comments: $in{'comments'}
EOD
#
close (MAIL);
}
# The following are Perl Routines to Manipulate CGI input
# Copyright 1994 Steven E. Brenner. Unpublished work.
# S.E.Brenner@bioc.cam.ac.uk full file: cgi-lib.pl
#ReadParse takes the data sent by the form and separates it
into fields, storing each field in the array %in
sub ReadParse {
 local (*in) = @_ if @_;
 local ($i, $loc, $key, $val);
 # Read in text
 if ($ENV{'REQUEST_METHOD'} eq "GET") {
 $in = $ENV{'QUERY_STRING'};
 } elsif ($ENV{'REQUEST_METHOD'} eq "POST") {
```

```
read(STDIN,$in,$ENV{'CONTENT_LENGTH'});
}
@in = split(/&/,$in);
foreach $i (0 .. $#in) {
# Convert plus's to spaces
$in[$i] =~ s/\+/ /g;
# Split into key and value.
($key, $val) = split(/=/,$in[$i],2); # splits on the first =.
# Convert %XX from hex numbers to alphanumeric
$key =~ s/%(..)/pack("c",hex($1))/ge;
$val =~ s/%(..)/pack("c",hex($1))/ge;
# Associate key and value
$in{$key} .= "\0" if (defined($in{$key}));
$in{$key} .= $val;
}
}
```

The following code is the corresponding form that this Perl program executes. It includes almost all the elements an HTML form contains: text fields, radio buttons, check boxes, and drop-down lists.

```
<FORM method="POST" action="http://www.domain/library/
form/cgi-bin/form.pl">
<UL>
<LI><FONT face="verdana, arial">Your name:
<INPUT type="TEXT" name="who" size="30" maxlength="30">
</FONT>
</LI>
<LI><FONT face="verdana, arial">Your email:
<INPUT type="TEXT" name="email" size="30" maxlength=
"30"></FONT>
</LI>
<LI><FONT face="verdana, arial">How would you rate this site?
<INPUT type="RADIO" name="rating" value="excellent"
>Excellent
<INPUT type="RADIO" name="rating" value="very good">Very
Good
<INPUT type="RADIO" name="rating" value="good">Good
<INPUT type="RADIO" name="rating" value="boring">Boring
</FONT>
</LI>
<LI><FONT face="verdana, arial">What would you like us to add?
<INPUT type="CHECKBOX" name="news" value="news">News
<INPUT type="CHECKBOX" name="weather" value="weather"
>Weather Updates <INPUT type="CHECKBOX" name="photos"
value="photos">Photos of our Staff <INPUT type="CHECKBOX"
name="calendar" value="calendar">Calendar</FONT>
```

```
</LI>
<LI><FONT face="verdana, arial">How did you find this site?
 <SELECT name="how">
<OPTION value="friend">A friend recommended it</OPTION>
<OPTION value="browsed">Surfed in from another site</OP-
TION>
<OPTION value="search">Via a search engine</OPTION>
<OPTION value="other">Other</OPTION>
</SELECT></FONT>
</LI>
<LI><FONT face="verdana, arial">Comments:
<TEXTAREA name="comments" cols="40" rows="5" wrap=
"virtual"></TEXTAREA></FONT></LI>
</UL>
<FONT face="verdana, arial">
<INPUT type="submit" value="Submit!">
<INPUT type="reset" name="Reset" value="Reset"></FONT>
</FORM>
```

The key part in the code is:

```
<FORM method="POST" action=http://www.domain/library/form/
cgi-bin/form.pl>
```

You should make sure that you include the proper pathname to the CGI script with the "action" attribute in the <FORM> tag. When you finish customizing the code, you can upload the program onto the cgi-bin directory. So it should be working. After the user clicks on the "Submit" button, the CGI program—form.pl sitting on the server will be called up. It processes the information sent by the user and delivers it to a specified mailbox.

Figure 3–14 CGI-Based Form

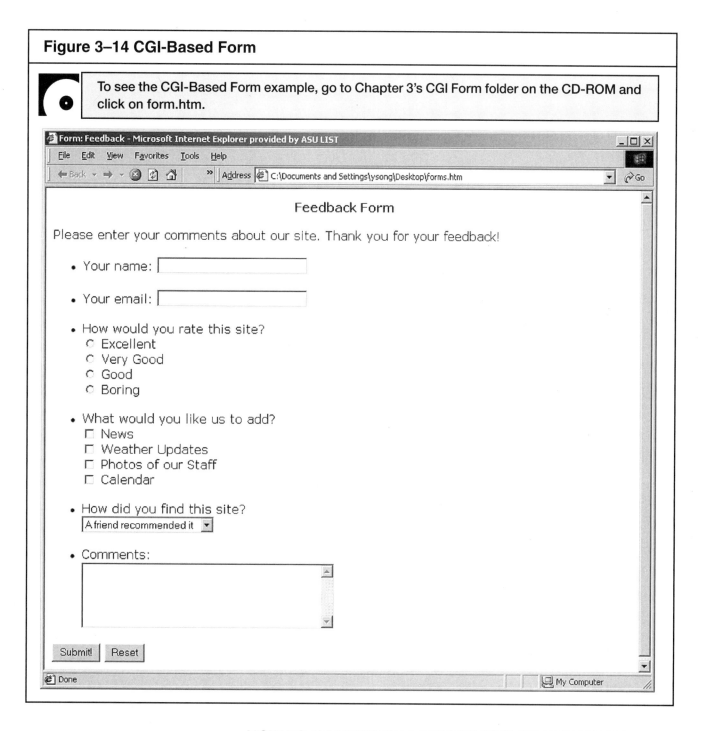

To see the CGI-Based Form example, go to Chapter 3's CGI Form folder on the CD-ROM and click on form.htm.

HOW TO MAKE YOUR LIBRARY SITE SEARCHABLE USING SWISH-E: A CGI-BASED PROGRAM

To make your library Web site searchable, you have to have a search engine. There are a few popular search engines such as

Google, Inktomi, and Alkaline. Here we are going to talk about SWISH-E used on Unix systems (SWISH-E for Windows NT systems are also available). SWISH-E stands for Simple Web Indexing System for Humans-Enhanced. Developed by Free Software Foundation, Inc., SWISH-E is a free CGI-based system for indexing and searching collections of Web pages. Two popular sites: The Berkeley Digital Library SunSITE and The Librarians' Index to the Internet both use SWISH-E. The program can be downloaded from *http://swish-e.org/*.

When indexing HTML files, SWISH-E can ignore data in most tags while giving higher relevance to information in header and title tags. Document titles are extracted from HTML files and show up in the search results. SWISH-E can automatically search your whole Web site in one pass, if it is under one directory. Moreover, you can narrow your search to words in HTML titles, comments, emphasized tags, and META tags.

To make SWISH-E work, you need to do four things. First, you need to create a configuration file. SWISH-E will read this configuration file to index your site. The next thing you should do is to run SWISH-E to index the site, in other words, to create an index file. The third thing to be done is to upload a CGI that will search the index file and return results. The last thing you need to do is to add a search form to your pages.

Let's look at the details of how SWISH-E works. The first step is to download (or copy) the following file to your own account from *www.cgi101.com/help/swish.conf*.

Once you download the file, you need to change three things in it:

- IndexDir /home/yourusername/public_html
- IndexFile /home/yourusername/public_html/swish.index
- IndexName "Site Index"

In other words, the paths to your Web directory should be fixed.

You have to replace/home/yourusername/public_html with the actual (full) path to your Web files.

After you have saved your conf file, you need to run SWISH-E to create the index file. SWISH-E will read the configuration file to determine which pages should (or should not) be indexed. This can be done from the Unix command line like:

```
/usr/local/bin/swish-e-c /home/yourusername/public_html/
swish.conf
```

If everything is fine, SWISH-E will create the index file at the location specified by the IndexFile directive in the conf file. Keep in mind, you will also have to use Unix command: chmod 644 to make swish.conf readable by your CGI. (For more details about Unix, check with your systems administrator or read a book on Unix.)

The next step is to upload a CGI to the cgi-bin directory on your server that will search the index file and return results. And here is the CGI to handle the actual search. The words after the "#" sign explain the functions of the code and the changes to be made:

```perl
#!/usr/bin/perl
# Kira's simple SWISH-E search CGI
use CGI::Carp qw(fatalsToBrowser);
# You'll need to change this to the document root of your
Webspace.
# for personal accounts, change it to /home/yourusername/
public_html.
# If you're running your own server, it should be the path to your
# document root for the server, e.g. /home/htdocs
$docroot = '/home/yourusername/public_html';
# This also must be changed; if you've used your personal ac-
count path
# above, you should change this to /~youruserid so the Webserver
can
# properly translate the URL for your files. For non-personal
pages,
# just set this to blank.
$prefix = '/~yourusername';
print "Content-type:text/html\n\n";
# customize this section as appropriate for your site
print <<EndHTML;
<html><head><title>Search Results</title></head>
<body>
<h2 align="CENTER">Search Results</h2>
EndHTML
read(STDIN, $buffer, $ENV{'CONTENT_LENGTH'});
@pairs = split(/&/, $buffer);
foreach $pair (@pairs) {
($name, $value) = split(/=/, $pair);
$value =~ tr/+/ /;
$value =~ s/%([a-fA-F0-9][a-fA-F0-9])/pack("C", hex($1))/eg;
$value =~ s/~!/ ~!/g;
$FORM{$name} = $value;
}
$keystring = $FORM{'keywords'};
if ($keystring =~ /^([\w\-\. ]+)$/ ) {
```

```perl
$topic = $1;
} else {
&dienice("Bad keyword: '$topic'. Please don't use commas or
non-alphanumeric characters.");
}
@results = '/usr/local/bin/swish-e-w "$topic"-f /home/
yourusername/public_html/swish.index';
$ct = 0;
foreach $i (@results) {
# results are returned in the form:
# relevance path title filesize
# separated by spaces.
# comments start with #, and the last line starts with a ., so we're
#ignoring those:
if ($i =~ /^#/ or $i =~ /^\./) {
# errors start with 'err', so we'll pass those on to dienice:
} elsif ($i =~ /^err/) {
$i =~ s/^err/Error/;
&dienice($i);
#
} else {
($start, $title, $size) = split(/\"/,$i);
($perc, $url) = split(/ /,$start);
$perc = $perc / 1000 * 100;
$percstr = sprintf("%3.1f\%",$perc);
# since the "url" returned is really the full unix path to the file,
# you need to translate this to a proper Web url. Change the
docroot
# and prefix variables as described above.
$url =~ s/^$docroot/$prefix/;
print "<a href=\"$url\">$title</a>—$percstr <br>\n";
$ct = $ct + 1;
}
}
if ($ct == 0) {
print "No results found.<p>\n";
}
&do_footer;
sub do_footer {
# customize this section as appropriate for your site
print <<EndFoot;
<p>
$ct results found.<p>
</body>
</html>
EndFoot
}
sub dienice {
my($msg) = @_;
```

```
print "<h2>Error</h2>\n";
print $msg;
&do_footer;
exit;
}
# the end.
```

Once you make changes to the CGI file and upload it to your server, you need to add the following form to your Web pages:

```
<FORM ACTION="http://www.librarydomain/cgi-bin/search.cgi"
METHOD="POST">
<INPUT TYPE="text" name="keywords" size=30>
<INPUT TYPE="submit" VALUE="Search">
</FORM>
```

Now your library Web site should be searchable.

On the whole, the arcane CGI code seems to be overwhelming. But there is still something you can figure out using your common sense without in-depth knowledge of the language. Compared with the field variables above, most of CGI script is too complicated to understand without some basic understanding of the language. A detailed explanation of it requires at least one whole chapter, which is beyond the scope of this book. If you really want to understand the nuts and bolts of CGI and Perl in order to use more advanced features of the technology, read *Creating a Power Web Site* by Gail Junion-Metz and Brad Stephens. In this book there are detailed discussions about the use of CGI technology in a library setting. You may also want to check with your library systems administrator about how to download, configure, and run CGI programs on your servers.

4 DESIGNING WEB GRAPHICS

The World Wide Web is a visually based component of the Internet. Because people are more visually oriented, the use of graphics is an enormous part of what makes the Web so appealing. To some extent, a Web site is like an electronic brochure. Setting up an attractive library Web site also requires some good-looking images and a sense of graphical design. Graphics not only enhance the page, but they characterize that library and help to tell the library's story by illustrating different types of resources and services, or by providing a virtual library tour. In a library site, graphics can be used as background, mastheads, seals, logos, pictures, or drawings of the library. They can also be used as navigational icons such as Home, Previous Page, Next Page, Back, clickable Imagemaps, and so on. Another type of graphics is library-related illustrations: library maps, floor plans, shelving diagrams, etc. In addition, animations and 3D graphics may help make your library site more attractive.

One can create images in several ways, for instance, with a digital camera, by scanning an image, or creating one with a painting or drawing program. Because of the bandwidth problem, developers should try to make image files smaller so that downloading time can be short. The best solution is to find a way to optimize download speed for Web graphics without compromising quality.

FORMATS

Generally speaking, there are two graphic types: bitmap and vector. Each of these types has its own graphic formats. Bitmap graphics include GIF, JPEG, Photoshop, PCX, TIFF, Macintosh Paint, Microsoft Paint, BMP, and PNG. The bitmap graphic programs used by the majority of Web developers are Adobe Photoshop, Macromedia Fireworks, and JACS Paintshop Pro. Bitmap graphic is also called raster graphic. It is a graphic image represented by pixel data, which define a specific arrangement of colors of the screen dots. If you enlarge a bitmap graphic, you will see that the graphic is formed by little squares.

Figure 4–1 Bitmap Image

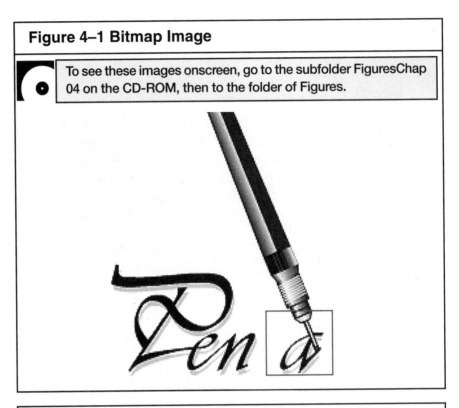

To see these images onscreen, go to the subfolder FiguresChap 04 on the CD-ROM, then to the folder of Figures.

Figure 4–2 Bitmap Image Enlarged

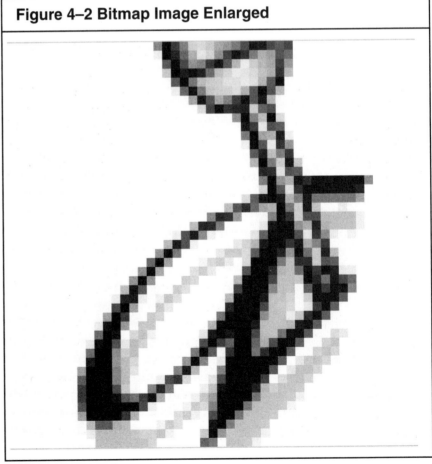

Vector graphics refer to images created in shapes and lines, called paths. The files of vector graphics are comparatively small while the quality is very good. The most popular vector graphic programs are Adobe Illustrator, Macromedia Freehand, and Macromedia Flash. If you enlarge a vector graphic, you will see that the graphic's edge is as smooth as it is before. Vector-based images and animations retain high quality even though they change shape from time to time.

Figure 4–3 Vector Image

To see this image onscreen, go to the subfolder FiguresChap 04 on the CD-ROM, then to the folder of Figures.

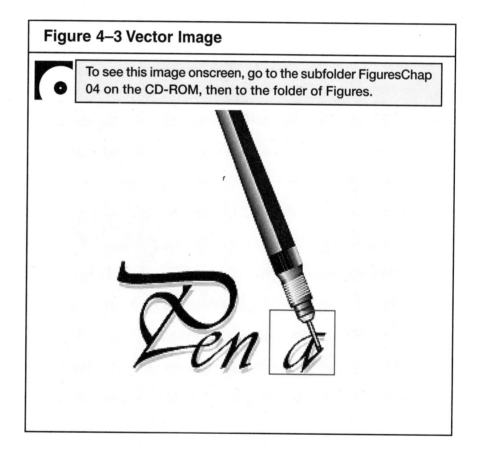

Figure 4–4 Vector Image Enlarged

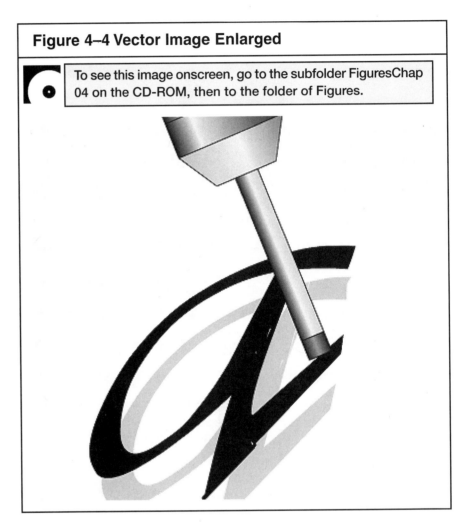

To see this image onscreen, go to the subfolder FiguresChap 04 on the CD-ROM, then to the folder of Figures.

The major bitmap image formats used on the Web include GIF, JPEG (JPG), and PNG. GIF stands for Graphics Interchange Format. GIF is one of the two most popular Web graphic file formats. GIF images display up to 256 colors. It is the best format for illustrated graphics such as background tiles, banner ad graphics, line art, and icons. With line art, a GIF may appear sharper while keeping a smaller size than a JPEG since there is no loss of quality in GIF format. But GIF images can only show a limited range of colors, and may not be good for color photographs.

JPEG means Joint Photographic Experts Group. It is the preferred format for full-color and black-and-white graphic images. Graphics in this format allow for more colors than GIF images. Usually JPEG is used for smoothly varying images such as photos, gradated graphics, images with lots of colors and fine detail, or scanned images. These two formats support options for progressive rendering where a crude version of the image is sent first and progressively refined. The best way to find which format is appropriate is to try both compression techniques for each of your graphics and see which renders the smallest file size and the best image quality.

PNG refers to Portable Network Graphics. Pronounced as "ping," it is used for lossless compression and displaying Web images. PNG supports images with millions of colors. PNG can create background transparency with no jagged edges. Like GIF, PNG is good for graphics art involving flat areas of color, lines, and text. The cons are that older browsers do not support PNG, and PNG's file size is bigger than that of JPEG and GIF.

Besides the formats mentioned above, SVG is a potential competitor of GIF, JPEG, and PNG. SVG stands for Scalable Vector Graphics, which, like Macromedia Flash, uses vectors to describe a form. Its major distinction from Flash is that SVG is based on XML. This would certainly guarantee the uniformity of the graphics on media and different kinds of screens. The revolution in wireless communication enabled people to browse the Web using a handheld device. The growth of the Web means that Web pages must be suitable for display on other media types such as cell phones. SVG is exactly what the portable device needs because SVG files are small, it can be displayed on all media quickly. Moreover, it is text based, and the illustrations can be indexed. The vector-based files guarantee high-resolution prints as well. On the whole SVG represents the future of the Web graphics.

Putting an image online is easy. All you have to do is to use the <IMG> tag. Suppose you have an image file called "mypicture.jpg" in the same folder/directory as your HTML file. It is 200 pixels wide by 150 pixels high. You embed the image file using the code:

```
<IMG SRC="mypicture.jpg" WIDTH="200" HEIGHT="150">
```

In the code above, the IMG SRC (image source) attribute names the image file. The WIDTH and HEIGHT attributes define the size of the image to be displayed on your Web page. For people who don't want to see or can't see the image, you need to put a description so that they can read it in absence of the image. You can add a short description as follows using ALT (alternate) attribute:

```
<IMG SRC="mypicture.jpg" WIDTH="200" HEIGHT="150"
ALT="My Picture">
```

When the browser reads the code, it will display the ALT description, "My Picture." For complex images, you can give a longer description using the LONGDESC attribute and an HTML file:

```
<IMG SRC="mypicture.jpg" WIDTH="200" HEIGHT="150"
ALT="My Picture" LONGDESC = "mypicture.html">
```

COMPRESSION

Compression is a technology for reducing the size of an actual file. By this technology, image data is scaled down in size, consuming less storage space and requiring a narrower bandwidth or shorter download time. Compression algorithms will re-encode your graphic file's data into a smaller, more compact chunk of the same data. This usually works best with GIFs and JPEGs.

There are two kinds of compression: lossy compression and lossless compression. Lossy compression is a technique used to make file sizes smaller by casting away some pixel information or details from the original and uncompressed images or videos. By reducing the quality of a video or a picture when you save it, you can shrink the file size. JPEG is a good example for lossy compression. A JPEG compresses to a smaller file than a GIF, taking less time to download, but it takes longer to decompress and display. Lossless compression is a technique that does not rely on omission of pixels from the original and uncompressed images or videos. This technique is used for GIF images.

Theoretically, lossy compression should lead to unnoticeable loss of image quality. But in reality, JPEG compression imposes a loss of image quality, which may be quite noticeable (depending on the settings in your image conversion program, and your visitor's hardware). Tools like Adobe Photoshop, ImageReady, and DeBabelizer can help you to reduce image file size by compression.

WEB GRAPHICS TOOLS

ADOBE PHOTOSHOP

Adobe Photoshop is the most popular graphics program with Web developers. This program allows designers to create original artwork, correct color, retouch, and composite scanned images. Photoshop provides powerful painting and selection tools. It also has features such as multiple layers, special effects filters, lighting effects, etc. Besides creating buttons and graphics, you can use Photoshop to create the Web page layout. All you should do is to begin in Photoshop with a new project at 640 x 480, or your desired resolution target. Draw out everything in the whole front page of the Web site such as menus, buttons, header graphics, text spaces, and so on. It ought to look like what you want the

Web page to look on the Web. You'd better create a new layer for all the important elements of the page because you can change and move them around easily. When you are drawing all the components, you can plan the coding in your mind.

Figure 4–5 Photoshop Working Environment

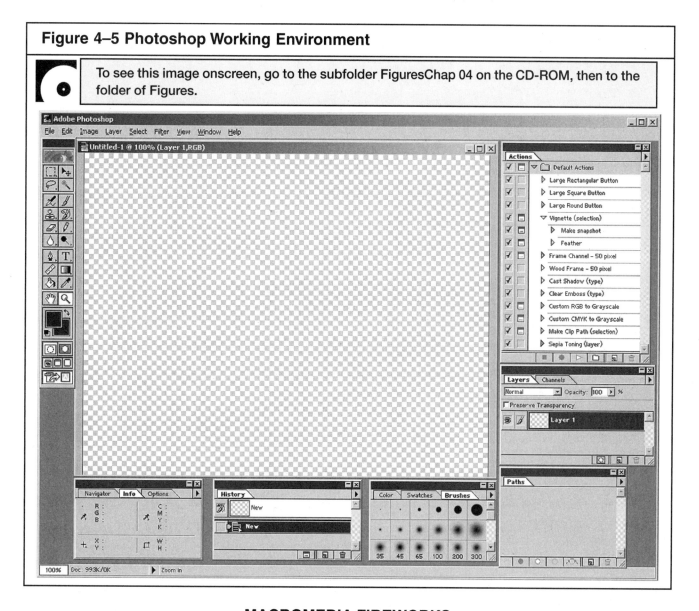

MACROMEDIA FIREWORKS

Macromedia Fireworks is designed especially for Web graphics creation. It has similar features as Photoshop. One advantage over Photoshop is that it allows you to move individual elements around in a single layer. Instead of selecting a layer and moving the element in that layer, you just highlight the element and move it.

Figure 4–6 Fireworks Working Environment

To see this image onscreen, go to the subfolder FiguresChap 04 on the CD-ROM, then to the folder of Figures.

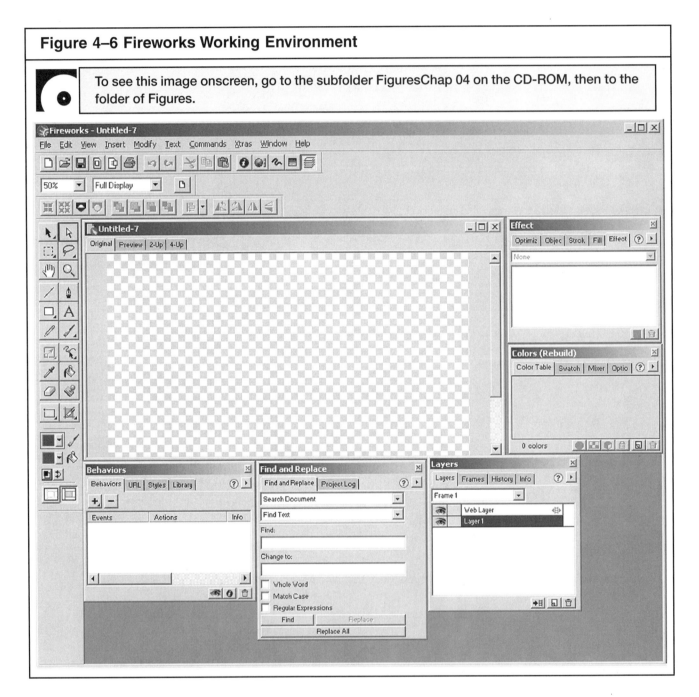

JACS PAINTSHOP PRO

JACS Paintshop Pro is the least expensive program yet quite powerful. Its graphics tools are similar to those of Photoshop and Fireworks. One neat feature is that you can capture part of a screen shot by dragging and dropping a specified area within the window onto the program and do editing.

ADOBE ILLUSTRATOR

Illustrator is designed for vector graphics creation. It is especially good for charts, tables, and graphics for statistics presentation.

Figure 4–7 Adobe Illustrator Working Environment

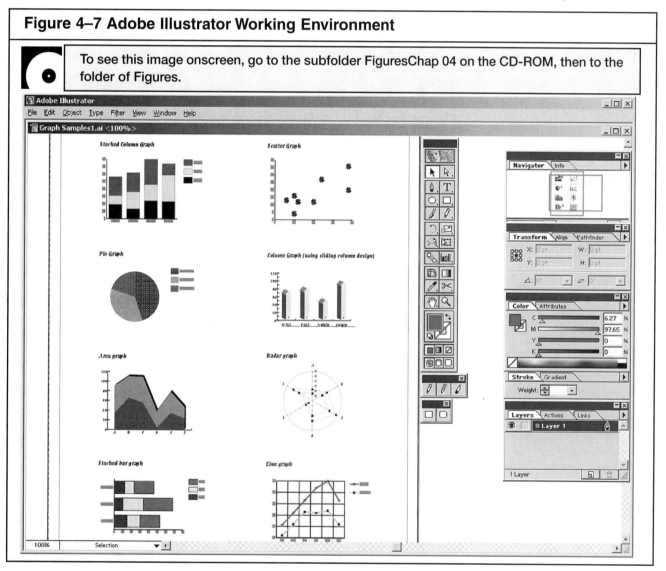

To see this image onscreen, go to the subfolder FiguresChap 04 on the CD-ROM, then to the folder of Figures.

RULES FOR REDUCING DOWNLOADING TIME

Graphics carry much more information than text, so a screenful of graphics comes up considerably slower than a screenful of text. Web sites that are optimized for slower connections are being rewarded with higher volumes of traffic. For the time being, many companies and educational institutions use T1 or faster connections; however, the general browsing public is connected via modem-based SLIP and PPP connections. For graphics of huge size, loading time is so long that the users with 28.8 or slower modem connections would just turn away. As with every aspect of Web development, you are dealing with tradeoffs, which typically pit content against performance. You have to find a way to skimp on your page size without sacrificing quality. The following are some general rules and tips for handling graphics.

REDUCE THE NUMBER OF GRAPHICS

No matter how great your graphics look, they should not overpower the page. Putting graphics on a page is like putting makeup on your face—you ought to bear in mind that there is a time when you have to stop. Avoid using graphics where text will do the job. Bear in mind that huge chunky headings are redundant graphics. Try to keep them simple and small. Try to keep all the graphics in one page under 50K in file size.

REUSE GRAPHICS

You can also reuse graphics if there is more than one page. Most browsers can cache images, which means the browsers will download and keep a copy of the images on the computer's hard drive or RAM. Once an image is cached, that image is available to be reused. So if a button graphic is used to represent the forward button, then that same graphic should be used for the same function on every page on the site. You should put the button image file in an image folder on your server and have all the pages that need the forward button linked to the image file in that folder. In this way, you can save time on downloading. The consistent use of a graphic such as a button will also allow users to recognize that graphic and know what a particular image will do on every page.

MINIMIZE THE NUMBER OF COLORS

For GIFs, you can reduce the number of colors. This can make the size of the graphics smaller. To make sure your graphics look the same on different computers, you should use a 216/256 color palette in your graphic programs.

Figure 4–8 216 Web Safe Colors

To see this image onscreen, go to the subfolder FiguresChap 04 on the CD-ROM, then to the folder of Figures.

00FFFF	00FFCC	00FF99	00FF66	00FF33	00FF00
00CCFF	00CCCC	00CC99	00CC66	00CC33	00CC00
0099FF	0099CC	009999	009966	009933	009900
0066FF	0066CC	006699	006666	006633	006600
0033FF	0033CC	003399	003366	003333	003300
0000FF	0000CC	000099	000066	000033	000000
33FFFF	33FFCC	33FF99	33FF66	33FF33	33FF00
33CCFF	33CCCC	33CC99	33CC66	33CC33	33CC00
3399FF	3399CC	339999	339966	339933	339900
3366FF	3366CC	336699	336666	336633	336600
3333FF	3333CC	333399	333366	333333	333300
3300FF	3300CC	330099	330066	330033	330000
66FFFF	66FFCC	66FF99	66FF66	66FF33	66FF00
66CCFF	66CCCC	66CC99	66CC66	66CC33	66CC00
6699FF	6699CC	669999	669966	669933	669900
6666FF	6666CC	666699	666666	666633	666600

Figure 4–8 *(Continued)*

6633FF	6633CC	663399	663366	663333	663300
6600FF	6600CC	660099	660066	660033	660000
99FFFF	99FFCC	99FF99	99FF66	99FF33	99FF00
99CCFF	99CCCC	99CC99	99CC66	99CC33	99CC00
9999FF	9999CC	999999	999966	999933	999900
9966FF	9966CC	996699	996666	996633	996600
9933FF	9933CC	993399	993366	993333	993300
9900FF	9900CC	990099	990066	990033	990000
CCFFFF	CCFFCC	CCFF99	CCFF66	CCFF33	CCFF00
CCCCFF	CCCCCC	CCCC99	CCCC66	CCCC33	CCCC00
CC99FF	CC99CC	CC9999	CC9966	CC9933	CC9900
CC66FF	CC66CC	CC6699	CC6699	CC6633	CC6600
CC33FF	CC33CC	CC3399	CC3366	CC3333	CC3300
CC00FF	CC00CC	CC0099	CC0066	CC0033	CC0000
FFFFFF	FFFFCC	FFFF99	FFFF66	FFFF33	FFFF00
FFCCFF	FFCCCC	FFCC99	FFCC66	FFCC33	FFCC00

Figure 4–8 *(Continued)*

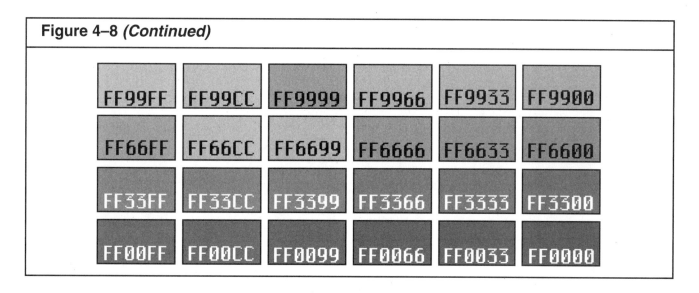

For color palette indexed formats such as GIF and PNG, always remember that the lower the bit depth, the smaller the file. If you use 640 x 480 24-bit color images, you will need about 900K of disk space, which is too big for even those who use cable connection for loading files. Most of the computers support 16-bit or higher color depths, however, people using the old 8-bit machines will see your subtle color gradations as dithering chunks of color. To avoid these problems and make sure your graphics look the same on different computers, you need to do all your work in a 256-color palette in your graphics programs. The 256 colors are considered to be Web safe. When you use your graphics applications, remember to check the color adjustment settings to reduce image file sizes. Image applications such as Adobe Illustrator, Adobe Photoshop, JACS Paintshop Pro, and Macromedia Fireworks include tools that can help you with the color palettes, and other features, which allow you to optimize your graphic's file size without losing its quality.

Figure 4–9 Photoshop Interface: Optimizing Graphics File Size

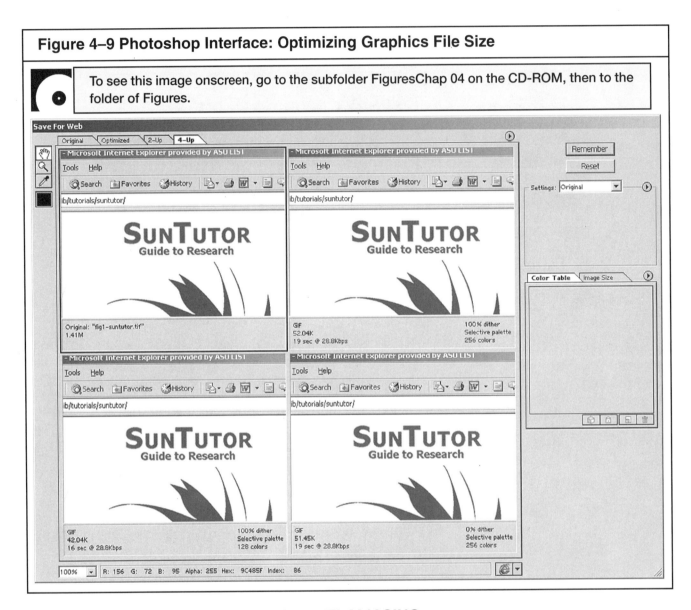

To see this image onscreen, go to the subfolder FiguresChap 04 on the CD-ROM, then to the folder of Figures.

USE OF ANTI-ALIASING

You can minimize jagged edges on graphics through anti-aliasing, a process that creates the visual effect of smooth edges between contrasting colors. You can do this by mixing the colors of the border pixels into two or more interim colors. Most image applications have this feature.

REDUCE ANIMATION

Animated graphics take longer to download than normal graphics. Use them cautiously.

PRELOADING GRAPHICS

For pages that require the users to navigate sequentially such as an online guide, you can preload the graphics of the next page on the current page and show them as 1 pixel x 1 pixel graphics at the bottom of the page. These graphics cannot be seen on the current page. When the viewers read the current page, the graphics are being loaded without being noticed. Once they go to the next page, the graphics should show up right away because they have been downloaded and stored on the user's machine.

USE OF ALTERNATE TEXT

While an image is loading in the browser, you can provide text indicating what the image contains by using the attribute ALT: <ALT= "text">. Browsers usually display a box the size of your graphic containing only your ALT text while downloading the image. You can use alternate text to engage your users. The alternate text will give them something to read while waiting.

USE OF INTERLACED GIFS

Interlaced GIFs allow the users to see a low-resolution version loading first. Then they will see the image displayed in growing degrees of resolution. Interlaced GIF files are a bit larger than that of regular GIFs, however, they provide your visitors with something to look at while being loaded. Use this technique cautiously. Some think the effect is annoying and it is hard to tell when the picture is actually ready to be viewed.

USE OF LOW RES ATTRIBUTE

You may want to create a low-resolution version of your graphic and use the "LOW RES" attribute in the image element. What happens is that the low-resolution version of your graphics will be downloaded before the loading of the image with higher resolutions. This is helpful when you have high quality full-color JPEG images or big Imagemaps to put on your page.

THUMBNAIL

For an online picture gallery, or things of that nature, you can use thumbnails. A thumbnail is a smaller version of a graphic. Usually a link connects the thumbnail to the larger version. By taking a glance at the thumbnail, the user can determine if the graphic with more detail is worth seeing.

WARNINGS

Let your users know how big the image sizes are by giving them a warning such as "This graphic is 100 K and may take more than 30 seconds to download for slower connection."

TEXT COLOR AGAINST BACKGROUND COLOR

For those using a dark background image and light color text, it is better to make the background color similar to the dark background image by defining the background color in the BODY element. Browsers show your text on the default gray background color while loading your background image. Since your text color is light, the users have to wait for the background image to load before they can read your text. If you make your background color dark, they can read it straight away.

IMAGE SLICING

Big, complex graphics for Web pages can produce large files, which take a long time to download over the Internet. However, often these large graphics contain areas of flat color or little detail. To reduce the amount of data to download you can slice the image into sections, which can be downloaded separately. In other words, one image can be divided into smaller parts that are reassembled on a page within HTML tables (you have to set table borders to zero). The advantage is that areas of flat color or little detail can be saved at a lower quality (as a 2-color GIF) than complex areas, which can be saved at a higher resolution. The 2-color GIF file takes less time to download, but it means you can still have high detail areas within your image. There are two potential disadvantages to this approach: the browser has to understand <IMG BORDER> tags to create a seamless image, and there will be more load on your Web server due to additional requests. If the online traffic is busy, a Web server may not bring back all the pieces.

To do slicing, you can draw your guides, merging layers, and cutting up the images in Photoshop. Then open them in ImageReady and optimize them there. An editor like Dreamweaver can write the HTML and JavaScript that puts the slices together. Software such as ImageReady can automatically segment design pages into graphics, HTML, and JavaScript code. You can also use Fireworks to slice and save the images for you. Fireworks can write all the necessary HTML code, so you can just copy it into your Web page.

Figure 4–10 Image Slicing in Fireworks

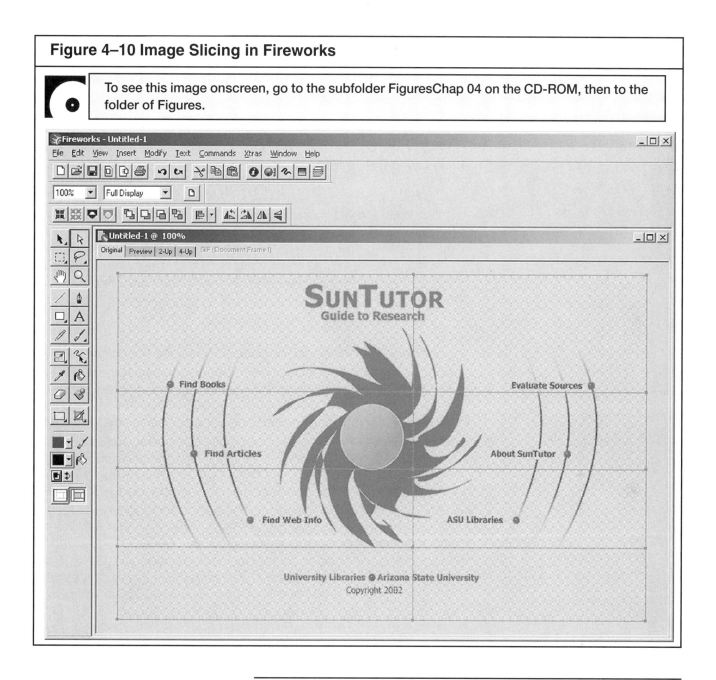

To see this image onscreen, go to the subfolder FiguresChap 04 on the CD-ROM, then to the folder of Figures.

BACKGROUND IMAGES AND COLORS ON LIBRARY WEB PAGES

You can use any graphics programs to create background images. Some graphics programs can make seamless tiles; in other words, the join between tiles should be indiscernible. For a left-border effect, you may want to create a graphic about 16 hundred pixels (most monitors are not that wide) wide and 5 pixels tall. If you create a graphic 10 hundred pixels wide, and the computer screen is wider than 10 hundred pixels, the background image would tile horizontally.

There are some design considerations regarding background images. Using Web safe colors is very essential. Some pages cannot be read because of the color choice. Bear in mind that computers of individual users are different from that of the designer.

Also keep in mind that too elaborate a background image makes the text unreadable. Sometimes a plain color behind the text is the best choice. You also need to consider that some users turn the image loading off. For these viewers, if you define a background color similar to your background image color, the page will still look close to what you want them to see. Selection of a background color is a kind of art. Looking at other people's sites will give you some ideas of what a good Web site background color is.

Although the majority of designers believe that no color is the best color, the selection of colors depends on the nature and content of your site. For an academic library Web site, a plain background color or image is good enough, while for kids' library Web sites, even a flamboyantly colored background can be justified.

Remember that text and images should contrast well with the background color. When you use images on your site, try to avoid using high-quality images such as art or photographs against a textured, dark, or lively colored background. Use white, a light shade of gray, or beige. You should stick with the same background, because it reduces download or reload time, especially since the browser will cache the background. The background serves as a continuity signpost. Keeping the same background on all of the pages on the site sends an easy message to the visitors that they are on your site.

To define the text color, background color, and background image on your page, you can use the code below:

```
<BODY BACKGROUND = "background.gif"
BGCOLOR= "#000000"
TEXT= "#ffcc66"
LINK= "#ffff99"
VLINK= "#ffcc33"
ALINK= "#ff0000">
```

The BODY tag has a BACKGROUND attribute to define the URL of a graphic, which is used as a background for the document. The image will be tiled as the background of the page. In the case when users turn the image loading off, the BGCOLOR will also be used, which, if specified similar to your image color, will make the page look like your intended color. LINK= "#ffff99" VLINK= "#ffcc33" ALINK= "#ff0000" define the color of the link in original, visited, and active state, respectively. It is important that the colors of links in different states also match that of a background or a background image.

IMAGEMAPS

WHAT ARE IMAGEMAPS?

Imagemaps refer to graphics that launch certain actions, leading the users to specified pages when clicked on in certain areas. In other words, an Imagemap is an image on the Web that leads to multiple links, depending on which part of the image one clicks. For example, you might have an image representing a library on your homepage, with a "book shelf" image that when clicked links the user to a page that represents the book section in the library. Clicking the reference desk image might take users to another page representing the reference section, and so on. Imagemaps are useful, but you should be careful when you use them. Some Web users are not familiar with graphical icons; they may not even know that they need to click on the image to get to certain sections in a page. So it might be necessary in some cases to put descriptive terms beside or on these graphics. For example: "Help" beside a question mark, "CDs" beside the CD-ROM symbol, or "Sports Books" beside a football.

There are two kinds of Imagemaps: server-side and client-side. They allow you to change a portion of a graphic into a clickable area or hotspot defined by coordinates. The server-side Imagemap is CGI script-based and more complicated because you need a Web-server package with Imagemap support built in. Each time you click the Imagemap, you make a request to the server, which will compare the defined coordinates to a list of anchor points in the map definition file and direct the browser to the designated Web page. Client-side Imagemaps are built in the HTML documents. In other words, the map definition is described right in an HTML document (not a CGI script) and interpreted locally by the browser without calling up the server. These Imagemaps function the same way their script-based counterparts do. There is no doubt that the client-side Imagemaps is the way of the future.

The following is an Imagemap example from the homepage of Arizona State University Libraries. The graphic buttons are images, which serve as links.

Figure 4–11 Imagemap: Arizona State University Libraries

To see the Imagemap example, go to Chapter 4's Imagemap folder on the CD-ROM and click on Imagemap.htm.

The code for the client-side Imagemap in the homepage of ASU Libraries is as follows. You can see how the coordinates are specified to define the positions of the hot spots.

```
<MAP name="bar-f">
<AREA shape="rect" alt="Online Catalog" coords="62,0,130,18"
href= "http://catalog.lib.asu.edu">
<AREA shape="rect" alt="Indexing and Abstracting Databases"
coords=
"136,0,199,18" href="/lib/resources/indexabs.htm">
<AREA shape="rect" alt="Library Resources" coords=
"206,0,287,18" href=
"/lib/resources/resources.htm">
<AREA shape="rect" alt="Library Services" coords=
"294,0,362,18" href=
"/lib/resources/services.htm">
<AREA shape="rect" alt="Help using the Library" coords=
```

```
"369,0,410,18" href= "/lib/help/help.htm">
<AREA shape="default" nohref>
</MAP>
```

Imagemaps can also be used for library floor plans or maps of library locations. The following are some examples.

Figure 4–12 Imagemap: A Floor Plan of Arizona State University Libraries

To see this image onscreen, go to the subfolder FiguresChap 04 on the CD-ROM, then to the folder of Figures.

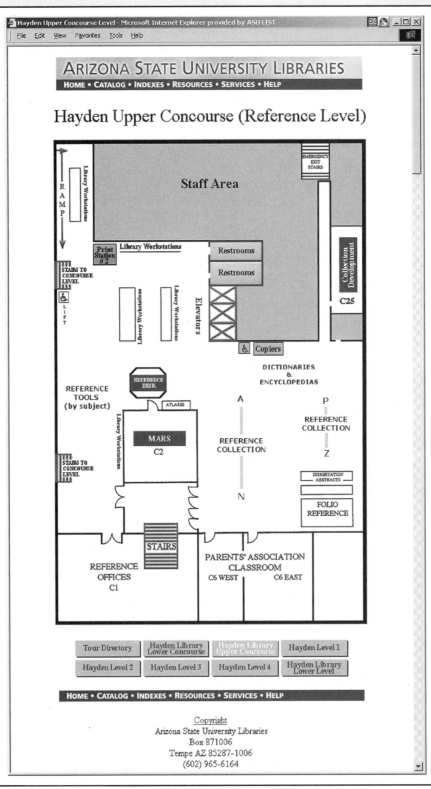

Figure 4–13 Imagemap: A Map of Cleveland Public Library Locations

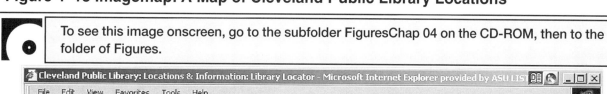

To see this image onscreen, go to the subfolder FiguresChap 04 on the CD-ROM, then to the folder of Figures.

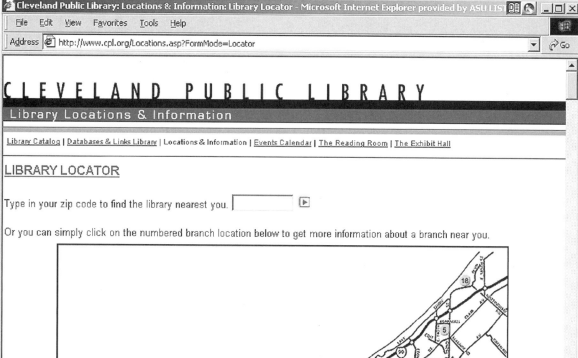

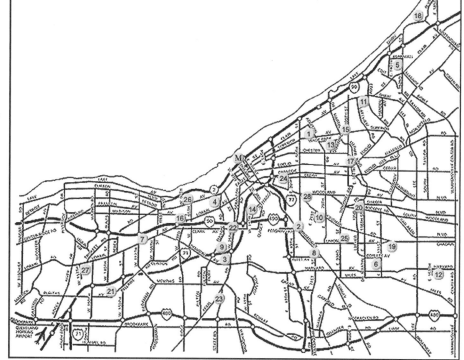

M. Main Library

1. Addison
2. Broadway
3. Brooklyn
4. Carnegie West
5. Collinwood
6. East 131st Street
7. Eastman
8. Fleet
9. Fulton

11. Glenville
12. Harvard-Lee
13. Hough
14. Jefferson
15. Langston Hughes
16. Lorain
17. Martin L. King, Jr.
18. Memorial-Nottingham
19. Mt. Pleasant

21. Rockport
22. South
23. South Brooklyn
24. Sterling
25. Union
26. Walz
27. West Park
28. Woodland

CREATION OF IMAGEMAPS

Before the development of Imagemap editors, creating Imagemaps required the use of complex HTML code for defining the different sections of the image, as well as programming definitions of the actions that should have taken place when each section was clicked. Now the Imagemap editors have relieved us of doing the complicated work. There are a few stand-alone Imagemap editors. The most popular one is Mapedit.

Mapedit is a WYSIWYG editor for creating an Imagemap. You open the image file that you want to turn into an Imagemap, and then define different sections of it as hotspots. Mapedit has tools for defining circles, rectangles, and polygons. It also allows you to create irregular-shaped sections on the map. You outline a section, adding as many points as necessary to make an outline smooth. After you specify a hotspot, you type the URL. A page with that URL should be opened when a visitor clicks there. When you have defined the entire map, you can save it either as a server-side or a client-side Imagemap. Then you send the Imagemap file to your Web server together with your HTML files and graphics files. To help you prevent making mistakes, Mapedit provides test and trial functions. Selecting Test/Edit from its Tools menu, you can click on all the hotspots in the image. When you click on a link section, the URL associated with it will be displayed and the entire area of the hotspot will be highlighted.

Web editors such as Macromedia Dreamweaver also have built-in Imagemap creation tools, which function pretty much like Mapedit. The following figure shows an Imagemap creation tool built in Dreamweaver.

Figure 4–14 Dreamweaver Imagemap Creation Tool

To see this image onscreen, go to the subfolder FiguresChap 04 on the CD-ROM, then to the folder of Figures.

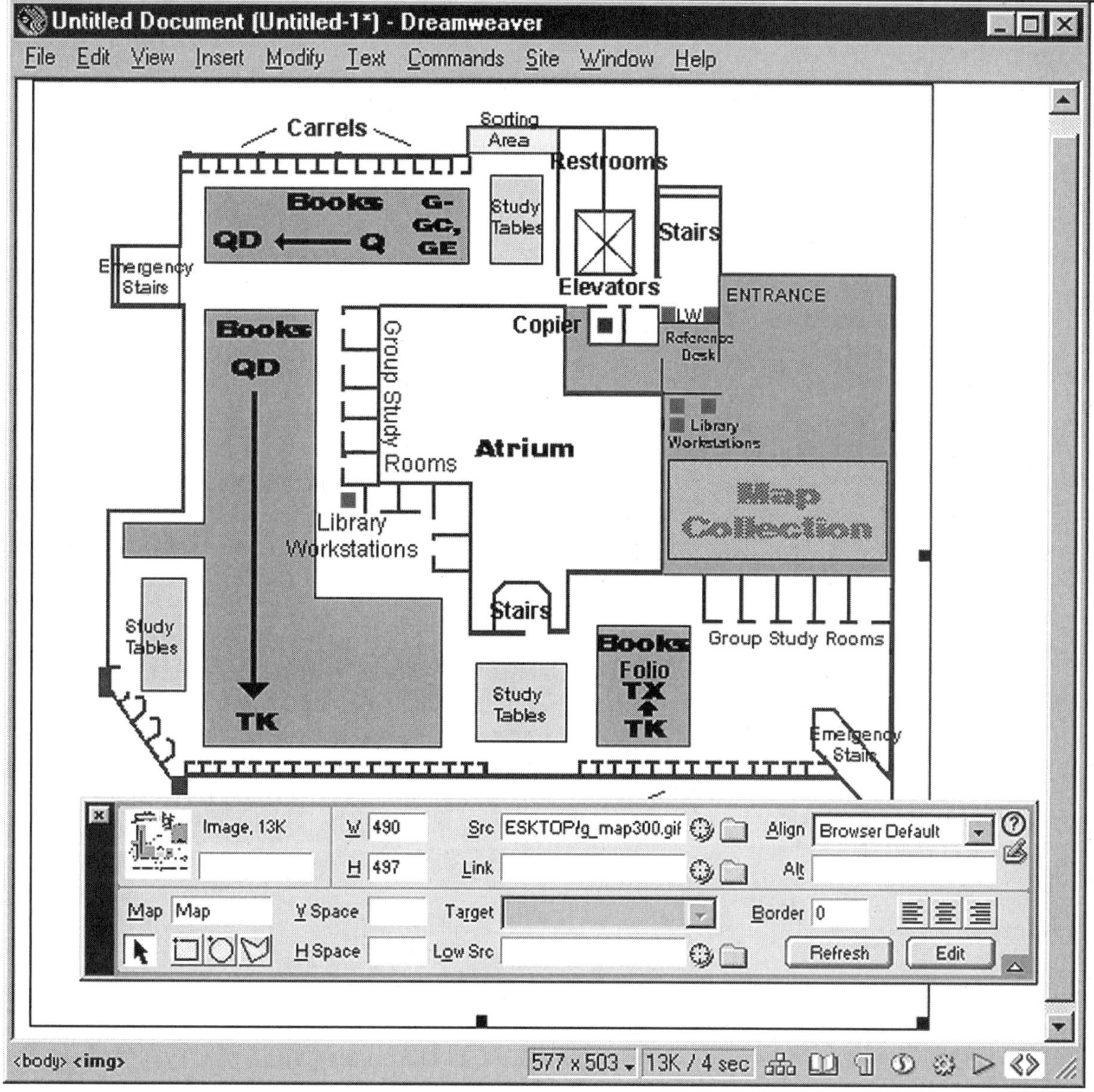

DOWNSIDES OF IMAGEMAPS

There are some downsides of Imagemaps, which you might want to take into account.

- Because the words on the Imagemap are not underlined, it is difficult to tell if they are links.
- Imagemaps take more time to download due to their size.
- Imagemaps give no clue about what has been seen and what hasn't since the links won't change color after being visited. This makes it harder for navigation.

- Because of limited space, it is hard to include more items in the Imagemap, especially when you want to include both icons and text in the map. This will result in a relatively simple page.
- Making changes in an Imagemap for updating is more time consuming than a page with regular text links.

ANIMATIONS

GIF ANIMATIONS

Animated GIF is a GIF graphics file with two or more frames or images displayed in a timed sequence to create the appearance of motion. The series of images can then loop to convey the desired information. The easiest way to create GIF animations is to use a graphics package: GifBuilder (Macs) or GIF Construction Set (PCs). Graphics programs such as Adobe ImageReady and Macromedia Fireworks provide easy-to-use tools for creating animated GIFs. When you build an animation, you put each image in a separate frame. All of the images of the animation are exported to an animated GIF file. By changing the content of successive frames, you can make an object appear to move across the canvas, get bigger or smaller, rotate, change color, fade in or out, or change shape. You can use these and other techniques to put together a sophisticated animation that tells an entire story or depicts a realistically moving object, such as a library logo or a banner.

Creation of a GIF Animation

There are a few steps to create a GIF animation using programs such as Fireworks.

- Create a new document in the program.
- Draw or locate the GIF files you will use to construct the animation.
- Put them in the order you wish them to appear.
- Using the Frames Panel, add multiple frames to the document.
- Place objects on separate frames. In other words, load the files one frame at a time.
- Set the frame delay.
- Optimize the image
- Export the document as an animated GIF. (This is done by first going to File>Export Preview. In the Format drop-down list, select Animated GIF. Then click the Export button.)

Figure 4–15 GIF Animation Creation Using Fireworks

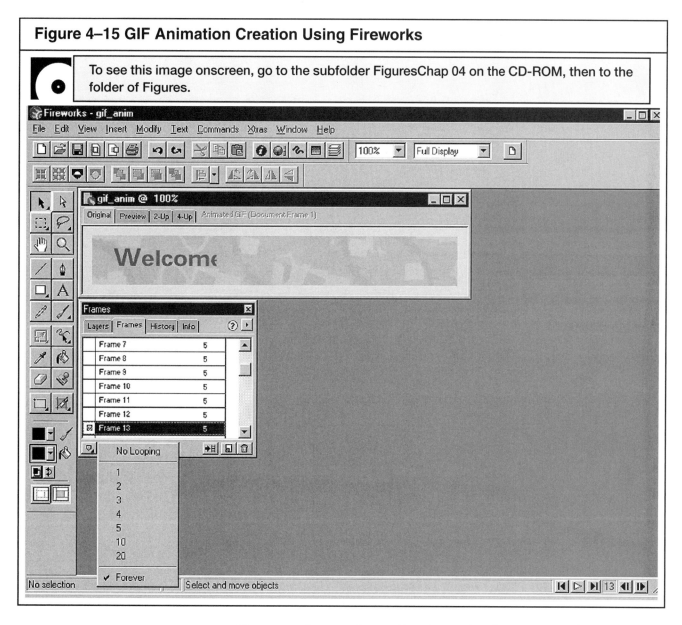

To see this image onscreen, go to the subfolder FiguresChap 04 on the CD-ROM, then to the folder of Figures.

You can also use ImageReady to develop animated GIFs. However, it is important to know that with ImageReady, you handle the layers on each of the different frames. When you create a new frame, you have to make a new layer. On each frame you have to make a change in the layers themselves for frame-by-frame animation. You are manipulating all your frames in all your layers in the same window. There seem to be too many elements to deal with in the ImageReady working environment. On the other hand, Fireworks has a grid system, and layers cut across all frames. When you are in a frame, you can place items in different layers. Fireworks provides you with flexibility to spread all kinds of graphics through your frames, as opposed to having this huge layer palette for every frame element.

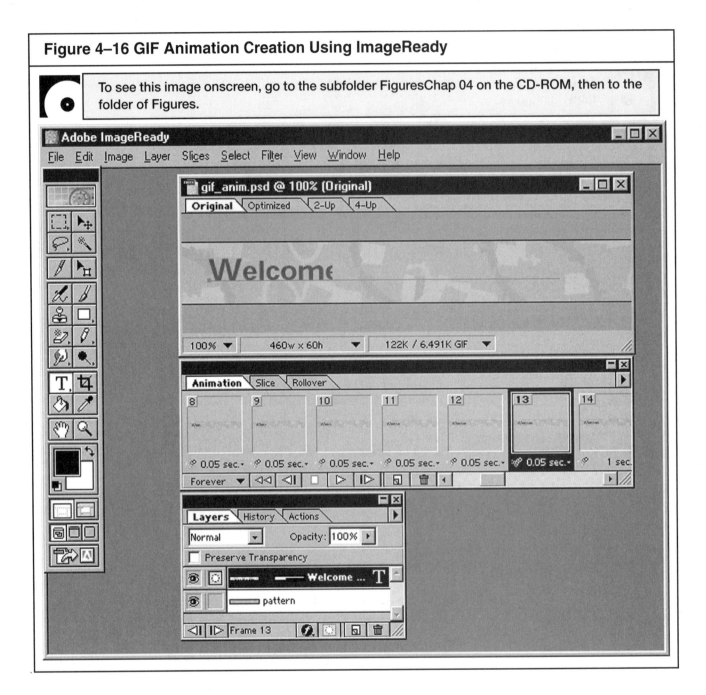

Figure 4–16 GIF Animation Creation Using ImageReady

To see this image onscreen, go to the subfolder FiguresChap 04 on the CD-ROM, then to the folder of Figures.

Editing a GIF Animation

First, you open up the GIF images in the program you choose. Then you can optimize their color palettes for viewing on the Web. You can specify the animated GIF's attributes such as the height and width of the animation and the height and width of each image within it. You can decide whether the animation should loop forever or for a set number of times, or how long each section of the action should last. You can also preview the effects of your creation as you work.

FLASH ANIMATIONS

Flash animations are vector-based images created with Macromedia Flash. They appear to be animations, but are, in reality, a series of image files displayed one frame after the other to give you the illusion of motion. Since it is vector-based, a Flash file is very small and loads fast. But you need a plug-in (free download from Macromedia Web site) installed on your browser to view Flash files. The newer versions of Netscape and Internet Explorer (4.0 and above) have Flash helper application built in.

SIMPLE 3D TEXT CREATION

Creating 3D text may not be as hard as you have thought. Here are some tips for creating simple 3D texts using Microsoft Word and Photoshop:

1. Open Microsoft Word.
2. Click on Insert>Picture>Word Art.
3. Choose the style that you would like to use.
4. Select the font size that you want to use.
5. Type the text.
6. Click once on the text to select it.
7. Click on Edit>Copy.
8. Open Photoshop.
9. Click on File>New.
10. Change the graphic size and click OK.
11. Click on Edit>Paste.
12. Go to File>Save for Web.
13. Click on OK.
14. Give the file a name and click on Save.
15. Your 3D text JPG (GIF) is ready to be placed in your Web page.

Figure 4–17 Simple 3D Text Creation

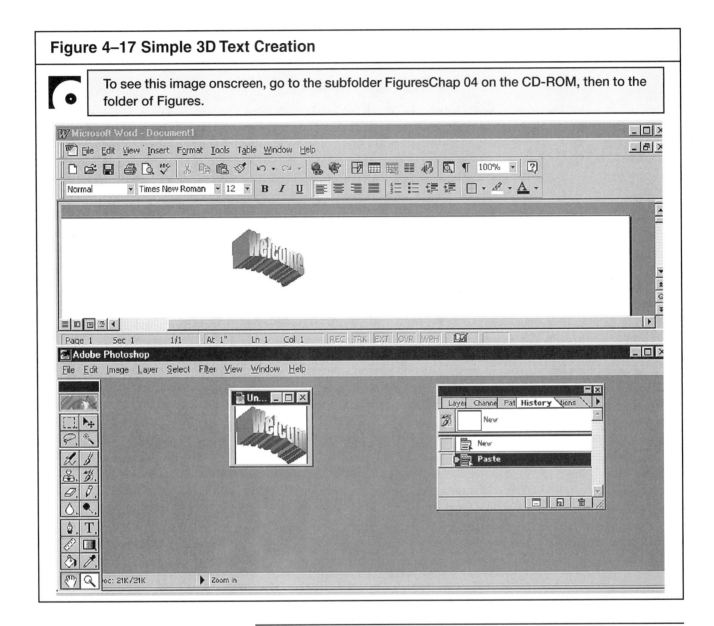

To see this image onscreen, go to the subfolder FiguresChap 04 on the CD-ROM, then to the folder of Figures.

ADVANCED 3D PROGRAMS

Will the Web remain flat? No, emerging technologies and tools are changing the landscape of the Web. Right now there is too little 3D on the Web because of lack of bandwidth. However, there is an alternative for creating "fake" 3D. In the market, there are two powerful 3D programs: Cinema XL4D and 3DStudio Max. These programs have the capabilities to create high quality 3D models. To reduce the file size, the 3D files are converted to Flash-based graphics with a Flash export filter (Illustrate for 3DStudio Max from *www.digimation.com*). For more information, check this Web site and 3DStudio Max Web site: *www.discreet.com*.

5 EXPLORING INVENTIVE WEB FORMATS AND MULTIMEDIA

Besides HTML and some basic Web tools, there are other delivery formats and multimedia on the Web that can be used for creating better library Web sites. This chapter focuses on the use of the applications such as Adobe Acrobat, Shockwave, Flash, Authorware, online video and audio. These applications to some extent greatly extend the content delivery and multimedia aspects of the Web by allowing functions that popular browsers like Netscape and Internet Explorer do not accommodate.

The Adobe Acrobat format, famed for its capabilities of retaining the original document layout, is widely used for online e-journal databases such as JSTOR. It is also good for displaying online guides, manuals, or documents containing forms, tables, charts, etc. Shockwave, Flash, Authorware are powerful tools developed by Macromedia that can be used to create dynamic interfaces, interactive online tutorials, quizzes, or games for library Web sites. Online video and audio can be used for creating library audio-visual tour and instruction. It can also be used for developing audio-visual archives containing collections of music, oral history, movies, documentaries, video courses, etc.

PDF

PDF is an acronym for Portable Document Format. This file format was created with Adobe Systems. PDF files can be downloaded from the Web and viewed page by page, if the user's computer has the necessary Adobe Acrobat Reader plug-in installed. Acrobat Reader can be downloaded free from Adobe's own Web site (*www.adobe.com*). This software gives you instant access to documents in their original form, independent of computer platform. With the Acrobat Reader, not only can you view any PDF file, you can also navigate, print, and present it. No matter what software program is used to make the printed materials, producing a PDF file will allow anyone with the Adobe Acrobat Reader to read and print the document in the identical form it was made. Because PDF documents retain the formatting used by the author, they are used widely. Most of the e-journals and databases of e-journals such as JSTOR in libraries contain PDF documents.

There is one thing you should keep in mind when using PDF. PDF currently is not very accessible to patrons using screen readers. So an explanation in HTML format might be needed to accompany a PDF document. And you should make the most essential information available in a format accessible to all people.

Adobe's Acrobat Capture software can be used for creating PDF files. You can find information about creating Adobe Acrobat PDF files at: Tips & Techniques—Take Your Publications from Paper to Web: *www.adobe.com/epaper/tips/acrpaper2web/*.

MICROSOFT OFFICE FORMATS

Presenting materials in different formats will provide various kinds of information in their original display types and increase the usability of your Web site. You can easily put MS Office based documents online such as word processing files (MS Word), spreadsheets (MS Excel), and slide presentations (MS PowerPoint) with the conversion tools built in the newer versions of MS Office Suite. You can also download the tools from Microsoft Web site. After you have downloaded them, they will show up as options in the software toolbars. Database software such as Access or FileMaker Pro has features that allow the databases to be placed on the Web and accessed via a Web interface. Figure 5–1 shows a PowerPoint presentation on the Web. You can also integrate music or narration into your online slideshow, making it a real multimedia presentation.

Figure 5–1 PowerPoint Presentation on the Web

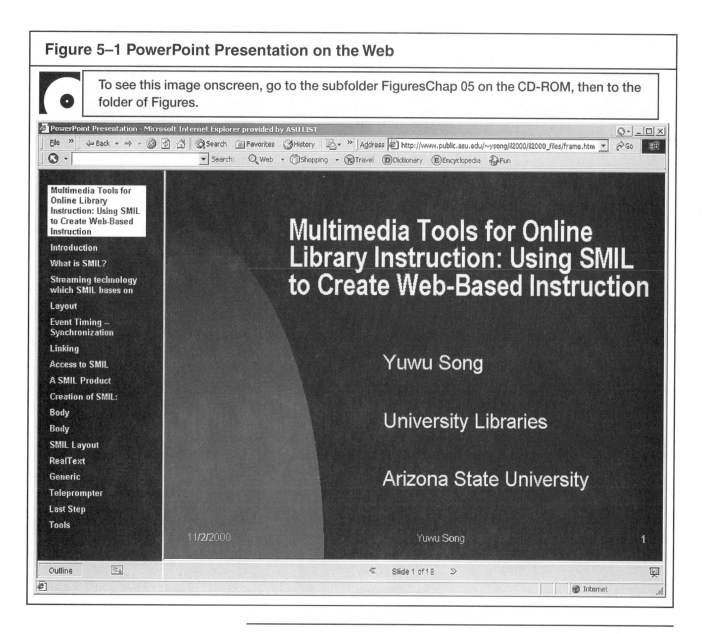

To see this image onscreen, go to the subfolder FiguresChap 05 on the CD-ROM, then to the folder of Figures.

FLASH

Flash, formerly called FutureSplash, is a product of Macromedia. Flash is a file format used for the delivery of vector-based images through a Web page or Web site. Flash files do not have pixels like GIF or JPEG images. Instead, they are created with lines and shapes and can include animation and interactivity. Flash files are small compared with pixel-based images. Although it was developed only a few years ago, it has become very popular with many developers in the Web community. The Flash program creates small, fast, vector-based drawings. To see Flash files on the Web requires the download and installation of the Flash plug-in from the Macromedia Web site (*www.macromedia.com*). For newer versions of browsers such as version 4 and above, Flash plug-ins are built in by default.

Unlike GIF89a or Shockwave, Flash uses streaming technologies: Flash files stream onto a document and begin to play as they download. Since Flash animations are vector-based, the Flash graphics are scalable. One can enlarge or "zoom" the images without sacrificing the image quality. Text is incorporated into the Flash animation in such a way that a designer doesn't have to worry about if a user has the fonts in his or her computer system. You can also incorporate audio into Flash products. Flash is a frame-based animation creation program. You make animation frame by frame using the drawing tool and other tools. It can be used to create Web interface and online animation such as logos, banners, interactive quizzes, games, slide shows, and so on.

After you created your Flash product, you should save it as a .fla file. Before you put it online, you have to export the file as .swf. Then you insert the .swf file in your Web page. Keep in mind, once a Flash file was exported, it cannot be edited anymore. If you want to make any changes, you have to go back to the original .fla file. It is very much like a PSD file in Photoshop exported into a GIF or JPG. Generally speaking, putting a Flash file on the Web page is like putting an image on the page. You use <EMBED> tags to refer to the Flash file. To insert a Flash file (movie.swf) in your page, use the following HTML code:

```
<EMBED SRC="movie.swf" pluginspage="http://
www.macromedia.com/shockwave/download/"
width="300" height="300">
</EMBED >
```

The graphics below show the working environment of Flash.

Figure 5–2 Flash Program Interface 1

To see this image onscreen, go to the subfolder FiguresChap 05 on the CD-ROM, then to the folder of Figures.

Figure 5–3 Flash Program Interface 2

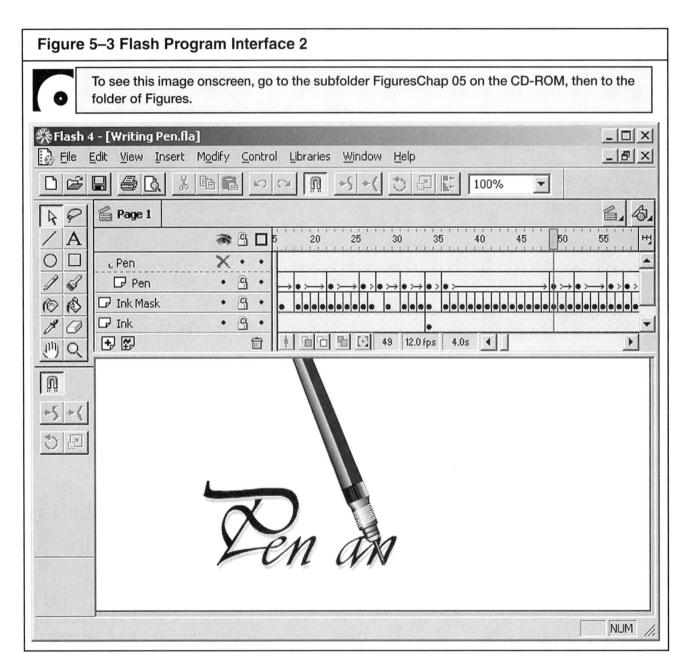

To see this image onscreen, go to the subfolder FiguresChap 05 on the CD-ROM, then to the folder of Figures.

Below is an example of Flash: a customized version of a library organization chart developed by Malaika Boyd. Users can click on one link and have the branch blocks displayed one by one like an animation film. The Flash document offers a complicated chart and provides the viewers with flexible viewing while having only a size of 25.9 k!

Figure 5–4 Chart Created with Flash 1

To see the Flash example, go to Chapter 5's Flash folder on the CD-ROM and click on flashchart.htm.

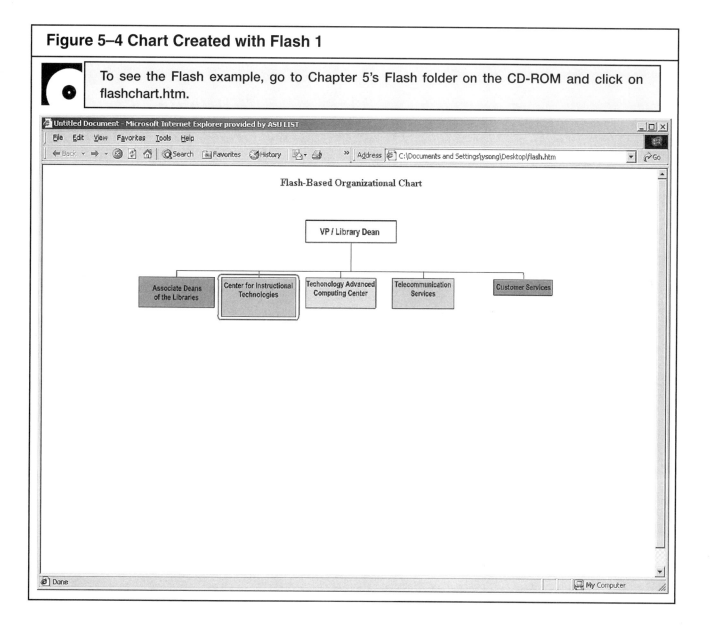

Figure 5–5 Chart Created with Flash 2

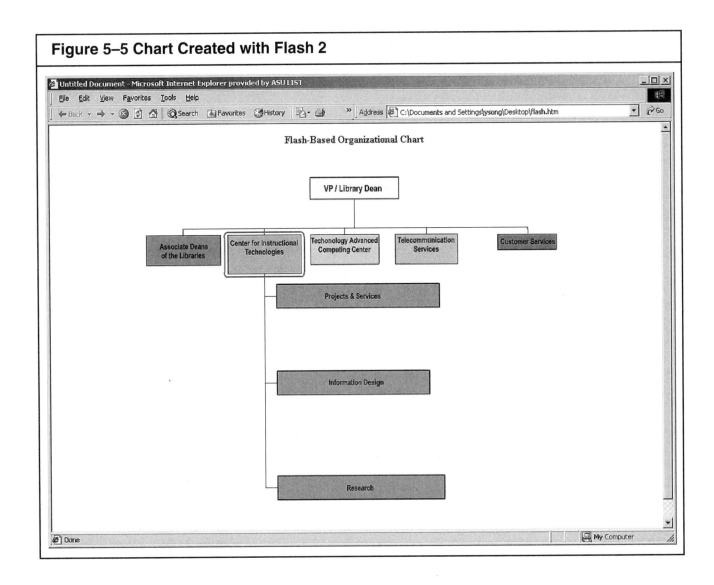

Another example of Flash applications is Texas Information Literacy Tutorial (TILT) developed by University Libraries of the University of Texas at Austin. This product displays the full potential of Flash with animation, interactivity, audio, etc.

Figure 5–6 Library Online Application Created with Flash (TILT): University Libraries, University of Texas at Austin

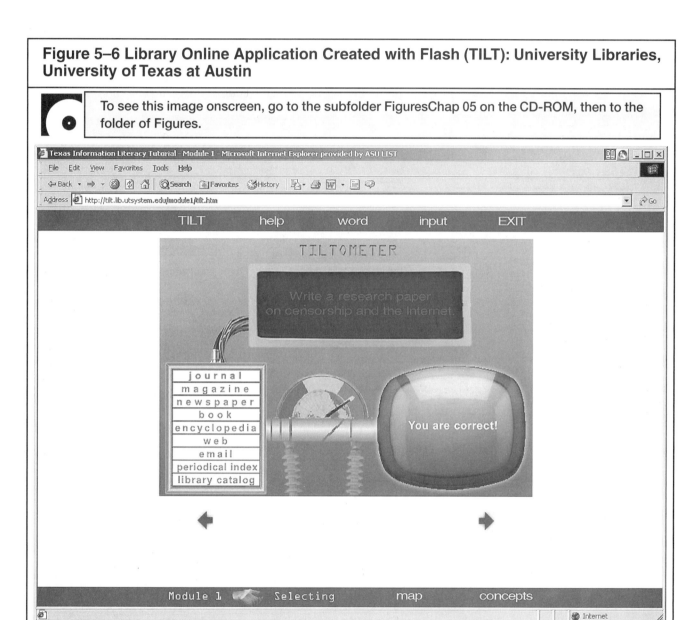

To see this image onscreen, go to the subfolder FiguresChap 05 on the CD-ROM, then to the folder of Figures.

Flash can be used to create animation with loop or without loop. The graphic below "Finding Articles," is an example of Flash animation with loop. It has a spotlight effect, which may enliven your Web site. The source code is included in the CD-ROM for this book.

Figure 5–7 Flash Animation: Finding Articles

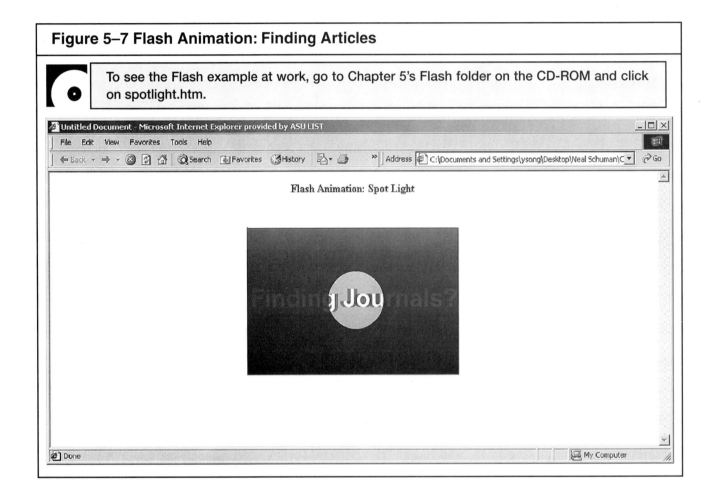

To see the Flash example at work, go to Chapter 5's Flash folder on the CD-ROM and click on spotlight.htm.

Flash can be used for interface design. Start Squad Web site designed by State Library of North Carolina is a good example.

Figure 5–8 Start Squad Web Site

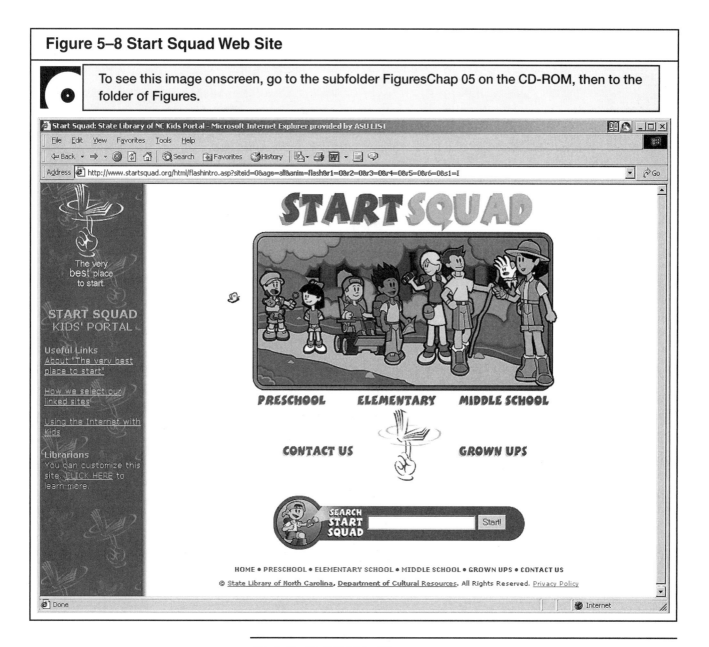

To see this image onscreen, go to the subfolder FiguresChap 05 on the CD-ROM, then to the folder of Figures.

SHOCKWAVE

Shockwave movies are interactive movies created with Macromedia's multimedia program: Director. This application is very powerful, but it is a little bit hard to learn how to use it. Shockwave is used mainly for interactive CD-ROMs. However Shockwave movies can be put on the Web and accessed with a Shockwave plug-in. To incorporate a Shockwave movie into a site, use the following HTML code:

```
<EMBED SRC="movie.dcr" pluginspage="http://
www.macromedia.com/shockwave/download/"
width="300" height="300">
</EMBED>
```

Here, "movie.dcr" is the name of the Shockwave movie file with Director's file extension .dcr. The "pluginspage" refers the users to the appropriate URL to get the Shockwave plug-in if they do not have it. Like in a graphic insertion, the "width" and "height" tags define the size of the movie. You can also insert a Shockwave movie file into your page by choosing "Insert Media>Shockwave" from the Insert Menu in Macromedia Dreamweaver.

AUTHORWARE

Macromedia's Authorware is a program that can be used to create highly interactive online applications such as tutorials and quizzes. Authorware provides features for creating sophisticated navigation, animations, and interaction. The drawback is that the learning curve for Authorware is steep and, moreover, users need to download another plug-in from Macromedia's Web site. Authorware files have an extension: .aam. To embed an Authorware product (authorware.aam) in your Web page, use the following code:

```
<EMBED SRC="http://www.domain/authorware/
authorware.aam"
pluginspage="http://www.macromedia.com/shockwave/
download/index.cgi?P1_Prod_Ver$ target="_top"
type="application/x-authorware-map" width="800"
height="500">
```

The University of Vermont Library developed an Authorware-based online tutorial for library instruction. Karl Bridges, the librarian/Web developer of this product, is quite willing to share with you his codes. With the Authorware software, you can easily customize the codes to create your own interactive applications. Or you can use the codes for learning purposes. For further information, contact Karl Bridges at: kbridges@zoo.uvm.edu.

Figure 5–9 Online Library Tutorial Created with Authorware: University Libraries, University of Vermont

To see this image onscreen, go to the subfolder FiguresChap 05 on the CD-ROM, then to the folder of Figures.

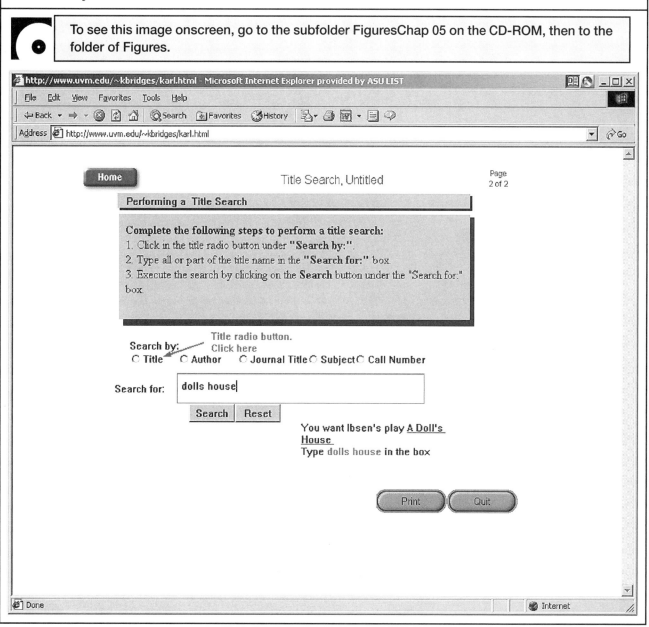

Figure 5–10 Authorware Development Environment

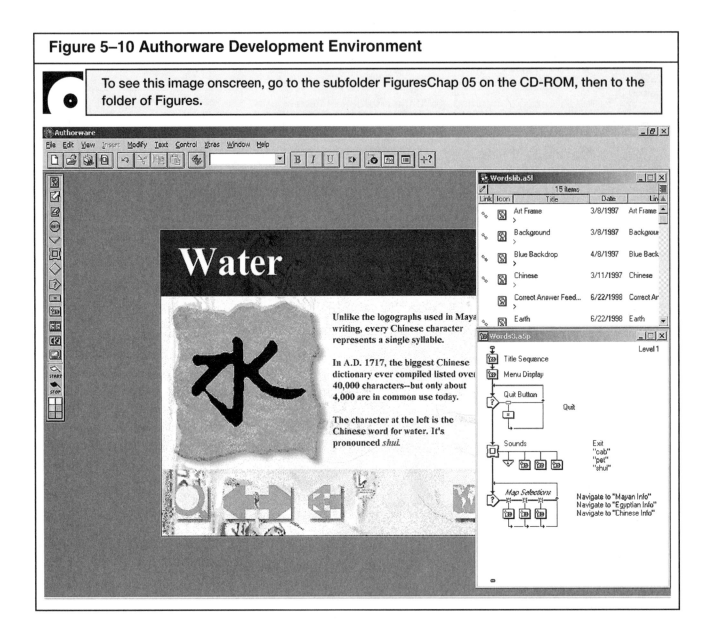

To see this image onscreen, go to the subfolder FiguresChap 05 on the CD-ROM, then to the folder of Figures.

VIDEO

Online video is an important but difficult aspect of multimedia development on the Web. In recent years, online video production and distribution have become feasible with the development of new technologies: high-quality and low-priced digital video, powerful desktop PCs, inexpensive and easy-to-use video editing software, and a new distribution channel on the Web characterized by broad band DSL and cable modem access.

VIDEO: TRADITIONAL VS. STREAMING

To further explore the online video world, it is necessary to get familiar with streaming technologies and applications. Until the emergence of streaming technology, the Web was relatively a quiet place. Traditional audio and video files are usually large and take a long time to download. With a telephone modem connection, it usually takes half an hour to download a one-minute video clip.

Streaming, as the word suggests, plays like a continuously flowing water stream. It is different from conventional files that must download in whole. Time is the most important factor for streaming. Streaming is done with encoding techniques and streaming players that allow the users to play the video while simultaneously downloading it. Using a process called buffering, the player downloads into the user's machine a small portion of the audio/video before beginning playback. In other words, instead of picking up and sending a whole reservoir of data at once, streaming files send the first part of an audio/video down the "pipe" first. While that is playing, the rest of the data flows down, getting in time to be played.

By today's "TV broadcast quality" standards, the quality of the online video is still poor. While streaming video quality is not yet well acceptable at modem speeds, it has reached true usability at bandwidths well within the capacity of many school networks. Now the streaming technology is improving fast. Researchers and developers have shown great interest in this field. It looks like TV quality, even DVD quality video on the Web will appear more likely sooner than later.

With streaming technologies, content authors can create, deliver, and play streaming media files in a streaming format such as RM, MOV, and ASF. Streaming video can be used in the language lab, for electronic delivery of video reserves, or for storage and delivery of lectures. It can also be used to Web-cast live events and to provide access to video collections in libraries or archives. As far as online teaching is concerned, no doubt there are advantages for an Internet-based video course over traditional video tape based courses and in some cases advantages over a classroom because online video provides searching and indexing, assessment, and the ability to view or review a lecture "on-demand." There are two forms of streaming video on the Web: progressive streaming (on demand) and real time streaming (live or in real time). The later is more like traditional live TV broadcasting while the former is downloadable "on demand."

Progressive streaming takes a compressed video file and downloads it to your computer via HTTP, the widely used Web protocol on Internet. Real time streaming (also called Webcasting or Netcasting) usually broadcasts to your local machine directly from a server. The "real time" streaming creates a video stream of a live event or archived files in real time. These files begin to download and play at the same time. Because of bandwidth limitations, real time video streaming files have to be smaller than those of the downloadable files. So, the video and sound quality of real time streaming is not as good as that of on-demand downloadable videos.

Real time streaming uses streaming media protocols such as RTSP (Real Time Streaming Protocol) or MMS (Microsoft Media Server Protocol). For these protocols, a special streaming server is required. Comparatively speaking, progressive streaming is the easiest way for novices, as you need no special streaming server. You can use a standard Web server to upload your compressed video files. Generally, progressive streaming works best for videos under ten minutes, such as movie trailers. The "real time" streaming is better for longer videos and live event broadcast.

As far as compression and encoding are concerned, the streaming encoders use lossy compression techniques to reduce file sizes. You compress the file by dropping certain digital information from the file. Developers can encode files at different rates, different screen sizes for best playback at different networks speeds. When delivered in the real life, there are a few files for each clip that are aimed at a specific data transfer rate. The end user chooses a file according to his/her connection speed, and the requested file is optimized for that speed.

Since the mid-1990s, a few different audio/video streaming technologies have been developed. The major players in this field are:

- Apple QuickTime: *www.apple.com/quicktime/*
- Audioactive: *www.audioactive.com/*
- Emblaze: *www.emblaze.com/*
- Liquid Audio: *www.liquidaudio.com/*
- Macromedia Shockwave: *www.macromedia.com/ shockwave/*
- Microsoft Windows Media (formerly called NetShow): *www.microsoft.com/windows/windowsmedia/default.asp*
- RealNetworks RealMedia: *www.real.com/*
- Vosiac: *www.vosaic.com/*

One big problem with so many streaming audio/video technologies is the proliferation of incompatible platforms. More than eight different applications and plug-ins have to be uploaded to your machine to view or listen to all the formats on the Web. With the development of streaming technologies in recent years, three players among all of the above have emerged as industry leaders: Apple's QuickTime, RealNetworks' RealMedia, and Microsoft Windows Media.

In technical terms, QuickTime, RealMedia, and Windows Media are called architectures or platform formats. An architecture is a package of software allowing data to be traded in a standard format, which is used for the client machine to interpret the compressed file. Architectures in digital video support file, storage, and playback formats, and let the developers use whichever codecs (compression/decompression device) they prefer. Now let's take a look at the three major streaming video architectures.

Figure 5–11 QuickTime Player

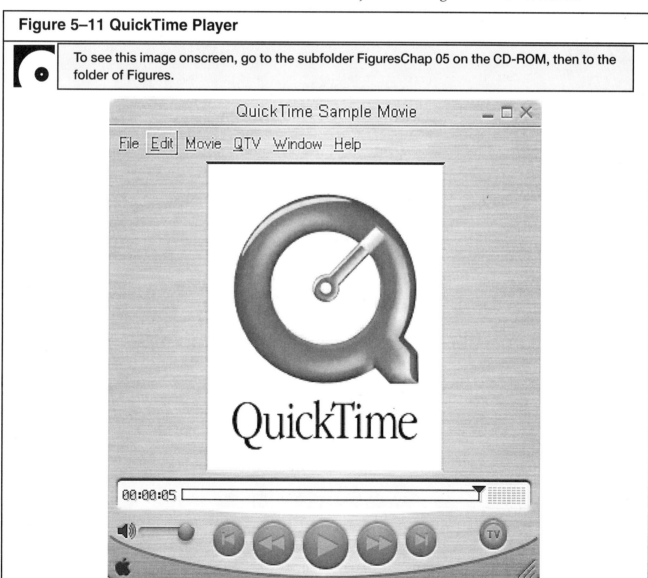

To see this image onscreen, go to the subfolder FiguresChap 05 on the CD-ROM, then to the folder of Figures.

APPLE'S QUICKTIME

Developed by Apple, QuickTime is a simple cross-platform architecture (for Macintosh, Unix, and PC). It has become the earliest industry standard for multimedia software platform. Its format is MOV. Apple adopted Sorenson Video technology for audio-video compression. QuickTime codecs and the player are available free. Right now QuickTime is the only driver that plays MOV files. QuickTime Streaming Server is based on RTSP. It is an open standard and can be used on multi-platform servers from UNIX to NT. And the best part is that it is free. Some believe that as Apache is to Web servers, QuickTime streaming is to video servers.

QuickTime is versatile. It can be used for delivery of media everywhere: Internet, CD-ROM, DVD, kiosk, and presentations. It works with every major file format for images, including JPEG, BMP, PICT, PNG, GIF, and animated GIF. It plays MP3 and also supports MIDI, the classic Web music format. Moreover, it supports the W3C Synchronized Multimedia Integration Language (SMIL) standard as a meta file format. SMIL documents set up the layout and timing of multimedia content, including images, text, audio, and video. It is a powerful tool for multimedia presentations. For detailed information about SMIL, look at Chapter 6, Investigating Advanced Web Technologies.

QuickTime possesses great interactive capabilities (similar to what a DVD video can do). It also supports the major standards for progressive Web streaming and real time streaming including HTTP, RTP, and RTSP. QuickTime's all-embracing features make it quite user-friendly. QuickTime's "Movie Alternates" feature allows developers to produce multiple versions of a film. Besides delivery, it can be used for editing and production of digital videos. QuickTime supports different kinds of digital video formats such as AVI, AVR, MPEG–1 formats and OpenDML MiniDV, DVCPro and DVCam camcorder formats.

There are a few versions of QuickTime. In 1999, Apple made public its QuickTime 4.0, which supported real time Web-casting. The recent QuickTime 5.0 did not seem to have big breakthroughs, although it is easier to use and has a well-designed interface. One new feature is the support for Macromedia Flash 4 products.

Generally, QuickTime has been quite popular with hardware and software developers, and multimedia content providers who produce and publish multimedia products in different formats. Apple's new Mac machines are bundled with FireWire, a digital conversion device, and iMovie, a nonprofessional video editing/ encoding program. This makes online video creation a breeze for common folks. For professional video editing, Apple's Final Cut Pro is a very powerful application.

Figure 5–12 RealPlayer

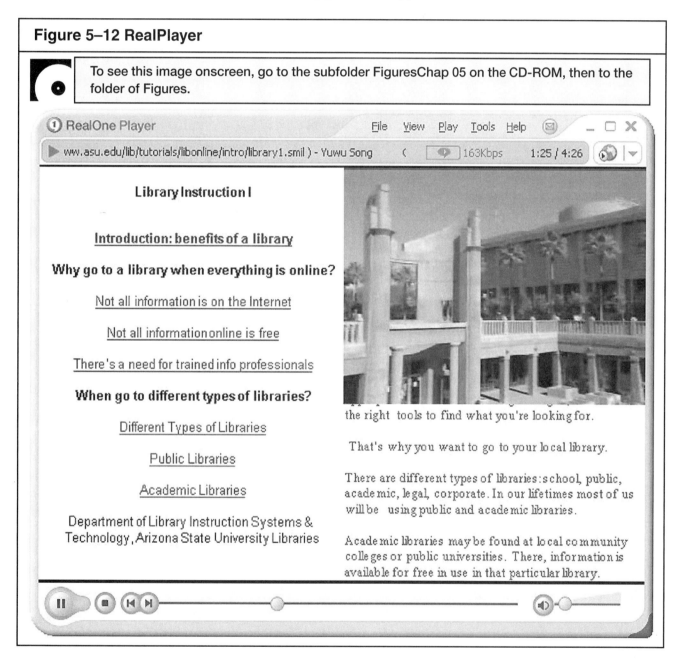

To see this image onscreen, go to the subfolder FiguresChap 05 on the CD-ROM, then to the folder of Figures.

REALMEDIA

RealMedia (RealVideo or Real for short) is developed by RealNetworks. It is a network oriented, streaming media platform. RealNetworks has been the pioneer in the field of multimedia on the Web. Its RM (real media) video format has become the acknowledged format in the Web community. RealNetworks' playing software, RealPlayer (RealOne) is widespread all over the Internet. For compression and decompression, RealMedia uses Real G2 Codec technology developed by RealNetworks. After RealMedia files are compressed into the RM format or other format, they cannot be edited or recompressed.

Currently, RealVideo is the most popular video format used on the Web. There are two other Real formats: RealAudio (streaming audio) and RealFlash (streaming Flash animation). They are also very popular with users. RealNetworks recently released version 8, but you have to purchase the server software to use it. The cost after software purchase is decided by connection usage. RealMedia supports both RTSP server-based "true streaming" and serverless "HTTP streaming." With a RealNetworks' server one can have better delivery performance and scalability advantages. For the time being, RealNetworks is the only company producing Real servers for the distribution of RealMedia files. RealMedia is most suitable for network delivery of audio, video, and other media types such as Macromedia's Flash products. It is not designed for CD-ROM or DVD delivery because of the high CPU requirements at higher bandwidths.

RealNetworks' newly published RealProducer 8.5, a production/encoding software, facilitated the production of real media files. One of its features is SVT (Scalable Video Technology). This technology allows slow computers to display video signals without decoding all the original data. It scans the whole video and then chooses the best compression rate based on bandwidth. Like QuickTime, RealPlayer supports the SMIL standard as a meta file format. As good and entrenched as RealPlayer may be, it does not have the close relationship with the operating systems enjoyed by Windows Media Player, which is obviously a drawback for RealNetworks' products.

Figure 5–13 Windows Media Player

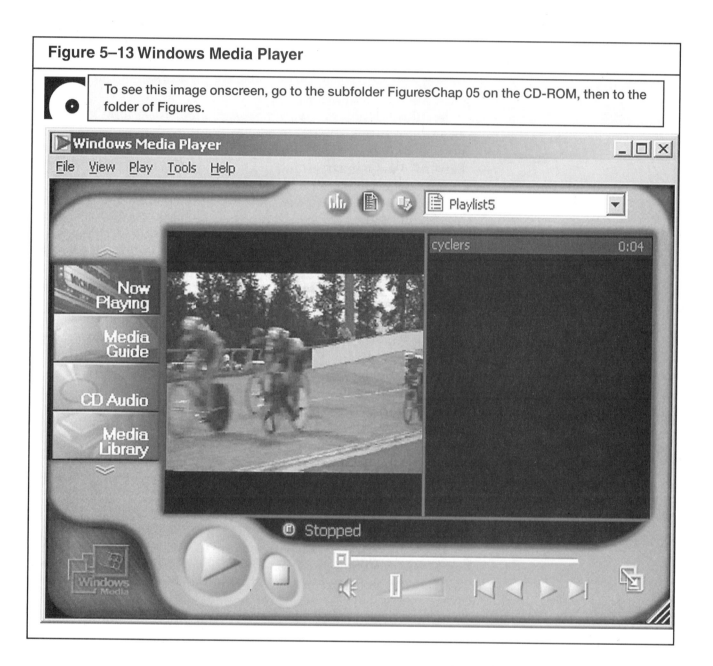

To see this image onscreen, go to the subfolder FiguresChap 05 on the CD-ROM, then to the folder of Figures.

MICROSOFT'S WINDOWS MEDIA

Microsoft's Windows Media (formerly called "NetShow") is Microsoft's answer to the development of streaming media architectures. Windows Media is also widespread and is currently in version 7. Although Windows runs its own proprietary server protocol, Microsoft Media Server Protocol (MMS), instead of the standard RTSP, it is free and it runs on the widely available Windows Server Platforms.

Like Real, Windows Media concentrates on network delivery of video and audio. Windows Media allows server-based "true streaming" as well as serverless "HTTP streaming." The standard file for Windows Media is Active Streaming Format (ASF). In Windows Media software package, there are Windows Media Tools for creating streaming media, Windows Media Services for hosting and delivering streaming media, and Windows Media Player for playing streaming media.

Windows Media servers support what is called "intelligent streaming"—it delivers the most suitable version of content to users based on the available Internet bandwidth between the server and the user. In other words, this technology is capable of providing continuous delivery of media even if there is a bandwidth problem with the networks. If problems show up, the media server will send less video data accordingly. If the available bandwidth decreases more, the server will automatically reduce video quality more, until only the audio is left for transmission. ASF files provide more than one version of the video track for both high and low bandwidth connections.

Windows Media Encoding Utility 8.0 beta, published in December 2000, represents a major improvement in quality, media type support, and other features. It contains compression and encoding systems for Windows Media Audio 8 and Video 8. Windows Media Video 8 uses the most advanced MPEG–4 video compression technology. Compared with the previous version, Windows Media Video 7, it increased the compression rate by 30 percent. It provides near DVD quality display at 500 Kbps (resolution: 640 by 480, 24 frames per second, rate equal to that of a regular film).

In the Windows Media software package, there is one useful component: Windows Media Rights Manager, which can be used for content piracy protection. No doubt this software component is very important for managing online multimedia materials.

All of the three technologies can be used for real time streaming or archived on-demand streaming. For the time being, no consensus about which is the best has been reached among professionals. However late Windows Media did come, it seems to be catching up and surpassing other attractive technologies. It is predicted that Microsoft's ASF (Advanced Streaming Format) will probably make it possible to encode files that will be playable on systems from different developers. But that has not taken place yet.

Although Windows Media Player has a much smaller market share than RealPlayer, Microsoft enjoys the advantage provided by the Windows operating system. Microsoft plans to incorporate Windows Media Player into future generations of the operating system. This will no doubt have a great impact on RealPlayer's market dominance. Microsoft and Real may start a media player war like the war between Internet Explorer and Netscape.

QuickTime still enjoys popularity with IT professionals. Many professionals believe QuickTime offers the best quality, as well as the elegant interface that Apple products are famous for. And the QuickTime VR looks very promising. However, convincing as QuickTime 5 is when playing local media, many Windows users and developers just don't want to deal with streaming QuickTime anymore, possibly due to their preference for the operating systems.

In the real world, to reach the greatest number of audiences, some developers put all the three formats on the Web. Each architecture plays on all platforms but ease of use varies on each platform. Recently, three companies—Generic Media (*www.genericmedia.com*), Vingage (*www.vingage.com*), and anyStream (*www.anystream.com*) spearheaded an initiative to solve the media player problem. The latest breakthrough is the ability to identify the player when a user first requests a media stream. With this factor established (along with, in some cases, the user's connection speed), an optimized edition of the stream can be delivered—normally in QuickTime, Real, or Windows Media format. With these developments and dreams in mind, the users are more eager to see the day when there is ubiquitous streaming media for all users, regardless of connection speed, media format, or device.

VIDEO SOURCES FOR THE WEB

To create online video you first need to have video sources. There are a few types of video sources.

- Your own captured video. Computers with interface cards (video capture cards such as those produced by Osprey) can be used for capturing video from a VCR, camera, camcorder source, or a digital camcorder using mini DV tapes (NTSC). Some computers have a video-capture feature as standard. For the originally shot digital video, you need to input the video source onto your Mac or PC hard drive using a FireWire (IEEE1394), a device to transfer digital video files. Without a doubt, you get the best results using a digital video camera hooked up to your computer via FireWire.
- Your own processed video. Using a video editing software

such as iMovie, Final Cut Pro, or Premiere, you can make a video by dragging and dropping images, effects, and transitions over a timeline and let the software make a video sequence of the results. You can fade (zoom) into or out of a still graphic, make a transition to another graphic, and move a graphic within an image around the screen with text. There are many possible ways for you to make a video without a video or animation source.

- CD-ROM video clip and video libraries. Some computer stores sell CD-ROMs of royalty-free video.
- The Internet. The Web is full of sites with video clips for downloading. Pay attention to the restrictions for reuse.

VIDEO EDITING

After you have your video sources ready, you can edit videos using professional level video editing tools such as Apple's Final Cut Pro, Adobe's Premiere, Media100, Avid, EditDV, or Microsoft's Moviemaker. Apple's Final Cut Pro has great appeal for professionals due to its elegant interface design and powerful features. However, only people with Apple computers can use it. Adobe Premiere is a popular program. It is a cross-platform video-editing package that has become the tool of choice for low- to mid-end video editing. The software Media 100 provides cross-platform, professional level quality tools. Avid offers a base but powerful range of features, with an interface designed for ease of use, but it is more expensive.

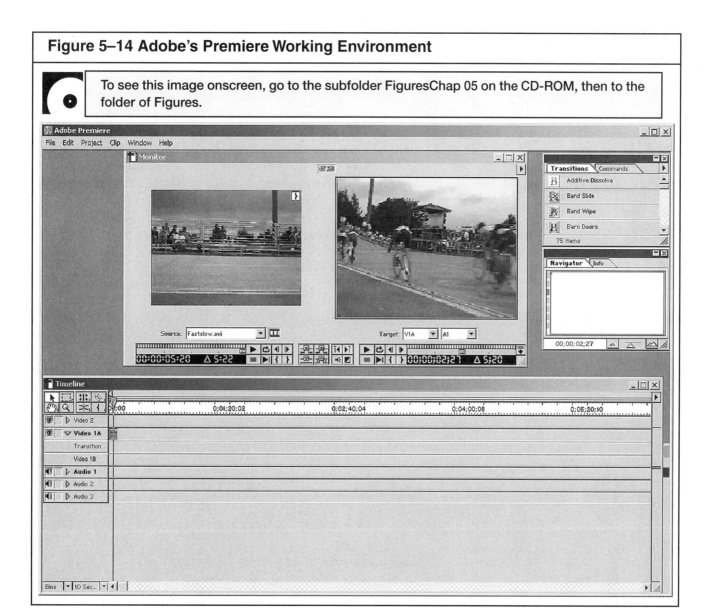

Figure 5–14 Adobe's Premiere Working Environment

To see this image onscreen, go to the subfolder FiguresChap 05 on the CD-ROM, then to the folder of Figures.

To edit a video file, you first open the folder of the source files, then you drag and drop individual clips onto a timeline and edit them by cutting, pasting, and adding special effects. Next, you stitch the clips together using transition. Finally, you save and export the edited clip to a folder on your desktop.

COMPRESSING AND ENCODING

At this stage you use a bundled video editing tool or a dedicated video compression tool. Digital video files are big. Five minutes of uncompressed video will consume one gigabyte of space on your hard drive, and no one has the patience to download or stream a video that large. So compression of the video files will optimize the video while retaining the highest quality possible for distribution on the Web. Here you need to know codec. Codec means compression/decompression, and it is the software to compress huge video or audio files into much smaller files that can be sent out online. You will choose a codec according to the video format (mov, rm, or asf) you are using. For example, QuickTime uses Sorenson Video 3 codec from Sorenson Media for QuickTime Video compression. Real Video 8 codec runs in conjunction with Real Server. Codecs generally come bundled with your video editing software or with compression suites such as Media Cleaner. You will probably use one of the following codecs for video compression:

- Sorenson Video
- RealVideo
- Windows Media Video
- MPEG

Many video content creators use Media Cleaner Pro from Terran Interactive as their full-service compression/encoding suite. Usually codec software comes with popular video editing tools such as Final Cut Pro. There are a few things you need to think about before compressing/encoding video for the Web:

1. Who is your audience?
2. What kind of Web connection might they have (28.8k, 56k modem, ISDN, DSL/Cable, T1, or T3)?
3. What video format (QuickTime, Real, Windows Media) might be used?
4. What data rate is feasible?
5. What frame rate is suitable?
6. What is the media player window size you should use?
7. What kind of streaming is to be used: Progressive or Real-Time?

After you make your decision, you take your edited video clip and encode it to a video format—QuickTime, Windows Media, or Real Media—and compress the file size to output to the Web. You can use a compression suite such as Media Cleaner Pro or a video editing program to encode the files. You need to go through a series of check box options. This allows you to select your video format such as RM, your data rate such as 56k-modem, your frame rate (e.g. 15 frames per second; regular movies play at 24 frames per second), and the size of your video viewing area (320 x 240 pixels).

To reach the largest number of audiences, you need to make

tradeoffs. If you make a near VCR or DVD quality video with a high frame rate, a 640 by 480 viewing window, and a high data rate, you will get a high-quality video, which can be seen only by people with fast connections like T1 or above. If you take speed as your priority, the quality decreases. So striking a balance between video quality and connection speed that is acceptable for your audience is what you should take into consideration.

A SAMPLE SETTING FOR ENCODING

For 56k modem connection, you may want to use:

- Streaming Method: Real-Time Streaming
- Data Rate: 40 – 45 Kb
- Window Size: 160 x 120 pixels
- Frame Rate: 5–6 frames per second (Use 5 or 6 fps, then scaling up for bigger data rate and faster Web connection)

For better quality, you may want to try different settings and see if the results best serve your needs.

DISTRIBUTION TO THE WEB
QuickTime (nonstreaming)

Once you have a QuickTime video clip, you can choose to either have the video automatically play on the page or allow the user to download the video clip. To automatically play the video, use the following code:

```
<EMBED SRC="myvideo.mov" width=320 height=240>
```

To allow the user to download the clip, use the following code:

```
<a href="myvideo.mov">Download My Video.</a>
```

QuickTime (streaming)

QuickTime movie can be easily embedded into a Web page for streaming:

```
<EMBED SRC="rtsp://myserver.com/myvideo.mov" WIDTH=
"320" HEIGHT="240"
STARTTIME="05:00" ENDTIME="08:00">
```

RealMedia: RealPlayer

RealPlayer can be embedded in the Web page with a control panel for video distribution. Take serverless HTTP streaming for example:

```
<a href="http://myserver/myvideo.html">Embedded player with
control panel</a></p>
```

There is a standalone player version:

```
<a href="http://myserver/myvideo.rm">Standalone Player
Version</a>
```

Here, a hyperlink would need to be clicked by the user to download the movie and spawn an external application to play it. In this case, RealPlayer will be launched, which plays the video.

You can also use a SMIL version:

```
<a href="http://myserver/myvideo.smil">SMIL version</a>
```

Here RealPlayer will be launched, which plays the video controlled by SMIL.

Windows Media

To launch and control playback, Windows Media Player uses ASX files as meta files. The latest ASX format uses an XML structure. ASX files have tags that look like HTML. Rather than HTTP, the protocol used here is MMS (Microsoft Media Server Protocol). ASX in general is quite similar in structure to SMIL. One can make a play-list by putting a number of <Entry> sections in an ASX file. You can also include title, author, abstract information, and even links to Web sites. An ASX file looks like this:

```
<ASX version="3">
<Entry>
<Title>My Video</title>
<Ref href=mms://myserver.com/myvideo.asf/>
<StartTime value="02:00"/><Duration value="05:00"/>
</Entry>
</ASX>
```

TIPS ON CREATING VIDEO FOR THE WEB

There are a few tips on creating video for the Web:

- Start with the best possible video source.
- Use high-quality digitizing equipment.
- Always keep bandwidth in mind.
- Make sure that the audio and video tracks of your video clips are synched up. You may want to import the audio into a video-editing package, and sync up the tracks in the program.

- Think about using black and white colors, because you can greatly reduce the bandwidth of your video files.
- Try to limit your frame rate. If you decrease the video rate from 30 frames per second to 15 fps, you have effectively cut the size in half.

QUICKTIME VR

In recent years, Apple has put great efforts to develop other forms of streaming media technology such as QuickTime VR (QuickTime Virtual Reality). QTVR is an enhanced version of QuickTime. It is a form of online panoramic photography. You take pictures of a scene or an object from all angles (360 degrees), you then export the pictures into a stitching program to join the pictures together, and save it as a QT or MOV file. You then put it online as a QuickTime movie.

Figure 5–15 QTVR Development Environment

To see this image onscreen, go to the subfolder FiguresChap 05 on the CD-ROM, then to the folder of Figures.

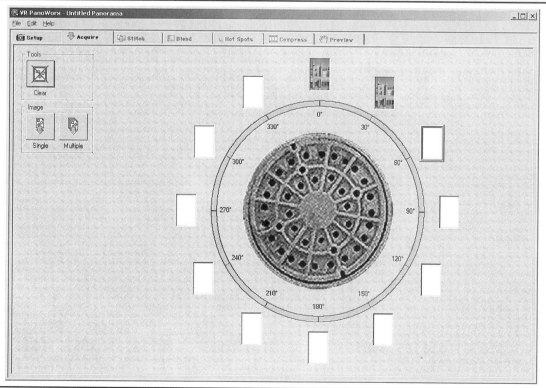

QTVR allows the users to navigate movies and actually move around within the movie by turning around, zooming in and out using the mouse. You can look at a place or an object such as a museum statue from different angles. This technology is good for putting up online museum exhibitions, visual tours of libraries and scenic spots, and displays of cars or other commercial products. QTVR files can be embedded in a Web page like a regular QuickTime movie:

```
<EMBED SRC = "QTVR.mov" width =100% height = 100% full
screen = yes >
```

AUDIO

Audio materials include music, sound, broadcast, speeches, conversations, interviews, oral history recordings, language learning materials, and so on. Due to technical problems such as lack of playback equipment, users have few opportunities to get access to audio materials in the old formats—audiocassette, reel-to-reel, or vinyl, plastic, etc. If the materials can be digitized and put online, they will be more easily available to users. Libraries have been involved in digitization and network delivery of audio. For music appreciation and instruction, or for foreign language instruction, it is a good idea for the instructors to put the audio materials online and let the students get access to them whenever they want. This will resolve the problems of equipment and formats, and the inadequacy of e-reserve of tapes and CDs. Online slide shows and movies also need audio. Products such as MS PowerPoint, Flash, Camtasia, or RealMedia based online slide shows and movies, if added with audio, can provide a new way for online exhibition or instruction. It is obvious that bringing audio to your library's Web pages can meet a number of important library needs.

Compared to video, audio enjoys some advantages. Audio files are smaller and download fast. And most of the computers have built-in audio players. That means you can play the audio right away after you download the file by clicking on the audio link. In general more modest requirements for computers and networks connection are needed for playing audio.

Audio can be recorded in traditional analog formats or digital formats such as .wav, .aiff, and so on. Audio files on a cassette tape or VHS tape are in analog formats. To put them online, you need to digitize them. You first need to transfer them to a computer through the USB or a FireWire port. Then you use applications such as SoundEdit 16, Bias Peak on the Mac, and Sound Forge on the PC to digitize the audio source files imported from the tapes. Once you set everything up, the production becomes a routine. All you need to do is to make sure that the compression settings are correct, the amplification is loud enough without distortion, and the digitization complete. Digital audio files are usually big. Compression technology such as MP3 has to be used to compress file sizes (about a tenth of its original size) while maintaining a maximum level quality over a network with lower bandwidth. The graphic below is the development environment of an audio editing software. To some extent, it functions like a video-editing program. You can treat parts of the media as objects, which you can cut, paste, delete, and so on. Figure 5–16 shows Samplitude (Digital Audio Editing Software) Working Environment.

Figure 5–16 Samplitude (Digital Audio Editing Software) Working Environment

To see this image onscreen, go to the subfolder FiguresChap 05 on the CD-ROM, then to the folder of Figures.

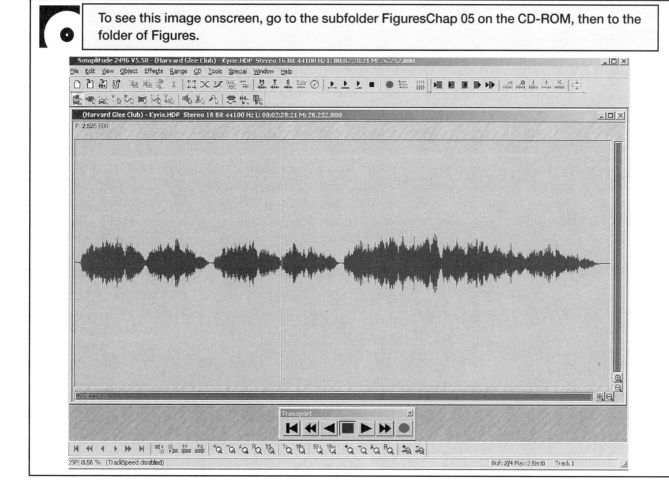

EMBEDDING SOUND IN WEB PAGES

Before you put audio files online, make sure that your server supports MIME types for MIDI, au, wav, aiff, or MP3 file formats. Once you have an audio clip, you can link to the clip with the traditional HREF tag, just as you would link to another HTML page:

```
<A HREF="music.wav">Please listen to my music.</a>
```

You can also use the "embed" tag by putting the following code in your Web page within <BODY></BODY> and it will automatically play a background sound:

```
<EMBED SRC="music.midi" autostart=true hidden= true>
```

The code above tells the browsers to begin playing the file immediately.

By showing the sound console, you can let the user pause, stop, and replay the sound or turn up or down the volume. The code is as follows:

```
<EMBED SRC= "MIDI/Classical/music.mid" width= 200 height=
60 loop=FALSE align= right >
```

Width and height attributes define the size in pixels of the sound console on your page. Loop=FALSE prevents the sound from playing endlessly. Align=right (or left) puts the console to the right (or left) of your page.

Keep in mind that CD-quality audio of one minute long takes up 10 Mbytes. Downloading will take one hour over a typical 28.8 Kbps modem. So you should make your background sound files small so they can be downloaded fast over a modem connection. Typical medium quality may be 22 Mhz, 16 bits. The best way to decide the file sizes is to listen to the same piece of sound using different software settings. Then you can decide which software settings are best to produce the best quality of sound with the smallest size.

THE STREAMING AUDIO

Like streaming video, audio can be streamed, too. The "streaming" audio can be played while it is being received. One can use RealAudio or Windows Media to stream for materials longer than 10 minutes. The streaming production applications are free. But for advanced streaming you need a streaming server. However, for simple streaming you can use the HTTP server to do the standard downloading (serverless streaming).

The RealAudio system developed by Real Networks does a good job delivering music and sound over a network in real-time. RealAudio is flexible to use. One has complete control over the sound. You can pause, move forward and back, and start or stop at any time. RealAudio formats are optimized for low- to high-speed connections ranging from 28.8 Kbps modems and ISDN to T1. RealAudio's encoding mechanism can reduce audio files of 10 minutes long to around 1 Meg. This is obviously good enough for even the traditional downloading. Now the RealAudio system has been incorporated into the RealVideo system and become the RealMedia system, called Real One, which plays both audio and video.

DESIGN CONSIDERATION

After you embed sound in your Web page, it will automatically play background sound when it is loaded. Take into consideration that the download time will be longer and also that the sound may be annoying to some people. You may want to offer a choice for people to turn the sound off. You may also want to let people know the length and size of the audio files.

HARDWARE CONSIDERATIONS

A dedicated area should be set up where people can get access to audio materials with headphones provided. Digital audio-visual facilities should be offered in the same way as traditional video or audio materials are used in an audio-visual lab.

SCREEN CAPTURING SOFTWARE: CAMTASIA

If a picture is worth a thousand words, then a moving picture is worth ten thousand words for explaining the complicated content on today's computers and the Web. Camtasia is a product that captures the action and sound from any part of the computer desktop and saves it to a standard AVI movie file or streaming video. Camtasia makes it a breeze to record, edit, and publish high-fidelity, compressed how-to videos for computer-based training, education, distance learning, technical support solutions, product demonstrations, and more.

Generally speaking, Camtasia is a suite of video-making tools: Camtasia Recorder, Camtasia Producer, Camtasia Player, and the audio program Dubit. You use Recorder to record video. Then you edit the video with Producer and add sound with Dubit. Camtasia Player is used to freely redistribute Camtasia movies to others. The Player will also play AVI files created by any other application.

CAMTASIA RECORDER

With Recorder, you can capture cursor movements, menu selections, pop-up windows, layered windows, typing, and everything else you see on your screen. You can use the ScreenDraw feature to draw on your desktop while recording a movie—just like television sportscasters. Camtasia's ScreenPad annotation feature allows you to add logos and graphics as you record your movie. You can apply real-time effects like cursor and object highlighting, graphic and image annotations, watermarks, time stamps, captioning, and audible mouse clicks. Moreover, you can move in for a closer look with Zoom, or pan the captured frame across the screen to show more detail.

CAMTASIA PRODUCER

Camtasia Producer is a nonlinear editor, which edits, trims, and joins AVI clips. You can add transition and watermark effects to any video. Producer allows you to incorporate an AVI file from another source and produce industry standard movie files, such as Microsoft Windows Media format, RealNetworks' RealMedia streaming format, or Animated GIFs.

ADDING AUDIO

You can narrate your Camtasia video while recording your movie. You can also use DubIt (bundled with Camtasia) to add narration and sound effects to a video while you view it.

Figure 5–17 Searching AltaVista: Video Created with Camtasia

To see this image onscreen, go to the subfolder FiguresChap 05 on the CD-ROM, then to the folder of Figures.

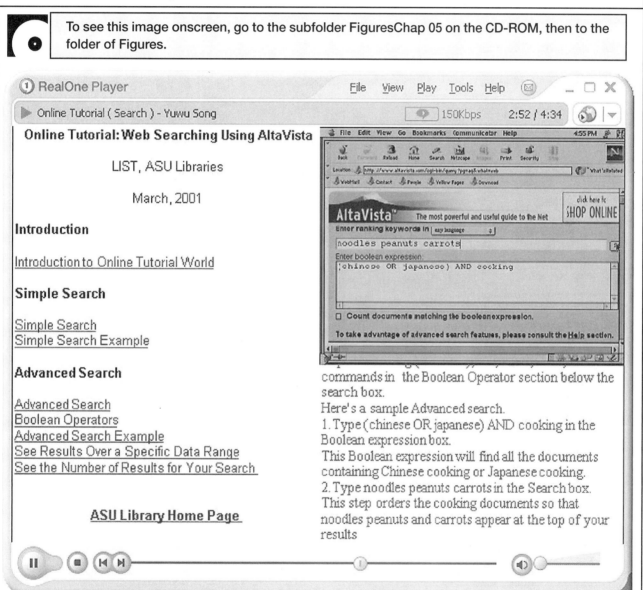

Figure 5–18 Camtasia Recorder

To see this image onscreen, go to the subfolder FiguresChap 05 on the CD-ROM, then to the folder of Figures.

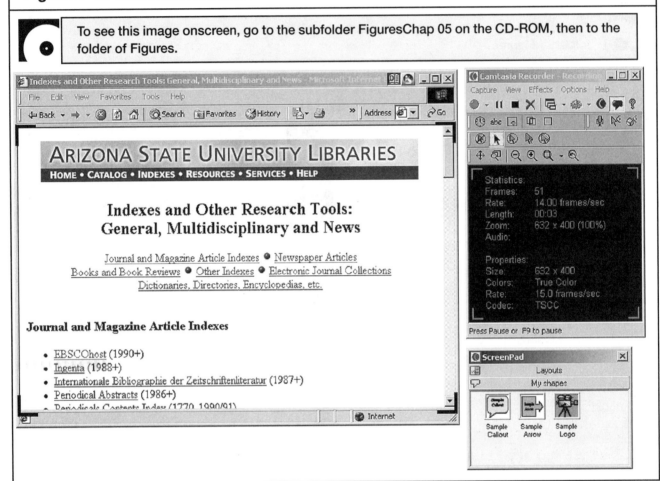

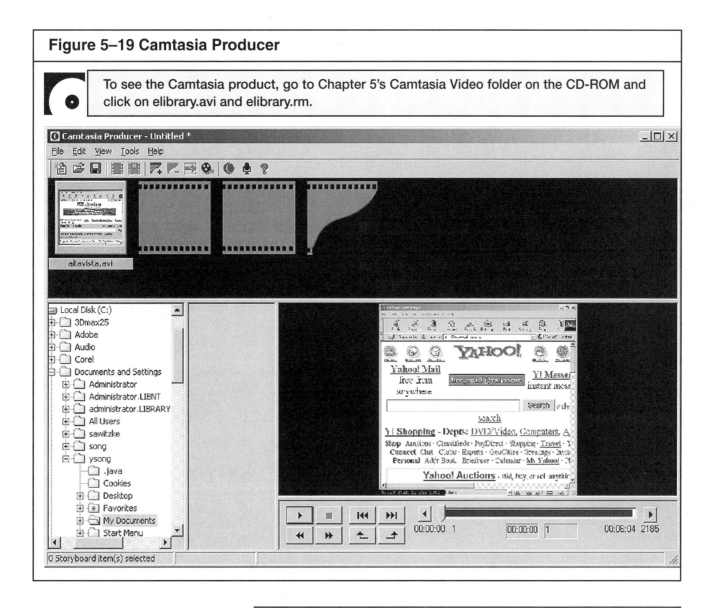

Figure 5–19 Camtasia Producer

To see the Camtasia product, go to Chapter 5's Camtasia Video folder on the CD-ROM and click on elibrary.avi and elibrary.rm.

LIBRARY MULTIMEDIA APPLICATIONS AND PRODUCTS

LIBRARY INSTRUCTION ONLINE VIDEO AT ARIZONA STATE UNIVERSITY (*WWW.ASU.EDU/LIB/TUTORIALS/LIBONLINE/*)

At Arizona State University, we converted VHS videos shot with a traditional video camera into digital formats. We used Apple G4s, a Sony DMA–200 digital converter, and Media 100 to do the conversion and then used Media 100 to edit the video. After

Figure 5–20 SMIL-Based Online Library Video Tutorial: Arizona State University Libraries

To see this image onscreen, go to the subfolder FiguresChap 05 on the CD-ROM, then to the folder of Figures.

this, we used Media Cleaner Pro v5 for compressing and preparing each video file for output to the Web as a RealMedia file (rm). We also used Camtasia to capture screen moving pictures of Web sites and databases. We then joined the Camtasia video with AVI clips digitized from regular VHS videos showing our instruction librarians teaching information literacy classes. The joined files were saved as .rm files. Finally we used SMIL (Synchronized

Multimedia Integration Language) to create the multimedia product interface including the layout, links to different sections in the video, and moving captions. For more details, see SMIL in Chapter 6, Investigating Advanced Web Technologies.

QUICKTIME VIDEO

This product is a QuickTime video: Introduction to the libraries at the University of California at Berkeley by University librarian Peter Lyman (*http://bmrc.berkeley.edu/video/lyman/*).

Another QuickTime video: Introduction to the Hayden Library at the Arizona State University (*www.asu.edu/lib/tutorials/test/libmov/libmov.htm*).

Figure 5–21 QuickTime-Based Video: University Libraries, University of California at Berkeley

To see this image onscreen, go to the subfolder FiguresChap 05 on the CD-ROM, then to the folder of Figures.

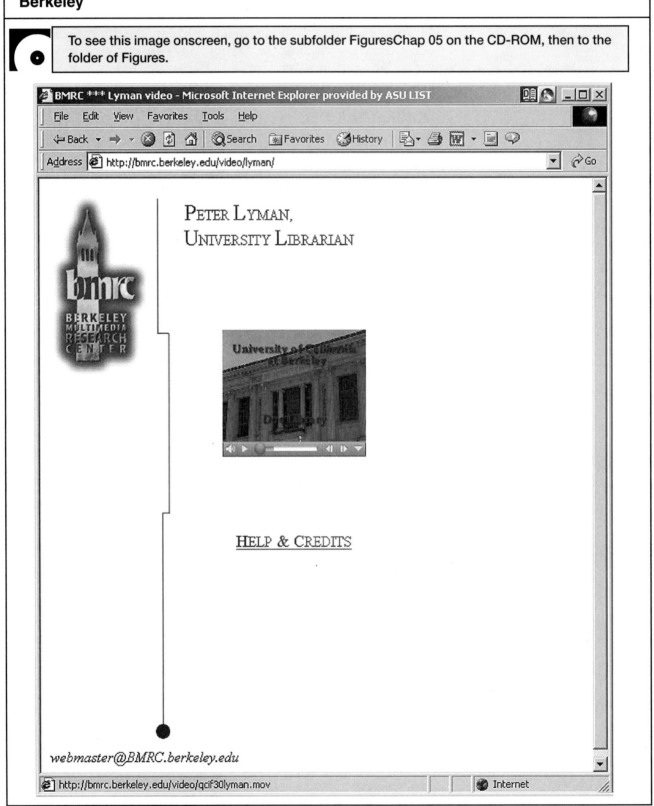

Figure 5–22 QuickTime-Based Video: Hayden Library at the Arizona State University

To see the QuickTime video, go to Chapter 5's QuickTime folder on the CD-ROM and click on libmov.htm.

MULTIMEDIA DIGITAL LIBRARY PRODUCT

The Texas Historical Society and the University Libraries of the University of Texas at Austin have created a very impressive multimedia digital library product, which not only includes text and pictures, but also scanned documents, as well as audio and video (*www.tsha.utexas.edu/handbook/online/multimedia.html*).

Figure 5–23 A Multimedia Digital Library Product: The Texas Historical Society and the University Libraries of University of Texas at Austin

To see this image onscreen, go to the subfolder FiguresChap 05 on the CD-ROM, then to the folder of Figures.

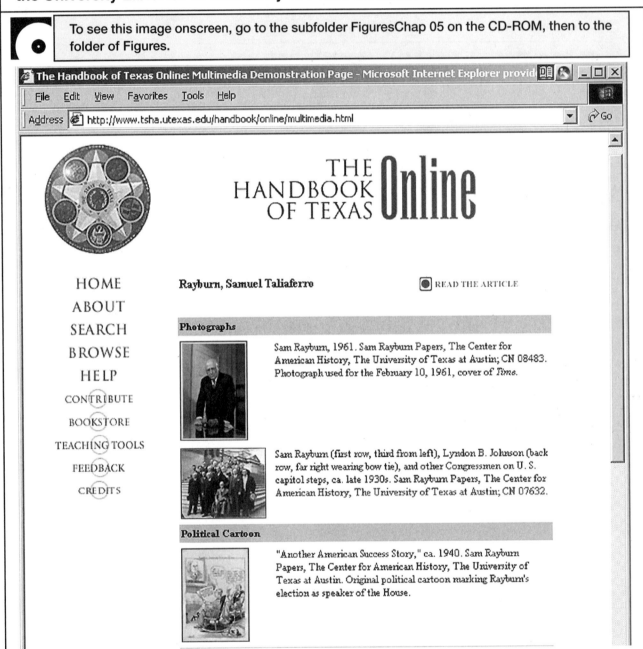

Figure 5–23 *(Continued)*

Documents

Letter from Lyndon B. Johnson to Sam Rayburn, January 6, 1939. Sam Rayburn Papers, The Center for American History, The University of Texas at Austin. Johnson congratulates Rayburn on the occasion of Rayburn's fifty-seventh birthday.

Letter from Lyndon B. Johnson to Sam Rayburn, May 13, 1939. Sam Rayburn Papers, The Center for American History, The University of Texas at Austin. Johnson thanks Rayburn for his counsel, remarking that Rayburn has been "like a Daddy" to him.

Audio

Audio

Audio tour (5:46) of the Sam Rayburn Library and Museum in Bonham, Texas. Sam Rayburn Papers, The Center for American History, The University of Texas at Austin.

(Real Player required)

Video

(low bandwidth)

(high bandwidth)

Mr. Speaker, Mr. Sam. Video (14:40), prepared by Mayah Productions in association with the Sam Rayburn House and the Fannin County Museum of History, 1995. Sam Rayburn Papers, The Center for American History, The University of Texas at Austin. Traces Sam Rayburn's life, especially his political career, in the Texas legislature and United States Congress. Mentions tourist attractions in Bonham, Texas, including the Sam Rayburn House, Sam Rayburn Library, and Fannin County Museum of History.

(Real Player required)

 COMMENTS?  BACK

top of page | about | search | browse | help | home - contribute - bookstore - teaching tools - feedback - credits

The *Handbook of Texas Online* is a joint project of The General Libraries at the University of Texas at Austin and the Texas State Historical Association.

Copyright ©, The Texas State Historical Association, 1997-2001
Last Updated: February 26, 2002
Comments to: comments.tsha@lib.utexas.edu

QTVR MOVIE: NATIONAL LIBRARY OF CANADA

This QTVR movie (see Figure 5–24) is a virtual library tour of the National Library of Canada (*www.nlc-bnc.ca/10/7/a7–7300-e.html*).

Figure 5–24 QTVR Movie: National Library of Canada

To see this image onscreen, go to the subfolder FiguresChap 05 on the CD-ROM, then to the folder of Figures.

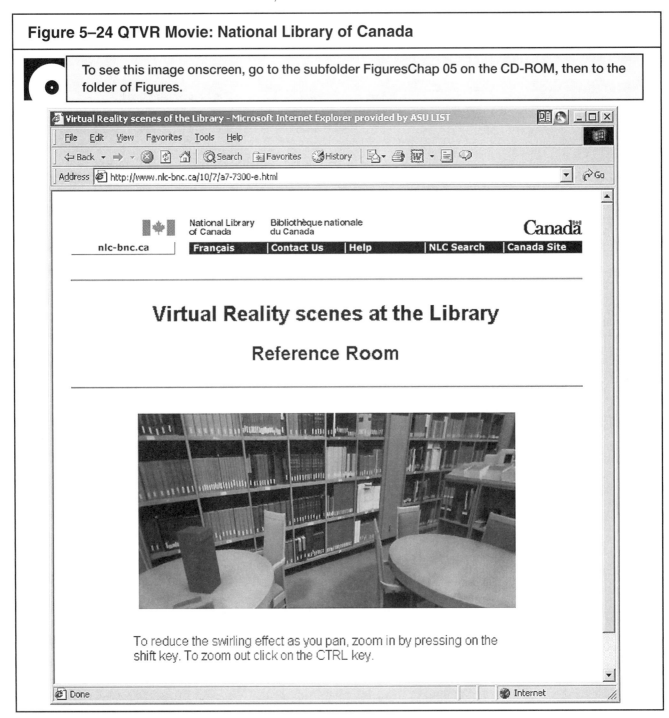

6 INVESTIGATING ADVANCED WEB TECHNOLOGIES

The Web tools and technologies introduced in the previous chapters are the most basic for you to develop a decent library Web site. However, more advanced technologies including Java, XML, SMIL, SGML, VRML, and database-driven Web technologies (ASP, PHP, Cold Fusion, and JSP) can help you create more sophisticated library Web sites featured by more interactivity, flexibility, and functionality. For example, Java Applets, such as animations or panoramic movies, can enliven your library site tremendously. SMIL provides a powerful tool for controlling and playing out library multimedia materials. For maintenance-intensive library Web sites, database-driven technologies offer great solutions. This chapter is intended for developers who have mastered HTML skills and are ready to tackle larger issues and more advanced tools and techniques of library Web development.

Some of these new technologies, though attractive, may not be suitable for regular library Web sites because of the bandwidth or plug-in restrictions. If, however, you are designing a Web site or Web-based application to be used on a library Intranet such as a library staff training Web site, you may have a valid reason for using one of these new technologies. The tightly controlled Intranet environment (hardware and software) eliminates many of the problems that would be encountered in using these technologies in the widely diverse Web environment.

JAVA

Java is a full-blown programming language like C or C++. It can be used to create general computer applications. Java has become quite popular because it was designed with the Web in mind. Java brings the greatest possibility for interactivity on the Web. It is robust, powerful, and platform independent; in other words, as a programming language it was developed so that its object modules can run on many different platforms. In a nutshell, Java adds advanced interactivity and multimedia functionality to the Web sites. The drawback of Java is that some Applets are loading slowly. This presents a problem for users with slow connection. On the whole, Java is a useful technology worthy of your investment.

A Java program for the Web usually comes in the form of "Applets" (small applications), Web-based programs that run when a user accesses the page. Java Applets are launched from a Web page, but they run independent of any HTML document and have much more powerful capabilities. Java Applets can do more sophisticated tasks than are possible using HTML, JavaScript, or server-based CGI. In contrast to CGI, when a Java-compatible browser accesses a Java-powered page, an Applet is copied to the browser's machine and executes there without calling up the server software to process. Java allows an Applet to have full client/server interaction between itself and a server. To some extent, the Applet is an independent application running within the browser. This local execution allows a greater level of Web interaction and multimedia effects, surpassing HTML restrictions or network bandwidth restrictions.

Java programs can be used to design site interface. They can also add to your site interesting features such as scrolling text, flipping images, crossword puzzles, animations, games, calculations, stock quotes, sports scores, weather conditions, chat, ad banners, and so on. They can be used to show step-by-step tutorial instructions, or run demonstration versions of computer software. Unlike Shockwave or Flash, you do not need a plug-in to play Java. This looks like a trivial point for veteran Web users, but for the beginners it can be a daunting proposition. The good news is that since the majority of browsers support Java, a Web developer can be assured that the site will be experienced as created.

Java interactivity goes far beyond rollovers and animations. The technology can be used in many Web-based applications. It is making more of a presence in the realm of library automation. Examples of Java applications in a library setting include full-blown Java clients in Millennium, Innovative's library automation system, and Java Applets in epixtech's WebPAC, a Java-based OPAC system. OCLC makes use of Java in its SiteSearch suite, which is a complex environment that contains a set of tools for creating interfaces to library resources.

To run a Java Applet, you need to download the HTML page containing the instruction (parameters) for the Applet to operate, and also the Applet files called class files. They are often with the extension .class and contained in compressed files such as ZIP. Java is an object-oriented language. The programmer needs special tools: compilers, linkers, libraries, debuggers, documentation, and so forth. Sun Microsystems, the developer of the language, provides the Java Development Kit at *http://java.sun.com.*

Although Java is well designed, due to its complexity the learning curve for Java is steep. Many people are intimidated by the thought of learning an object-oriented language such as Java. But as with all programming languages, it is not necessary to understand the semantics of programming so as to use the applications or tools that are created by that language. There are many Applets from the Web that you can download free and tailor for your Web site. One good site providing information about Java Applets is Gamelan: *www.developer.com/java/.* It has libraries of different Applets available for developers. By following the directions, you can customize Applets for your needs.

To use Java in your Web site, you need to put the Applet files on your Web server in the same directory as your Web page and add Java Applets to your pages with the <Applet> tag, which can include attributes for the Applet's height, width, and other parameters. You can also use the <object> tag instead of <Applet> in your HTML page.

For example:

```
<Applet code= "java_Applet.class" width = "300" height = "300">
<param name= "bgcolor" value= "green">
<param name= "font" value= "bold">
<param name= "url" value= "http://www.domain/library">
</Applet>
```

In this example, code defines the Applet file name, width and height specify the dimensions of the area where the Applet will show up. The param tags define how the Applets operate. For the Applets, the developers usually provide documentation about the ranges of parameter values. With this documentation, you can set the Applet's parameters properly. If the Applet is not in the same directory as your HTML file, you can reference it to a URL by "codebase" attribute. Other attributes you can use include "align" for horizontal alignment: left, right, center, and vspace and hspace (the vertical and horizontal white space around the Applet's writing area). Within the <Applet> tags, you can insert alternate text by including an ALT = "description" attribute. If the users' browsers cannot process the Applet, the alternate text will be displayed. If you have Macromedia Dreamweaver, you can incorporate them into your site by choosing "Insert Applet" from the Insert Menu in Dreamweaver. It is very much like inserting a graphic into your page.

JAVA-BASED ANIMATION

In this section, we will take a look at placing and using an existing Applet in a Web document. Java can be used to create animation. For Java animation Applets, the following site is a nice place to check: *www.anfyteam.com*. On this site you can download and use for free a couple of Java programs.

There is a "Lens Applet." This Applet can simulate a lens moving over any GIF or JPG image. You first download three files: AnLens.class, Lware.class, and anfy.class. You can create your own graphic (facet.jpg) using your favorite program and then replace facet.jpg with your graphic at: <param name=image value="facet.jpg">. You then change the values of the parameters to generate the kinds of lens effects you like. You can change the size of the lens, the speed of the movement of the lens, distortion, and so on. The range of values and code descriptions is listed below:

```
<Applet archive="AnLens.jar" code="AnLens.class"
width="320" height="256">
<param name="credits" value="Applet by Fabio Ciucci
(www.anfyteam.com)">
<param name="regcode" value="NO">; Registration code (if
you have it)
<param name="reglink" value="NO">; Optional URL link when
the Applet is "clicked".
<param name="regnewframe" value="YES">; Reglink opened
in new frame?
<param name="regframename" value="_blank">; Name of new
frame for reglink
<param name="statusmsg" value="Lens Applet">; Statusbar
message
<param name="image" value="facet.jpg">; Image to load
<param name="lenswidth" value="35">; Size of lens
<param name="distdval" value="10">; Diagonal distortion (5 ..
20)
<param name="distoxy" value="0">; XY distortion (–40 .. 40)
<param name="zoomfactor" value="5">; Zoom factor (0 .. 30)
<param name="interactive" value="YES">; Interaction ("ON" ..
"OFF")
<param name="distort" value="YES">; Distortion ("ON" .. "OFF")
<param name="spdx" value="2">; X speed (0 .. 8)
<param name="spdy" value="1">; Y speed (0 .. 8)
<param name="overimg" value="NO">; Optional image over
Applet
<param name="overimgX" value="0">; Over image X offset
<param name="overimgY" value="0">; Over image Y offset
<param name="memdelay" value="1000">; Memory
```

```
deallocation delay
<param name="priority" value="3">; Task priority (1..10)
<param name="MinSYNC" value="10">; Min. milliseconds/
frame for sync
Sorry, your browser doesn't support Java.; Msg in no java
browsers
</Applet>
```

The following code is a customized version of this Applet:

```
<center>
<p> <font color="#000000" face="Times New Roman, Times,
serif">
<Applet archive="AnLens.jar" code="AnLens.class" width=320
height=256 alt="java_lens">
<param name=credits value="Applet by Fabio Ciucci
(www.anfyteam.com)">
<param name=regcode value="NO">
<param name=reglink value="NO">
<param name=regnewframe value="YES">
<param name=regframename value="_blank">
<param name=statusmsg value="Lens Applet">
<param name=image value="facet.jpg">
<param name=lenswidth value="45">
<param name=distdval value="10">
<param name=distoxy value="0">
<param name=zoomfactor value="12">
<param name=interactive value="YES">
<param name=distort value="NO">
<param name=spdx value="1">
<param name=spdy value="1">
<param name=overimg value="NO">
<param name=overimgX value="0">
<param name=overimgY value="0">
<param name=memdelay value="1000">
<param name=priority value="3">
<param name=MinSYNC value="10">
Sorry, your browser doesn't support Java.
</Applet> </font>
</center>
```

Figure 6–1 shows the customized Java-based animation, which can be found at: *www.asu.edu/lib/tutorials/test/journal/journal. htm*. The Applet simulates a lens moving over a few periodicals, producing the effect that someone holding a magnifying glass is trying to distinguish a popular magazine from a scholarly journal.

Figure 6–1 Java-Based Animation: Arizona State University Libraries

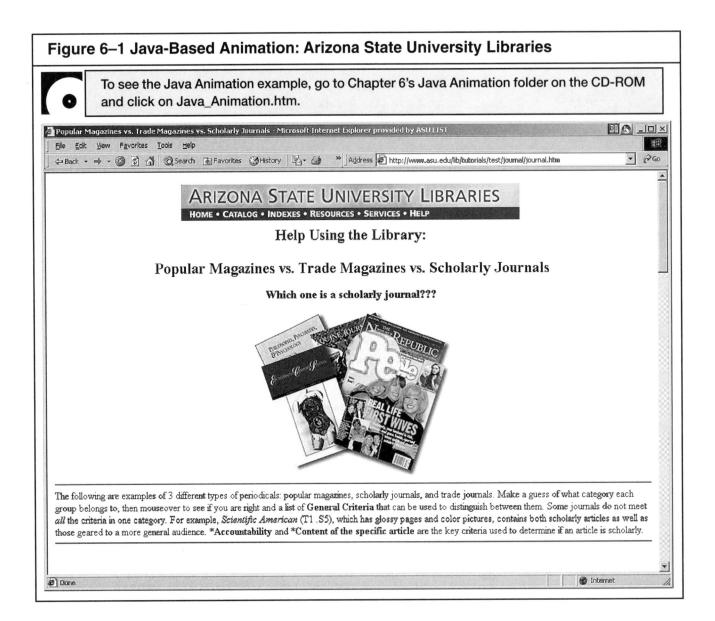

To see the Java Animation example, go to Chapter 6's Java Animation folder on the CD-ROM and click on Java_Animation.htm.

JAVA-BASED MENU

Rancho Cucamonga Public Library Web site (*www.rcpl.lib.ca.us*) contains a Java-based menu. It provides a nice-looking and effective navigation set. You mouse over a menu link; a submenu list with hyperlinks will pop up, prompting you to explore further.

Figure 6–2 Java-Based Menu: Rancho Cucamonga Public Library

To see this image onscreen, go to the subfolder FiguresChap 06 on the CD-ROM, then to the folder of Figures.

JAVA-BASED PANORAMIC MOVIE

Tempe Public Library Virtual Tour (*www.tempe.gov/library/360/ default.htm*) is a Java-based panoramic movie modeled after QuickTimeVR Movie. You can actually place yourself in this library in the various locations and actually look around by dragging along with your mouse. What is neat about this application is that you don't need a QuickTime plug-in to watch the panoramic movie.

Figure 6–3 Java-Based Panoramic Movie: Tempe Public Library Virtual Tour

 To see this image onscreen, go to the subfolder FiguresChap 06 on the CD-ROM, then to the folder of Figures.

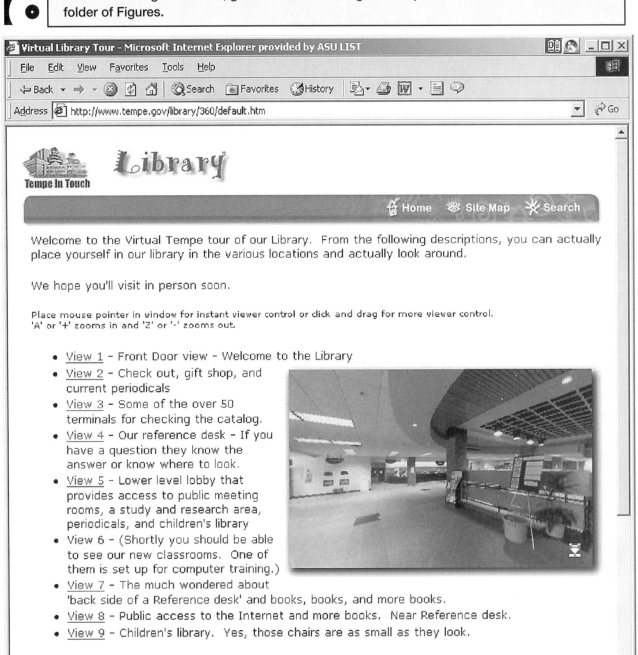

Virtual Library Tour – Microsoft Internet Explorer provided by ASU LIST

File   Edit   View   Favorites   Tools   Help

⇐ Back ▾ ⇒ ▾ ⊗ ⬆ ⌂ │ ⬛Search ⬛Favorites ⬛History │ ⬛▾ ⬛ ⬛ ▾ ⬛ ⬛

Address http://www.tempe.gov/library/360/default.htm

Welcome to the Virtual Tempe tour of our Library. From the following descriptions, you can actually place yourself in our library in the various locations and actually look around.

We hope you'll visit in person soon.

Place mouse pointer in window for instant viewer control or click and drag for more viewer control. 'A' or '+' zooms in and 'Z' or '-' zooms out.

- View 1 – Front Door view – Welcome to the Library
- View 2 – Check out, gift shop, and current periodicals
- View 3 – Some of the over 50 terminals for checking the catalog.
- View 4 – Our reference desk – If you have a question they know the answer or know where to look.
- View 5 – Lower level lobby that provides access to public meeting rooms, a study and research area, periodicals, and children's library
- View 6 – (Shortly you should be able to see our new classrooms. One of them is set up for computer training.)
- View 7 – The much wondered about 'back side of a Reference desk' and books, books, and more books.
- View 8 – Public access to the Internet and more books. Near Reference desk.
- View 9 – Children's library. Yes, those chairs are as small as they look.

Virtual Tour Listings

Done   Internet

JAVA TOOLS

One way around Java's high learning curve is to create your Java content in a software program that supports Java, and have the software convert the content into Java code for you. One tool is Symantec's Visual Cafe. It provides an extensive set of source code development tools. Visual Cafe seamlessly integrates visual and source views. Modifications made in visual view are immediately reflected in the source code. Changes to the source code automatically update the visual views. With Visual Cafe, you can assemble complete Java Applets and applications from a library of standard and third party objects without writing source code.

Figure 6–4 Symantec's Visual Café

To see this image onscreen, go to the subfolder FiguresChap 06 on the CD-ROM, then to the folder of Figures.

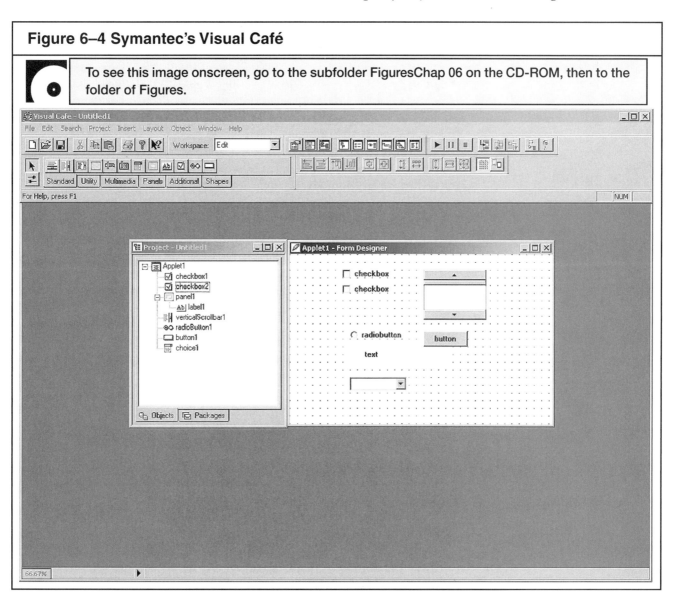

XML

XML, THE POWERFUL LANGUAGE

XML stands for Extensible Markup Language. It is a subset of the Standard Generalized Markup Language (SGML). XML is designed for distributing materials on the Internet. One of the greatest challenges in developing Web sites is the diversity of software and hardware that must be supported. "Portable" Web users want to have a quick and light version that they can view on a screen that is just 200 pixels wide and with only a 2-bit color depth, while Web TV users want a complete experience, with all the flashy graphics, animations, and multimedia.

The issue here is that although both types of users can see the same Web content, the page presentation must be customized for best viewing on the specific device or operating systems. To do this, traditional Web designers have to create different versions for different platforms, which is not realistic. Another way is to make a separation between the Web content and the form in which the Web content is presented. Theoretically speaking, in order to have a seamless interchange of data, it is necessary to require all database holders to use a single standard system instead of existing heterogeneous systems. The alternative for interchange of records between heterogeneous systems is to use a single industry-wide interchange format that serves as the single output format for all exporting systems and the single input format for all importing systems. Actually, SGML is designed as this single interchange format, while XML is developed as a simplified version of this format. We may refer to XML as SGML Lite. XML is different from SGML in that it has less complex formalisms of SGML. This ensures that an XML parser is simple enough to be embedded in Web browsers. XML can serve as a solution by combining structural information with a flexible, descriptive presentation.

XML can be used to pass data between unrelated programs, handling more of the processing load at the client machine instead of the server, presenting different views of data to different users, and adjusting content according to the historical preferences to different users. Because data computations can be performed without additional return trips to the server, this no doubt lifts the loads from the server and reduces the congestion on the net. Developments of XML will continue to separate content from container, thus opening up new possibilities for flexible display and intelligent manipulation of information. As far as libraries are concerned, XML has already been used in the fields of interlibrary loan, systems integration, cataloging and indexing, building collections and databases, data migration, systems interoperability, etc.

Like HTML, XML is a mark-up language. But it expands the functionality of HTML by allowing the users to create new tags, and making it possible for regular Web browsers to handle such user-made element types usefully. HTML enables universal methods for viewing data; but it does not provide universal methods for working directly with data. HTML has its own limitations:

- HTML is incapable of representing or differentiating between the multitudes of database fields in the mixture of documents making up the records.
- HTML is unable to represent the variety of structures in those documents.
- HTML has no mechanism for checking the data for structural validity before importing it into the target database.

XML is able to define and exchange structured data. By describing structured data in an extensible way, XML complements HTML, which is used to depict user interfaces. XML's ability to do these in a text-based format and deliver this data using standard Web protocol HTTP is very useful. It allows powerful applications, formerly found only on high-end databases, to be created naturally for the Web using a simple and open format.

AN XML EXAMPLE

When displayed in the browser, the HTML only gives a value to the name of author Shakespeare. To state it more emphatically, the name is coded for bold type.

The popularity of <B>Shakespeare</B>is...

The following XML descriptions tell us more about Shakespeare's function and a book about him. XML makes it possible to search the file for the terms: author and book.

The popularity of<author>Shakespeare</author>is...
The popularity of<book>Shakespeare</book>is...

This example shows that XML assigns a meaning to information, while HTML only describes the information display. The freedom XML provides for you to create your own tags and labels makes it possible to develop all types of documents, including Web pages, metadata, database files, and so on. The following is another example from an XML application, which shows how to make new tags for describing data in a flexible and extensible way.

```
<?xml version= "1.0"?>
<books>
<book>
<author>Peter Alexander
</author>
<title>Shakespeare
</title>
<place of publication>New York; London
</place of publication>
<publisher> Oxford University Press
</publisher>
<data of publication>1964
</data of publication>
<ISBN>0 471–88611–4
</ISBN>
<pagination>256
</pagination>
<price= "USA">$14.95
</price>
</book>
<book>
...
</book>
</books>
```

This XML-based record is very easy to customize. You can add or remove certain things. It can be used as an acquisition order or as a regular bibliographical record for an online catalog. You can add table of contents or descriptive information such as non-fiction, fiction, reference, etc. All of the metadata helps you to search, select, or sort information.

MAJOR STRENGTHS OF XML

The major strengths of XML include:

- XML is simple to use.
- It is media independent; writing something in XML means publishing it infinitely.
- XML's logical "content-descriptive" tags make it possible to check the quality of a document.
- XML allows structured data storage without the complexity of a database.
- XML allows you to search and select content. For ex-

ample: Give all books written by Shakespeare; give all books written about Shakespeare.

- Once the XML file has been read into an XML-capable browser, data can be manipulated without requiring contact with the server. For example: Give all books written about Shakespeare published after 1990; give all books written about Shakespeare published by Oxford University Press; give all reference books about Shakespeare.

A USEFUL WEB APPLICATION OF XML: LETTING THE USER DECIDE VIEW SELECTION

To understand how XML works, we'd better take a look at a real-world example. One of many potential XML applications is dynamic display of data. In real life users may wish to switch between different views of the data without requiring that the data be downloaded again in a different form from the Web server. As we know, HTML describes the appearance of data, while XML describes data itself. Since display is now separate from data, having this data defined in XML allows different views to be specified, resulting in data being presented appropriately. After data is sent to the client, data in XML format may be parsed and locally edited and manipulated, with computations performed by client applications. Now local data can be presented dynamically in a manner determined by client configuration, user preference, or other criteria.

Now, let's take a close look at an XML-based library's directory at: *www.asu.edu/lib/tutorials/test/sorter/sorter1.xml* (to see the application, you have to use an XML-capable browser such as Internet Explorer 5). To look for information in a directory, an average user might want to see just the subjects a librarian specializes in. But other users might want to know about who specializes in what. It is easy for them to get the information by sorting. Clicking on Subject Area or First Name buttons will give you a display of the information you want in alphabetic order. Take a look at Figure 6–5 and Figure 6–6.

Figure 6–5 XML-Based Sorter (Sorting by Subject Area): Arizona State University Libraries

To see the XML Application (Sorter) example, go to Chapter 6's XML Application (Sorter) folder on the CD-ROM and click on XML_APP_Sorter.htm.

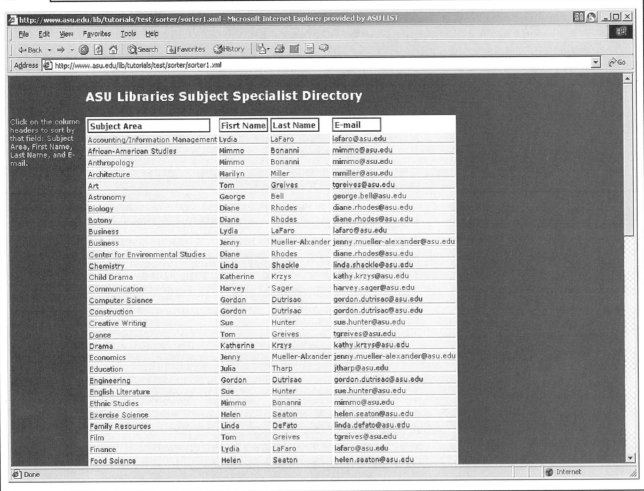

Figure 6–6 XML-Based Sorter (Sorting by First Name): Arizona State University Libraries

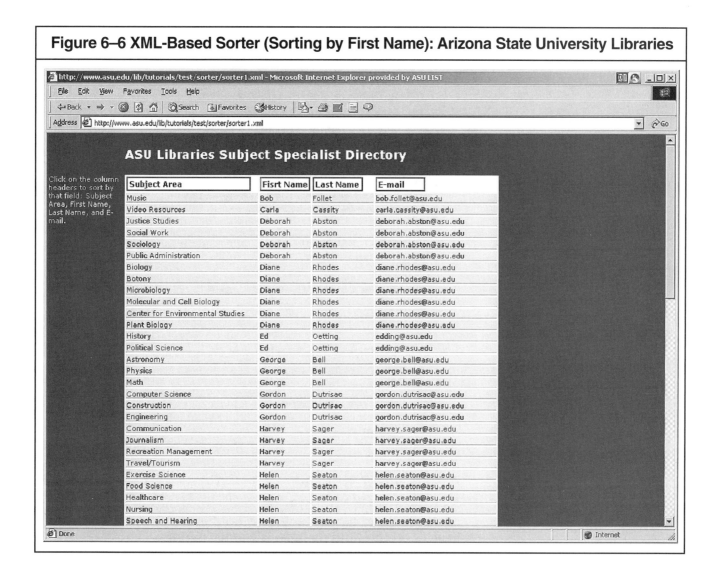

WHAT THE APPLICATION CONTAINS
This application contains three components: a schema, an XSL file, and an XML data file.

A Schema
Written in XML, a schema provides a method for XML to describe its own structure. It functions like DTD (Document Type Definition). It defines element names that indicate which elements are allowed in an XML document, and in what relationships. With a schema, the developers can also define attributes. The following codes were downloaded free from Microsoft Web site (*www. microsoft.com*) and customized according to the library's needs.

```
<?xml version="1.0" ?>
<Schema xmlns="urn:schemas-microsoft-com:xml-data"
xmlns:dt="urn:schemas-microsoft-com:datatypes">
<ElementType name="date" dt:type="dateTime"/>
<ElementType name="description"/>
<ElementType name="firstname"/>
<ElementType name="subject"/>
<ElementType name="lastname"/>
<ElementType name="email"/>
<ElementType name="directory" content="eltOnly">
<group minOccurs="0" maxOccurs="1">
<element type="description" />
</group>
<group minOccurs="0" maxOccurs="1">
<element type="date" />
</group>
<group minOccurs="1" maxOccurs="1">
<element type="specialist" />
</group>
</ElementType>
<ElementType name="specialist" content="eltOnly">
<element type="firstname" />
<element type="subject" />
<element type="lastname" />
<element type="email" />
</ElementType>
</Schema>
```

A Style Sheet: XSL file

As we know HTML pages use predefined tags, and the meaning of these tags is clear: <b> means bold font size and <hr> means a horizontal rule, and the browser understands how to display these pages. Using XML developers can use any tags, and the browser does not understand the meaning of these tags: <title> could mean an HTML page title or maybe a title of a person, or a book. Due to the nature of XML, we do not have standard ways to show an XML file. To show XML documents, we need to have a mechanism to describe how the document should be displayed. XSL is the exact tool that fits in here.

XSL (eXtensible Stylesheet Language) is a transformation language that defines rules for turning structured XML data to HTML, using an XSL processor. In other words, XSL can be used to define how an XML file should be displayed by transforming the XML file into a format that is recognizable to a browser. XSL can be used to generate CSS (Cascading Style Sheet) along with HTML as well. XSL can also add new elements into the output document, or remove elements. It can rearrange and sort the elements, and decide which elements to display. XSL consists of a method for transforming XML and a method for formatting XML documents. In the following XSL file, the part of the <SCRIPT>...</SCRIPT> defines rules for mapping structured XML data to HTML. The Cascading Style Sheet: <STYLE>... </STYLE> within the XSL file defines the appearance of the output just like a regular CSS in a Web page.

```
<?xml version="1.0"?>
<xsl:stylesheet xmlns:xsl="http://www.w3.org/TR/WD-xsl">
<xsl:template match="/">
<HTML>
<HEAD>
<STYLE>
BODY {margin:0}
.bg {font:8pt Verdana; background-color:#990033; color:white}
H1 {font:bold 14pt Verdana; width:100%; margin-top:1em}
.row {font:8pt Verdana; border-bottom:1px solid #CC88CC}
header {font:bold 9pt Verdana; cursor:hand; padding:2px;
border:2px outset gray}
.up {background-color:#DDFFDD;}
.down {background-color:#FFFDDD;}
</STYLE>
</HEAD>
<SCRIPT><xsl:comment><![CDATA[
function sort(field)
{
sortField.value = field;
listing.innerHTML =
source.documentElement.transformNode(stylesheet);
}
]]></xsl:comment></SCRIPT>
<SCRIPT for="window"
event="onload"><xsl:comment><![CDATA[
stylesheet = document.XSLDocument;
source = document.XMLDocument;
sortField = document.XSLDocument.selectSingleNode("//
@order—by");
]]></xsl:comment></SCRIPT>
<BODY>
<TABLE width="100%" cellspacing="0">
<TR>
<TD class="bg"/>
<TD class="bg">
<H1><xsl:value-of select="directory/description"/>
<xsl:apply-templates select="directory/date"/></H1>
</TD>
```

```
</TR>
<TR
<TD class="bg" width="120" valign="top">
<P>Click on the column headers to sort by that field: Subject
Area, First Name, Last Name, and E-mail.</P>
</TD>
<TD class="bg" valign="top">
<DIV id="listing"><xsl:apply-templates select="directory"/>
</DIV>
</TD>
</TR>
</TABLE>
</BODY>
</HTML>
</xsl:template>
<xsl:template match="directory">
<TABLE STYLE="background-color:white">
<THEAD>
<TD width="200"><DIV class="header"
onClick="sort('subject')"
>Subject Area</DIV></TD>
<TD width="80"><DIV class="header"
onClick="sort('firstname')"
>Fisrt Name</DIV></TD>
<TD width="80"><DIV class="header"
onClick="sort('lastname')"
>Last Name</DIV></TD>
<TD width="80"><DIV class="header"
onClick="sort('email')">E-mail</DIV></TD>
</THEAD>
<xsl:for-each select="specialist" order-by="firstname">
<TR>
<xsl:for-each select="change">
<xsl:if expr="this.nodeTypedValue &gt; 0">
<xsl:attribute name="class">up</xsl:attribute>
</xsl:if>
</xsl:for-each>
<xsl:for-each select="color">
<xsl:if expr="this.nodeTypedValue &lt; -1">
<xsl:attribute name="class">down</xsl:attribute>
</xsl:if>
</xsl:for-each>
<TD><DIV class="row"><xsl:value-of select="subject"/>
</DIV></TD>
<TD><DIV class="row"><xsl:value-of select="firstname"/>
</DIV></TD>
<TD><DIV class="row"><xsl:value-of select="lastname"/>
</DIV></TD>
<TD><DIV class="row"><xsl:value-of select="email"/></DIV>
```

```
</TD>
</TR>
</xsl:for-each>
</TABLE>
</xsl:template>
</xsl:stylesheet>
```

An XML Data File

This file contains basic information for this application such as references to the XSL file and the schema file, which are the heart and brain of the application. The XML file also holds the information of the element types: first name, last name, e-mail, and subject, which are to be formatted and displayed by the XSL file if the user clicks the switch button. These elements are, in other words, the individual items in a database.

```
<?xml:stylesheet type="text/xsl" href="sorter.xsl"?>
<directory xmlns="x-schema:schema.xml">
<description>ASU Libraries Subject Specialist Directory
</description>
<date>2000–06–13T15:56:00</date>
<specialist>
<firstname>Lydia</firstname>
<subject>Accounting/Information Management</subject>
<lastname>LaFaro</lastname>
<email>lafaro@asu.edu</email>
<color>–2</color>
</specialist>
...
</directory>
```

HOW XML WORKS

As far as we know, XML data does not contain information about how data, such as first name, last name, e-mail, and subject, should be displayed. So to show this data, either the Web server or the Web browser will need to move XML data into HTML for presentation, or alternatively transform XML data into HTML. Here the XSL file provides a declarative mechanism for describing a particular view of the data. The browser's XSL processor processes the instruction in the XSL file and presents the XML-based data in HTML format.

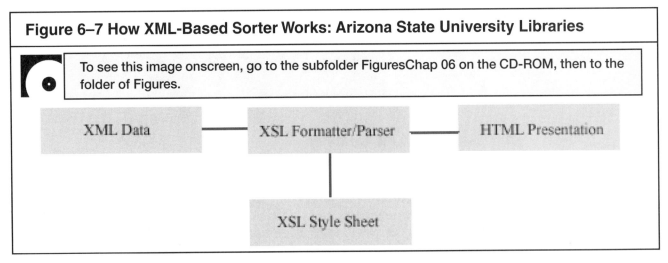

Figure 6–7 How XML-Based Sorter Works: Arizona State University Libraries

To see this image onscreen, go to the subfolder FiguresChap 06 on the CD-ROM, then to the folder of Figures.

XML Data — XSL Formatter/Parser — HTML Presentation

XSL Style Sheet

XML's ability to send and format structural data greatly expands the range of possibilities for client-side manipulation of the way in which data appears to the users. There are other potential applications of XML for data downloading and viewing as well. For example:

- A catalog librarian can have one view of the data; a library user can have another; accounts payable can have yet another.
- A stock price table containing information can be made to show current stock changes, and users' preferred categories by sorting: company name, stock prices in descending or ascending order, change of percentage, etc.
- A document with annotations can be changed from displaying only the text, to showing only the annotations, or to displaying both.
- A multiple-language document can be made to show just the ones in the language selected by the user.
- A weather report can be made to show cities, states, temperature, etc., by clicking a preference switch.
- A technical manual dealing with both the NT and 95/98 versions of the Microsoft operating system can be switched to look like a manual for NT only, or a manual for 95/98 only, just by the user's selection.
- By granular updates, XML embedded within an HTML page only downloads the changed elements without refreshing the whole page.
- Other useful user-specific view of data: the same data can be presented as a subset, depending on the user's role regarding the data; for instance, accountants see more details than the purchasers.

The short list above is only a fraction of possible uses of XML for dynamic viewing, while dynamic viewing is only the tip of the iceberg of XML applications.

OTHER USES OF XML

There are many other XML applications:

- SMIL (Synchronized Multimedia Integration Language) describes the layout and temporal behavior of multimedia presentations and the way media objects use hypertext links.
- MathML (Mathematics Markup Language) is a markup language for describing formulas of mathematics.
- CML (Chemical Markup Language) is a markup language for chemistry.
- BSML (Bioinformatic Sequence Markup Language) can be used to display information of genetic sequence.
- CDF (Channel Definition Format) describes metadata or "push channels" such as the URL, page summary, etc.
- WML (Wireless Markup Language) supports browsers for handheld computing appliances.
- DSML (Directory Service Markup Language) is a data model describing directory data such as name and address listings.
- XML-EDI (Electronic Data Interchange). This format, if included in XML, will make it possible to connect disparate systems that were only used in one institution.
- XML-QL (XML Query Language) allows SQL to work in XML documents.
- SDML (Signed Document Markup Language) provides a way to electronically sign one's signature and verify electronic documents.
- VXML (Visual XML) can help create sites in VRML (Virtual Reality Modeling Language) with a virtual 3D navigation set.
- TMX (Translation Memory Exchange) helps exchange language databases between software packages for language translation.
- XML-RDF (Resource Description Framework) provides better capabilities for processing metadata and searching.

In general, XML is becoming the standard method by which information of a variety of sources is encoded, delivered, and processed. XML's capabilities have revolutionized the ways people structure, transfer, and view data. XML is and will be bringing many benefits to our information-oriented society.

SMIL

SMIL stands for Synchronized Multimedia Integration Language, a new markup language being developed by a group coordinated by the World Wide Web Consortium (W3C). The first public draft of SMIL was released in November 1997. The specification defines SMIL as an application of XML that describes the layout and temporal behavior of multimedia presentations and the way media objects use hypertext links.

SMIL enables Web developers to deliver text, sound, images, and movies separately; meanwhile, it allows them to control spatial layout and hyperlinks, and to coordinate the timing of the media. In other words, you can use SMIL to place media elements wherever you want on the screen, synchronize those elements, display media following user-preferences, language, bit-rate, and so on. As a new and powerful Web format, SMIL will definitely change the scene of Web-based information delivery and human communication.

One of the greatest advantages of SMIL is synchronization. With SMIL, the designers can time events by programming several streams, images, and text elements into a kind of "schedule" for playback. For example, by adding a time line to a presentation, you can control when content is displayed and how transitions between various content types are handled. SMIL offers quite a few features for handling the timing of media playback. One can set duration for a media clip. For instance, you can assume that the file will play for three minutes. You can time events according to the time line for the entire presentation. You can let a media file begin ten seconds into the presentation and end 15 seconds into the presentation. You can decide what should take place at the end of the presentation. For example, you can remove all graphics or video clips from the display or you can freeze still images on the last frame.

For SMIL, each media object is accessed with a unique Uniform Resource Locator (URL). That means presentations can be made of objects arriving from more than one place and objects can easily be reused in multiple presentations. Part of the language's appeal is that elaborate multimedia productions could be created out of smaller, less bandwidth-intensive components. And by choreographing the interaction between and timing of different multimedia elements, designers could conserve bandwidth and speed transmissions.

SMIL also permits you to include hyperlinks in your presentation. In this way, media files can provide links to other presentations so that when a user clicks on the link, a new presentation starts. Links can also target specific regions within a presentation. Thus you could click on a video to start a different video within the same presentation. You can click links within a presentation that access other presentations or other media files. For example, a presentation on Web search engines could provide links to information on Yahoo and Google.

SMIL is a simple markup language, and while it may sound like a difficult task to do, working with SMIL should be very easy, particularly if you are familiar with HTML. It is nowhere near as complex as current scripting languages such as JavaScript or DHTML. SMIL statements are simple and can be entered with a text editor similar to those used to create HTML pages. It is designed so that SMIL can be used by anyone who knows basic HTML.

You can easily access SMIL presentations from the Web. When you do this, your browser launches a SMIL player, which in turn displays the presentation. To see SMIL in action, you need a compatible player plug-in. The most commonly used SMIL players are RealPlayer (from Real Networks: *www.real.com*) and GRiNS (GRaphical iNterface to SMIL: *www.oratrix.com/GRiNS/*). Once you download and install the player, you can view SMIL presentations.

A REAL WORLD SMIL APPLICATION: LIBRARY INSTRUCTION ONLINE TUTORIAL

Figure 6–8 shows an SMIL-based multimedia project developed at Arizona State University Libraries (*www.asu.edu/lib/tutorials/test/OnlineTutorial/onlinetutorial.smil*). It is a good example of what SMIL can do.

Figure 6–8 SMIL-Based Multimedia Online Library Instruction: Arizona State University Libraries

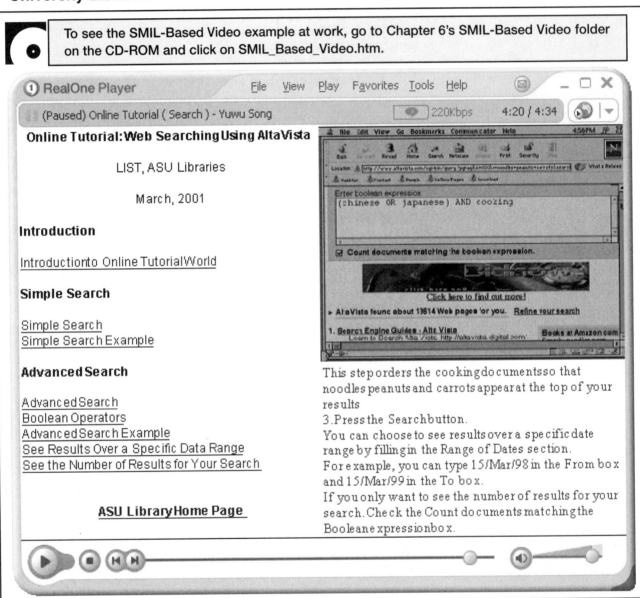

The project takes the form of an online tutorial for library instruction: Web Search Using AltaVista. It employs the interactivity of a Web-based interface to teach information literacy. Users will learn about the process of research on online sources. The tutorial is composed of a video clip with narration, a few indexed links, and a moving caption based on the narration, which explains how to do online search step by step. The video is produced with screen capture software: Camtasia developed by Tech Smith. It shows the interface of a Web database search engine (AltaVista) and the screen movements in a Web browser. It tells the users exactly where to type the query, what kind of keywords to type, and which buttons to click. The moving caption enhances understanding of the tutorial for people with hearing disabilities and international students who may have difficulty following spoken English.

The self-paced nature of the tutorial and multimedia approach to introducing students to new information strives to accommodate varying personal interests and learning styles. The users can jump around within the video clip by clicking the indexed links. In other words, they can go directly to one section of the video just by a click. They can also click and go to Web pages outside the presentation window. Moreover, users can do a live-guided exercise by opening a new window for the specified database and doing the exercise in that window while watching the streaming video. To view the SMIL file, you need a RealPlayer plug-in (free download at: *www.real.com*).

CREATION OF THE SMIL APPLICATION

Before you write SMIL, you need to consider the types of media you will use, the presentation's layout, and the time line for events within the presentation. There are some SMIL editors in the market that allow visual authoring environments. One is GRiNS (GRaphical iNterface to SMIL from *www.oratrix.com/GRiNS*). Real Networks also has some simple authoring tools for making presentations. You can also create SMIL by hand using any plain text editors such as Notepad.

Now let's look at how SMIL is structured in the SMIL application above:

SMIL Code (onlinetutorial.smil):

```
<smil>
<head>
<meta name="title" content="Online Tutorial" />
<meta name="author" content="Yuwu Song" />
<meta name="copyright" content="(c) March, 2001" />
<layout>
<root-layout width="640" height="420"/>
<region id="text_region" width="320" height="480" left="0"
top="0"/>
<region id="video_region" width="320" height="240" left="320"
top="0"/>
<region id="text2_region" width="320" height="240" left="320"
top="240"/>
</layout>
```

```
</head>
<body>
<par>
<textstream src="http://www.asu.edu/lib/tutorials/test/Online
Tutorial/table_of_content.rt" region="text_region" fill="freeze" />
<video src="http://www.asu.edu/lib/tutorials/test/OnlineTutorial/
video.rm" region="video_region" fill="freeze" />
<textstream src="http://www.asu.edu/lib/tutorials/test/Online
Tutorial/caption.rt" region="text2_region" fill="freeze" />
</par>
</body>
</smil>
```

Like HTML's start and end tags, SMIL is wrapped by thetags. SMIL's media object tags let you include various
media types in your presentations, and they are self-explanatory.
The <animation> tag supports animation technologies such as
Shockwave, which is used in a RealFlash file. The <audio> tag
supports audio formats such as AIFF or SND files. The <img>
tag is used for still images such as JPEG files or RealPix. The
<text> tag is used for static text files; the <textstream> tag is used
for streaming text files such as RealText. The <video> tag is used
with video clips. There is also a generic tag called <ref> you can
use for other media types.

The SMIL file is like a container that holds the other media
types mentioned above. It defines the positioning where the
RealText files will show up, and tells them when to start and stop.
It also defines the position of the video. There are three sections
in the file: the head, regions, and the body. The head section contains the meta information, including copyright information, author of the page, the title, and the date. The second part of the
head section defines the different regions, which control the layout in the RealPlayer window.

The presentation layout determines how you set up your screen.
A SMIL player has a window. When you plan to play multiple
media types simultaneously, you need to create regions or mini-
windows within the main window. The root-layout sets the height
and width of the entire presentation in pixels. This is the whole
player area, which will be divided into regions. Each region sets
specific areas in the presentation that media will play in. It is worth
noting that the basic SMIL layout element is otherwise remark-
ably similar to CSS (Cascading Style Sheets). Because the basic
layout language for SMIL is consistent with Cascading Style
Sheets, you can place regions using standard CSS techniques. You
can even assign IDs and z-order indexes to regions. This allows
you to create regions that overlap (and if you want, to reposition

regions much as you can do with objects in DHTML). Figure 6–9 shows how the code above defines the regions for laying out the elements of a synchronized presentation in a RealPlayer.

Figure 6–9 The Interface Layout for the SMIL-Based Multimedia Online Library Instruction: Arizona State University Libraries

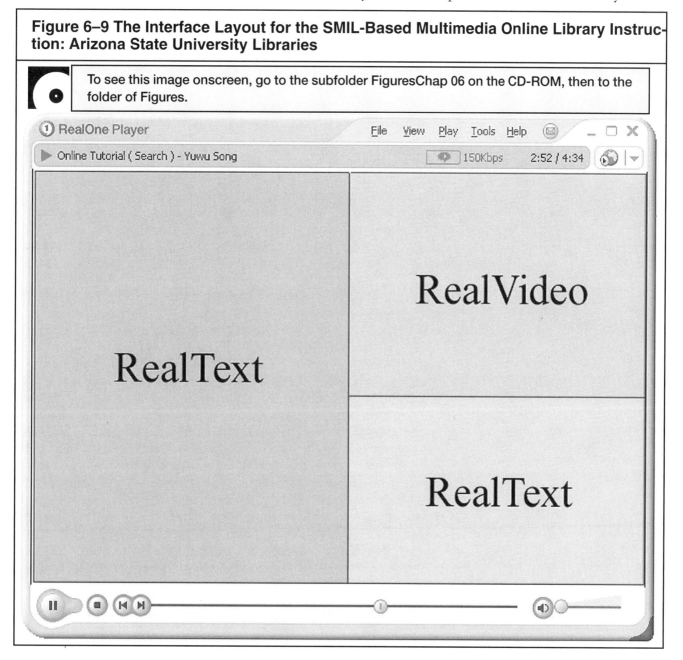

To see this image onscreen, go to the subfolder FiguresChap 06 on the CD-ROM, then to the folder of Figures.

In this example the main viewing area (identified with the <root-layout> tag) to 640 by 420 pixels is sized. Three regions within the viewing area: text_region, text2_region, and video_region are created. The text-region is positioned 0 pixels to the left and 0 down from the top of the main viewing area. The text2_region is placed 320 pixels to the right of the main viewing area's left edge and 240 pixels down from the top of the main viewing area. The video_region has variables of width="320" height="240" left="320" top="0."

One way of looking at the code for defining the regions is similar to the way you would lay out the cells in a table. Regions are like cells within an HTML table. You can decide the size and position of the window as well as the size and position of the mini-windows within it. Instead of specifying rows or columns like in a table, you use attributes such as left and top to control the position of the different regions. You use height and width attributes to define the size.

The RealVideo (a video file with rm extension) is played in the video_region. This area is defined as being located at left=320 and top=0. This places it against the top border, but 320 pixels from the left margin of the screen. The area is defined as being height="240" width="320." The text_region is where the RealText is displayed. There are two external RealText files (table_of_content.rt and caption.rt) that control how the RealText is laid out and when it should appear. The text_region is located at left=0 and top=0. This places it against the left margin, 0 pixels down from the top of the player. The text_region2 is at left=320, top=240.

SMIL offers two ways to play media elements: sequentially (one file right after another in a single region), where a few files: text, audio, or video files can play at the same time. Each line between the <par></par> tags is a media file which will play to a specified region. The <par> tags mean that media files will play simultaneously (in parallel). The <seq> </seq> tags mean that they will play sequentially. Fill="freeze" means that the final frame will stay visible when that media file is done.

The body of the SMIL file describes the order in which the presentations will appear. The <par> tags mean that the video_region, text_region, and text_region2 will be displayed in parallel. Keep in mind that the timing of the events for each element is controlled within their respective file types. This will be explained in the following sections.

Creation of RealText

There are other multimedia formats such as RealText and RealPix. These are the different Real media types that SMIL synchronizes and plays back. With RealText you can develop mechanisms for moving type, such as horizontal ticker tape, vertical scrolling news, and teleprompter. There is also a generic window type for placing static text on the player window.

Generic Text

Generic text is positioned on the screen at a certain place and can appear or disappear over time. The language is similar to HTML. You specify the height and width of the window as attributes, like you do for a graphic. You can create hyperlinks. You can jump around within the video clip by clicking the indexed links. The new elements in the file are <a href = "command:seek ()" target="_player">. This file sets the text that stays constant. This includes all the entries in their non-active state. The command: seek() function sets the clock time that the presentation will seek when that word is clicked. Like regular HTML, <a href= "http://www.asu.edu/lib" target="_browser"> lets you go directly to an external Web site: Arizona State University Libraries Web Site. Here is the code of the RealText file—table_of_content.rt:

```
<window type="generic" duration="266" height="480"
width="320" underline_hyperlinks="true" />
<font face="arial" font size=5 font color="orange">
<h3><center><b>Online Tutorial: Web Searching Using
AltaVista</b><br>
<br>LIST, ASU Libraries<br>
<br>March, 2001</center></h3></font><br>
<font face="Arial"><b>Introduction</b></font>
<font color="black" face="Arial" ><br>
<a href="command:seek(3)" target="_player"><br/>Introduction
to Online Tutorial World</a><br><br>
<font face="Arial"><b>Simple Search</b></font>
<font color="black" face="Arial" ><br>
<a href="command:seek(16)" target="_player"><br/>Simple
Search</a>
<a href="command:seek(28)" target="_player"><br/>Simple
Search Example</a><br>
...
<a href="command:seek(250)" target="_player"><br/>See the
Number of Results for Your Search </a><br>
<a href="http://www.asu.edu/lib" target="_browser"><br/>
<b><center>ASU Library Home Page </center></b></a>
</window>
```

Teleprompter

In a teleprompter, text appears line by line. We have a new element here: time control. The <time begin> tag tells each line what time it should appear on the screen. Time is measured from the start of the presentation. When a new line appears, another line is forced off the top of the screen. Here you specify time according to the video narration. Here is the code for caption.rt:

```
<window type="teleprompter" duration="266">
<font color="purple"><br/>
<time begin="4"/>Welcome to the Online Tutorial World.<br/>
<time begin="7"/>This tutorial will show you how to do simple
search and advanced search using AltaVista.<br/>
...
<time begin="264"/>Welcome to the Online Tutorial World.
</font>
</window>
```

When you create your multimedia production, you will likely be using a lot of media file formats. Keep in mind that you should save your RealText files using extension: .rt and your SMIL file using .smil. For the video, rm format is used, which is the standard RealNetworks format for video. After you complete your project, you should move the multimedia files and the SMIL file to the Web server. The server should be configured to handle multiple forms of media including text, audio, video, and animation, and they should understand hypertext links. If the server supports all the media formats such as ra, rt, rm, rp, smil, etc., you can view the presentation in your SMIL player.

To see the SMIL-Based Video example, go to Chapter 6's SMIL Based Video folder on the CD-ROM and click on SMIL_ Based_Video.htm.

SMIL-CONTROLLED ONLINE SLIDE SHOWS

SMIL can be used to create coordinated slide shows online. SMIL can control the time and space layout for the slide show. Like in the video, SMIL depicts the design layout and temporal behavior of slide presentations. SMIL's media object tags allow you to put various media types in your presentations. The <audio> tag is for audio files such as RMI, MIDI, MP3, or AIFF. The <img> tag is for graphics such as JPEG files or RealPix. The <text> tag is for static text files. You can mix any of the available media types in your slide presentations. The presentation layout determines how you set up your screen. Similar to the SMIL-based video, SMIL divides up the player window into regions. Each region sets specific areas in the presentation that media will play in. The following code is for the layout:

```
<layout>
<root-layout height="405" width="770" background-
color="black"/>
<region id="title" left="5" top="120" width="400" height="200"
z-index="1"/>
```

```
<region id="full" left="0" top="0" height="425" width="450"
background-color="#602030"/>
<region id="video" left="450" top="240" height="120"
width="315" z-index="1"/>
<region id="toc" left="450" top="0" height="405" width="255"/>
</layout>
```

The code below shows an example of event timing:

```
<par>
<audio src=http://www.asu.edu/lib/Webcom/yuwu/VisualTour/
smone2.rmi
 dur="400s"/>
<text src="http://www.asu.edu/lib/Webcom/yuwu/VisualTour/
toc.rt" region="toc"/>
<text src="http://www.asu.edu/lib/Webcom/yuwu/VisualTour/
song.rt" region="video"/>
<seq>
<!– This part displays the title screen and the caption with an
audio soundtrack–>
<text src="http://www.asu.edu/lib/Webcom/yuwu/VisualTour/
title.rt"
type="text/html" region="title" dur="35s"/>
<!– This section displays a slide show –>
<par>
<img src=http://www.asu.edu/lib/Webcom/yuwu/VisualTour/
map.rp
region="full" fill="freeze"/>
</par>
<!– This section contains the annotated slideshow –>
<par>
<switch>
<img src="http://www.asu.edu/lib/Webcom/yuwu/VisualTour/
slideshow.rp"
region="full" fill="freeze" system-bitrate="45000"/>
</switch>
</par>
</seq>
</par>
```

The <par> tags mean that media files will play simultaneously (in parallel). The <seq> </seq> tags mean that they will play sequentially. When the presentation starts, the text file toc.rt displays. The audio clip smone2.rmi also begins. Then the text file title.rt clip specified in the next line starts at 35 seconds into the presentation. Then the slide show begins. While the audio clip is playing, the text and slide shows are displayed. By adding a time line to a presentation, you can control when content is displayed and how transitions between various content types are handled. SMIL provides the sophisticated control that the protocol offers.

One feature of SMIL is that by setting choices, you can even serve up different versions of the production based on the available bandwidth. In other words, you can use the <switch> tag to get the player to use media files appropriate to the bandwidth.

```
<switch>
<img src="http://www.asu.edu/lib/Webcom/yuwu/VisualTour/
slideshow.rp"
region="full" fill="freeze" system-bitrate="45000"/>
</switch>
```

The presentation's bandwidth needs are optimized based on the speed of your computer's connection to the Internet. The media files used in the presentation will depend on whether you have a 28.8 modem or a high-speed connection such as a T1 line. This feature makes it possible for users to enjoy the presentation regardless of their connection speed. You can include low- and high-bandwidth choices. The <switch> tag tells the player it should make a choice. The bandwidth choices are made in the order listed; the highest-bandwidth choice should come first.

SMIL offers quite a few features for handling the timing of media playback. One can set specifically the duration for a media type. For example, assuming that the file will play for three minutes, you can time events according to the time line for the entire presentation. You can use special effects like fade-in, cross-fade, view-change, and wipe target in your slideshow presentation. For each special effect, attributes such as "start" specify the time to begin, the duration how long the picture lasts, and the source target of the picture. For example: <crossfade start="00:45" duration="00:08" target="5"/>.

The Virtual Library Tour presentation at Arizona State University Libraries is a good example for SMIL-controlled online slide shows.

SMIL Code for Online Slide Show (vt.smil):

```
<smil>
<head>
<layout>
<root-layout height="405" width="770" background-
color="black"/>
<region id="title" left="5" top="120" width="400" height="200"
z-index="1"/>
<region id="full" left="0" top="0" height="425" width="450"
background color="#602030"/>
<region id="video" left="450" top="240" height="120" width=
"315" z-index="1"/> <region id="toc" left="450" top="0"
```

```
height="405" width="255"/>
</layout>
</head>
<body>
<par>
<audio src=http://www.asu.edu/lib/Webcom/yuwu/VisualTour/
smone2.rmi
dur="400s"/>
<text src="http://www.asu.edu/lib/Webcom/yuwu/VisualTour/
toc.rt" region="toc"/>
<text src="http://www.asu.edu/lib/Webcom/yuwu/VisualTour/
song.rt" region="video"/>
<seq>
<!– This part displays the title screen and the caption with an
audio soundtrack–>
<text src="http://www.asu.edu/lib/Webcom/yuwu/VisualTour/
title.rt"
type="text/html" region="title" dur="35s"/>
<!– This section displays a slide show –>
<par>
<img src=http://www.asu.edu/lib/Webcom/yuwu/VisualTour/
map.rp
region="full" fill="freeze"/>
</par>
<!– This section contains the annotated slideshow –>
<par>
<switch>
<img src="http://www.asu.edu/lib/Webcom/yuwu/VisualTour/
slideshow.rp"
region="full" fill="freeze" system-bitrate="45000"/>
</switch>
</par>
</seq>
</par>
</body>
</smil>
```

RealText Code for the Table of Contents (toc.rt):

```
<window type=generic duration="6:30.0" scrollrate=0
height=250 width=375 bgcolor="#000000" link="#DDBBBB"
loop=true>
<time begin ="00:02"/><font size="5" color="white" face=
"times"><pos y="10"/>
<b>Visual Library Tour</b>
<time begin="00:05"/>
<font size="3" color="white" face="times">
<a href="http://www.asu.edu/lib/hayden/">Hayden Library</a>
</font>
```

```
<time begin="00:07"/>
<font size="3" color="white" face="times">
<a href="http://www.asu.edu/lib/music">Music Library</a>
</font>
time begin="00:9"/>
<font size="3" color="white" face="times">
<a href="http://www.asu.edu/lib/noble/">Noble Library</a>
</font> <br/>
<time begin="00:11"/>
<font size="3" color="white" face="times">
<a href="http://www.asu.edu/caed/AEDlibrary/">Architechture
Lib</a></font> <br/>
<time begin="00:13"/>
<font size="3" color="white" face="times">
<a href="http://www.lawlib.asu.edu/">Law Library</a></font>
<br/>
<time begin="00:15"/>
<font size="3" color="white" face="times">
<a href="http://www.asu.edu/lib/"><i><b>ASU Libraries</b>
</i></a> </font>
</window>
```

RealText Code for Title (title.rt):

```
<window type="generic" bgcolor="#602030" WIDTH="400"
HEIGHT="200">
<center><font size="6" color="white">
<time begin="00:20"><center><i><b>The Arizona State
xUniversity, University Libraries</b></i></font>
<font size="4" color="white"><br/>
<time begin="00:22">A Visual Library Tour
<time begin="00:26"><clear/>
<time begin="00:28"><pos y="50">Welcome and enjoy a visual
experience!</center></font>
<time begin="00:30"><font size="3" color="white"><i><b>
<p>– LIST, ASU<b/></i></font></center>
</window>
```

RealText Code for the Slide Show (map.rp):

```
<imfl>
<head duration="01:05" width="450" height="425" bitrate=
"13500" preroll="00:20" aspect="true" timeformat=
"dd:hh:mm:ss.xyz"/>
<image handle="1" name="hayden1.jpg"/>
...
<image handle="6" name="law.jpg"/> <fadein start="00:01"
duration="00:02" target="1"/>
<crossfade start="00:06" duration="00:15" target="2"/>
<viewchange target="2" start="00:25" duration="00:05"
```

```
srcx="290" srcy="139" srcw="118" srch="115"/>
<crossfade start="00:30" duration="00:02" target="3"/>
<wipe target="4" start="00:35" duration="00:08" type="normal"
direction="down"/>
<crossfade start="00:45" duration="00:08" target="5"/>
<crossfade start="00:55" duration="00:10" target="6"/>
</imfl>
</window>
```

RealText Code for the Slide Show (slideshow.rp):

```
<imfl>
<head duration="04:15" bitrate="20000" width="450"
height="425" aspect="true"
timeformat="dd:hh:mm:ss.xyz" preroll="80" />
<image handle="1" name="hayden.jpg"/>
<image handle="2" name="hayden2.jpg"/>
...
<image handle="23" name="hayden23micro.jpg"/>
<fill start="0" duration="00:01" color="#602030"/>
<fadein start="00:02" duration="0:03" target="1"/>
<crossfade start="00:10" duration="00:03" target="2"/>
...
<crossfade start="03:50" duration="00:05" target="23"/>
<fadeout start="04:10" duration="00:5" target="1"/>
</imfl>
```

RealText Code for the Caption (song.rt):

```
<window type="teleprompter" bgcolor="black"
duration="266"><font color="white">
<br/><time begin="36"/>Welcome to our library.
<br/><time begin="37"/>The Hayden Library is located on
Cady Mall.
...
<br/><time begin="264"/>Welcome to our library.
</font>
</window>
```

Figure 6–10 SMIL-Based Slide Show (A Virtual Library Tour): Arizona State University Libraries

To see the SMIL-Based Slideshow example, go to Chapter 6's SMIL-Based Slideshow folder on the CD-ROM and click on SMIL_Based_Slideshow.htm.

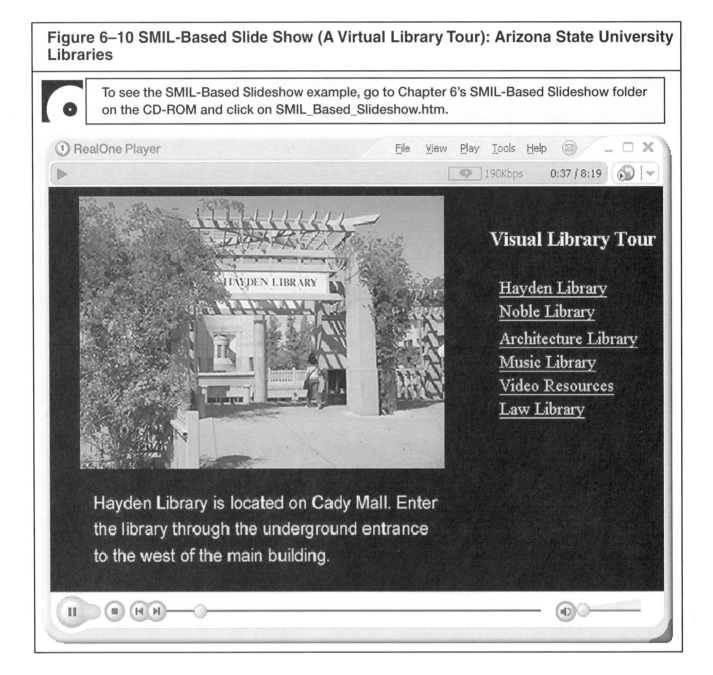

SGML

SGML stands for Standard Generalized Markup Language. As an open standard for information presentation, it can be used for publishing in its broadest definition: from single medium conventional publishing on paper to online multimedia database publishing. Due to its complexity, there are not so many SGML experts as those of HTML. However, it is useful to have a basic understanding of SGML since most of the Web markup languages such as HTML, XML, and SMIL are based on SGML and each of them can be called a subset of SGML.

The language was first developed in 1970 as GML (Generalized Markup Language) and evolved into both a national and international standard. SGML has been an international standard since October 1986 (ISO Standard 8879). It is widely accepted in the United States, Western Europe, and Japan and is used for a variety of business, industrial, and academic applications. SGML is frequently referred to as a meta language. This means that SGML is not a single language, but a language that describes other markup languages. In other words, SGML is the rules or framework for specifying particular markup languages. Markup by definition is the text that is added to the data of your files in order to convey particular information about that data. In a word processor, the markup is the proprietary codes that the software inserts into your text files to indicate which words should be printed in a certain font; which paragraphs should be centered; where page breaks occur; etc. In a database system, the markup is the proprietary codes, which indicate where one field or record ends, and another starts, and so on.

SGML produces files that can be exchanged between machines and applications in a straightforward manner. Those who use SGML include scientific and reference publishers, such as Elsevier, Springer-Verlag, and Oxford University Press. Organizations with large-scale information handling needs, like the International Standards Organization, the European Patent Office, the European Commission, and the U.S. Department of Defense also use SGML. All the major suppliers of Unix software and hardware have chosen SGML to deliver their next generation of documentation for publication on paper and as online materials. The latest version of the Oxford English Dictionary is an SGML document available both on paper and as a CD-ROM.

Within academia, the Text Encoding Initiative (a major international project) recommends SGML for the coding and interchange of any electronic text intended for scholarly analysis. The American Chemical Society and American Mathematical Society will be using SGML for all their electronic publishing needs. CERN (European Organization for Nuclear Research) and the publishing wing of the Institute of Physics have also adopted SGML.

SGML is more powerful than HTML. SGML tags delineate

the header, such as author, title, and affiliation. It also describes the body content such as chapter, figure, table, and equation structures (HTML cannot compile such mathematical characters). It is notable that SGML relies on the principles of descriptive markup—where the markup is used to indicate the nature, function, or content of the data in a file, rather than saying how that data should be processed. SGML can be used to encode semantics rather than syntax. Using SGML, a heading will be identified as a "heading" rather than a piece of text that has to be printed or displayed in "20 point Times Bold."

SGML is rigorous. The markup schemes that you write using SGML declare a set of rules which unambiguously state how the data must be marked up in order to be correctly structured. SGML-aware software can ensure that any markup in a file conforming to the appropriate set of rules thereby guarantee that the data in that file will be structured in a known way. If the set of rules you are working with declares that text labeled as a "subsection" can only occur within text labeled as a "section," SGML-aware software will ensure that this rule is obeyed during text creation and editing.

SGML is flexible. If you are given a file that contains data structured according to a known set of rules and in an unambiguous manner, you are free to use that information the way you like. You can format it for printing on paper or display it online. You can map the data to a database to create text archives, or import data from a database to create active documents. You can create new documents by extracting or combining information taken from one or more source files. You can incorporate your files into a hypertext or multimedia system. You can do all of these without altering the source file, which means you can process the same source information in many different ways simultaneously.

As a powerful tool, SGML makes it possible to reuse and share information. People working at different sites, using different editors on different machines, are able to produce SGML files that can be easily combined to produce a single document. Provided that you know the markup scheme that is used to create it, you can take any SGML file and process it however you see fit. Thus, several sites could download a copy of a document from an archive and each prints it off in their local house style. SGML is viewed with an SGML browser. Right now software is being developed that can turn SGML to HTML on the fly. This will eventually allow people to not only view and search the full text of documents, but to manipulate figures on the screen using a regular Web browser.

SGML can be created using any editor that can produce files

containing no application-specific codes (plain ASCII). Dedicated SGML software is available for virtually every platform or environment—with high-quality commercial software available for all the major machine types and operating systems (PC, Mac, UNIX, and so on).

VRML

VRML is short for Virtual Reality Modeling Language. The language was developed for designing 3D Web sites. Providing an exciting surfing paradigm, VRML allows the user to view, navigate, interact with, modify, and move around online three-dimensional worlds. On a flat computer screen, VRML displays three dimensions using visual depth, perspective, and shading. Unlike the traditional 3D imaging, VRML makes it possible for the user to move within the objects in a virtual scene. VRML has hit the market for a couple of years. Although it is thought to be the next great development on the Web, due to the problem of bandwidth the above picture is likely to be years away. Unlike Java and Flash, VRML did not become very popular. VRML is designed for multidimensional presentations on the Web. Maybe it will take more time for VRML to display its full potential.

Different from flat HTML pages, VRML permits visitors to walk through a Web site. It provides clues where they can go and where they've come from. This life-like spatial quality makes it more interesting for people to navigate. With VRML, it is easier to browse around without being lost among dozens of regular Web pages. As far as efficiency is concerned, a 3D page may be more powerful than a flat Web page because each 3D room has six 2D surfaces where one can put content. But VRML has some limitations; for example, users need more bandwidth to play VRML files. It is one of the major obstacles for VRML to become popular.

With VRML, you can design your own virtual world: develop virtual online photo galleries; you can provide users with access to your virtual news room or let distant learners take a virtual walk-through of your reading rooms. You can also have visitors tour your virtual museum, or invite exploration of your virtual 3D libraries. In the future, a "VRML/CGI/Java/DHTML" interface to databases might be created. The users can type a key word in a search box; the interface will have similar results grouped together and represented as different sized and shaped objects.

The locations and colors of the objects will serve as indicators of different characteristics of a result set. Users could put results sets together and resubmit the refined search.

VRML is composed of objects such as cube, sphere, bullet, and pyramid, which are called nodes and coded in ASCII. The description for a cube is very simple:

```
#VRML V2.0 ascii
Cube {height 3width 3 depth 3}
```

A VRML browser such as a Netscape plug-in Live3D will then display a 3 by 3 meter virtual cube on the computer screen. With VRML, you can specify attributes including position, color, light source, and camera perspective:

```
#VRML V2.0 ascii
Separator {
DirectionalLight {
Direction 0.0–1
}
PerspectiveCamera {
Position 0 8 15
Orientation 1 0 0 –0.4
}
Separator {
Translation {translation 3 2 3}
Material {DiffuseColor 1 0 0}
Cube {}
}
}
```

The following images from *http://animbase.enet.gr/anims.html* show a simple VRML in action. In this VRML world, you can do things such as walking, panning, turning, rolling, going to, studying, zooming out, etc.

Figure 6–11 VRML: Sample 1

To see this image onscreen, go to the subfolder FiguresChap 06 on the CD-ROM, then to the folder of Figures.

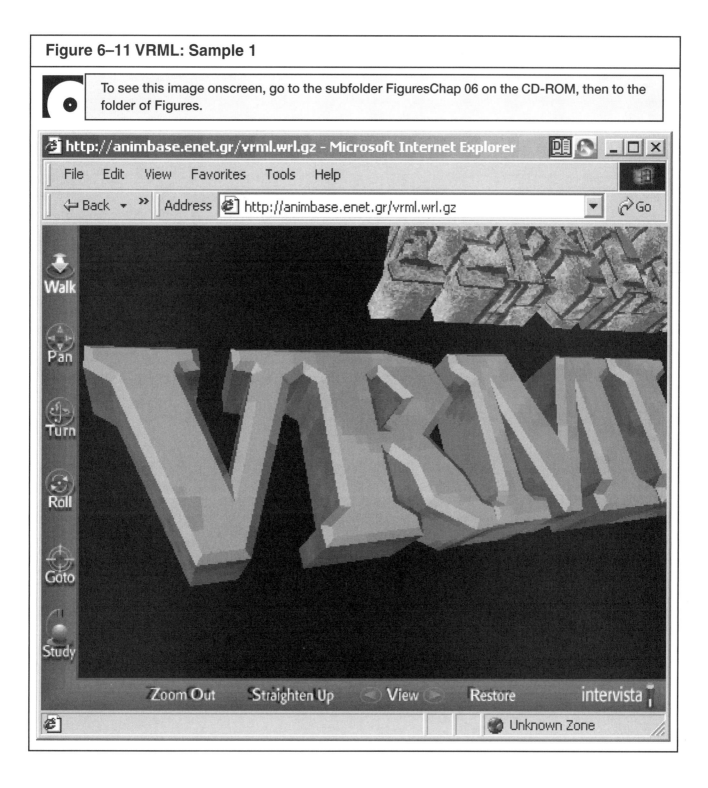

Figure 6–12 VRML: Sample 2

To see this image onscreen, go to the subfolder FiguresChap 06 on the CD-ROM, then to the folder of Figures.

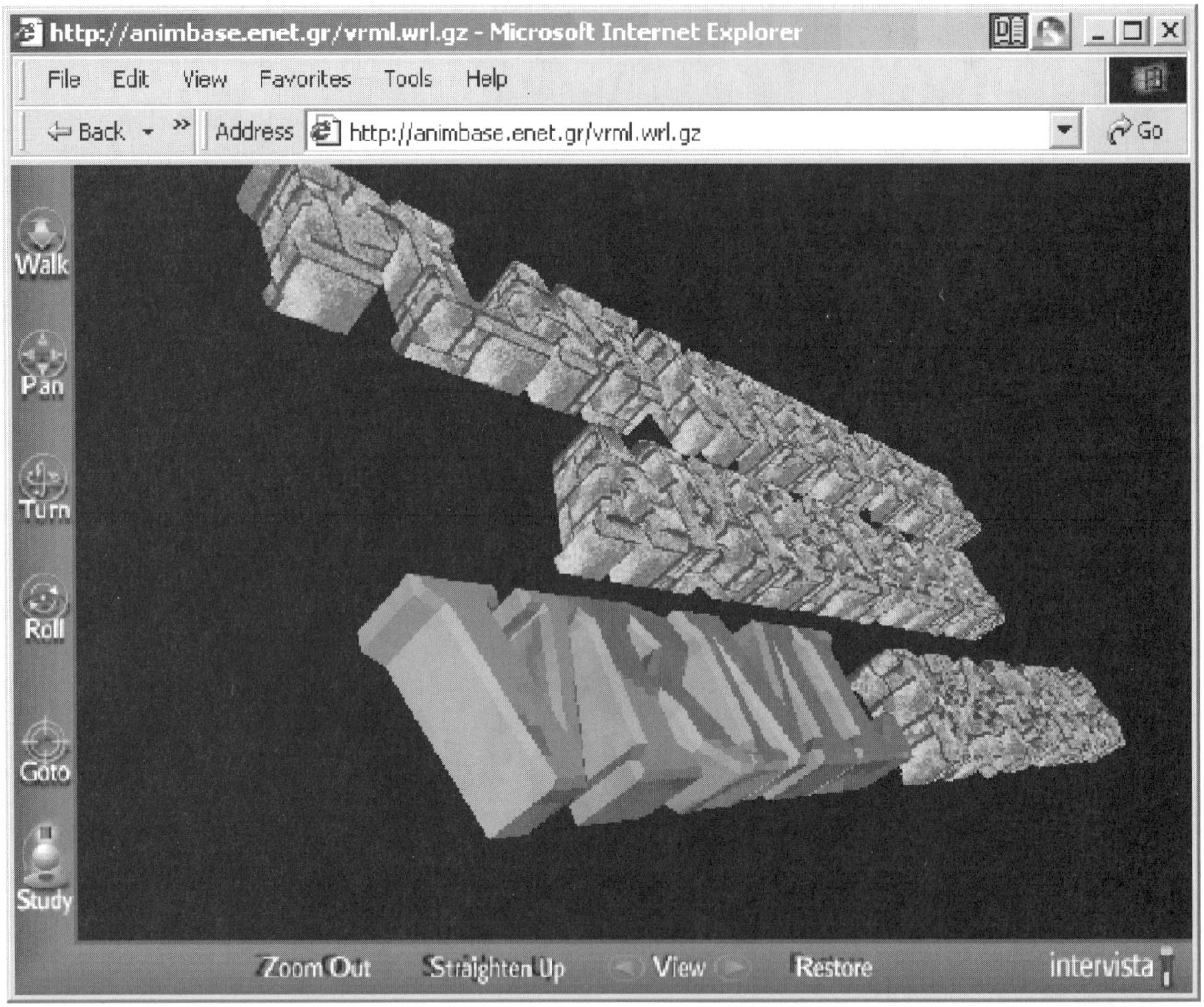

DATABASE-DRIVEN WEB SITES (ASP, PHP, COLDFUSION, AND JSP)

You may have already seen this scenario: a Web user enters a zip code into a Web form, and the server would query a database for information on the nearest library or the weather conditions, and present the results in HTML. This is a typical database-driven Web site. In this dynamic environment, information can be delivered on the fly from a relational database rather than through static coded HTML pages.

There are many reasons why libraries should develop database-driven Web sites. Library Web sites are composed of many lists of print and online resources, library services, guides, help pages, information about administration and personnel, etc. These resources are usually listed by title, subject, and media type. With new resources added or updated each day, the lists become bigger and bigger. The sheer volume of HTML-coded pages and the links they contain have become quite cumbersome to manage. Many sites feel locked into a dry, outdated design because rewriting those hundreds of HTML files to reflect a new design would take a long time. The traditional templates, validators, and link-checking utilities can only provide short-term solutions. It is clear that the old Webmaster model of Web site management has become inefficient due to lack of flexibility and scalability. Oftentimes, the content provider doesn't even know HTML. Not every library can afford to staff a full-time Webmaster, and most Webmasters have better things to do than copying Word files into HTML templates anyway.

Obviously, creating and maintaining the library Web sites becomes more and more difficult. How to provide fast delivery of information and how to maintain the functionality of links and consistency of look and feel of Web pages present great challenges for librarians. To make progress, libraries must stop viewing their Web sites as collections of HTML pages; they must change the paradigm and look forward to developing dynamic resources that can be used in highly individualized ways by users.

The solution to the problems above is database-driven Web sites. The conception is to develop something that is extremely convenient for an editor or an administrator to make updates to the content on the library Web site without having to edit HTML. When the site is growing larger and larger, it is time to stop managing it as a list of resources embedded in static HTML and to begin using the Web as an interface to a database. Commercial Web sites such as Amazon.com offer some very good examples of this model. Amazon.com is actually a Web interface to a large database system with customer and transactional information.

To understand the database-driven Web site, the paradigm of database-to-Web connectivity, and how content from a database is merged with and displayed in a Web page, you need to know a few concepts about the server, client, and the database. In the old paradigm of the Web, when a user clicks on a link, he or she is requesting a document to be sent from a server. The server replies by sending the requested HTML document to the user's browser. It is up to the browser to interpret and display the page. All the server does is to store and deliver requested files to the clients' machines.

In the new paradigm of dynamic database-driven Web sites, technologies such as PHP, ColdFusion, ASP (Active Server Pages), and JSP (JavaServer Pages) have added new features to Web functionality by inserting powerful scripts into the HTML. Instead of a static page, a Web site can become a real application. Besides the script component, the other main component of these technologies is server add-ins that execute these scripts. The server is now empowered to do more things. In other words, the functionality of the server has been expanded from just delivering HTML pages to the client computer to actively retrieving database content, handling conditional statements, and reacting to user input.

Before the development of ColdFusion, ASP, JSP, and PHP, CGI languages such as Perl played a big part in building Web interactivity on the server. However, CGI is not as easy to implement as the emerging technologies in terms of making database connectivity. Moreover, the shortage of local programming expertise often limits the use of the tool.

Besides CGI, Dynamic HTML (DHTML) and JavaScript have also been used to enhance interactivity. They both allow a Web page to change after it has been loaded in the browser, by using cascading style sheets and scripts; however, both tools deliver only a dynamic look, not dynamic content. FileMaker Pro and Microsoft Access 2000 are able to create databases on the Web as well, but they do not generate dynamic content either.

The new model, however, can produce dynamic content. It requires developers to achieve separation between their Web site's design and the content they plan to present. In this way, designers can work with each without disturbing the other. In other words, rather than writing an HTML file for every page of your site, you only have to write a page for each kind of information you want to present. Instead of copying and pasting new content into your page layouts whenever it comes, you create a simple content management system that allows your library content providers to post new content themselves without dealing with HTML.

To build a database-driven Web site, you need a bridge between the Web server and a database. The middle-ware we discuss here includes PHP, ColdFusion, ASP, and JSP. These technologies are designed to integrate databases and Web pages, allowing easier Web management and dynamic viewing and interaction. Since database-driven Web sites involve compiling Web server software, installing additional server components, changing file permissions, doing various kinds of configurations, and connecting databases, it is absolutely necessary for library Web developers to cooperate with the systems people in the library or consultants from outside in the technical fields.

There are many potential database-driven Web site applications. They can be developed and used to help users find various types of information. One good example for database-driven library Web sites is to implement site-wide subject searching, or browsing, that would have a single page pop up showing links to all kinds of electronic resources on a given topic, which are drawn from different places on the library Web site. The database-driven Web sites will provide multiple access points allowing users to view materials alphabetically by title and sort them by subject category, resource format, publication date, publisher, full-text availability, or access authentication. And the materials can be searched by keywords as well.

The following sections discuss a few of the most popular database-driven Web site technologies and some examples of database-driven library Web sites.

PHP

PHP is an open source server-side scripting language, developed by the Apache Software Foundation. It works with a variety of Web servers, but it is usually used with Apache. PHP code, similar to Perl, is put into the HTML documents using special PHP tags. PHP's advantage over Perl is that it is easier to include short bits of PHP code in a Web page to process form data or draw information from a database. You can compare PHP with a "plug-in" for your Web server that will allow it to do more than just send plain Web pages when browsers request them. Once embedded in your Web pages, PHP will enable a Web server to do things such as extracting up-to-the-minute information from a database and insert it into a Web page before delivering it to the user's browser.

Here is a simple example from *www.Webmasterbase.com/examples/today.php?*

```
<HTML>
<HEAD>
<TITLE>Today's Date</TITLE>
</HEAD>
<BODY>
<P>Today's Date (according to this Web server) is
<?php
 echo( date("l, F dS Y.") );
```

```
?>
</BODY>
</HTML>
```

When you click the link on the Web page, you will see the date displayed on the screen:

Today's Date (according to this Web server) is Tuesday, March 12th 2002.

If you view the code source in your browser, all you will see is a regular HTML file with the date in it. The PHP code (the code between <?php and ?>) has been interpreted by the Web server and converted to normal text before sending it to your browser. The beauty of PHP is the server-side execution without the Web browser knowing anything about it.

The concept of a database-driven Web site is to let the content of a Web site sit in a database, and for that content to be dynamically taken from the database to output Web pages for people using a Web browser to see. On one side, a client's browser asks for a page, on the other side you have the content of your site in a database such as MySQL that only understands how to respond to the SQL (Structured Query Language) queries. The PHP serves as a bridge between the two sides. With PHP, you can create the presentation structure of your site (page layouts) as "templates" in regular HTML. You use some PHP code to connect to the database to retrieve and display content.

What happened in the example above includes a few steps:

- The client's Web browser requests a Web page using a standard URL.
- The Web server recognizes that the requested file is a PHP script, and starts the installed PHP plug-in.
- Some PHP commands begin to hook up to a MySQL database and ask for the content in the Web page.
- The MySQL database talks back by sending the requested content to the PHP plug-in.
- The PHP plug-in stores the content into PHP variables, then uses the "echo" function to create it as part of the Web page.
- The PHP plug-in sends a copy of the HTML it has produced to the Web server.
- The Web server sends the HTML generated by the PHP plug-in to the client browser.

The steps above show how PHP works. The advantage of using PHP is obvious. For instance, you can build a content management system with a database administration interface, allowing authorized staff to view, manage, and change the information (organizing them into categories, tracking their authors, adding or deleting content) stored in the database. You can do this without having to deal with the complicated SQL syntax and the ins and outs of HTML behind the scene. So creating new information is just like regular data entry—filling in forms or checking boxes. In so doing, you will solve the problems of continually putting new content into an HTML page template, and producing an unmanageable mass of HTML files. The key is that you have separated HTML from the data it displays.

To redesign your Web site, you only need to make the changes to the HTML contained in the PHP files. Since all records are displayed using that single PHP file, a change to one file such as font or background will be completed in the page layouts of all records. With PHP, you can create a content management system easy enough for anyone with a Web browser to use.

For more information about PHP, go to the official Web site of PHP: *www.php.net*.

COLDFUSION

Developed by Allaire, ColdFusion offers a well-integrated Web-based database development environment, including a client base on the HTML editor HomeSite that lets developers quickly design Web applications. ColdFusion uses its own markup language: ColdFusion Mark-up Language (CFML), which is integrated into the HTML coding of pages. It accesses the database via either a native database interface or using a standard protocol, Open Database Connectivity (ODBC), and a common database query language: SQL. Like PHP, it handles queries to the online database and sends the results to the Web browser in HTML. The new functions allow people without knowledge of HTML to interface with a database server and do text formatting. With a few clicks, you can create a database-driven Web site by publishing your database online, and doing editing online such as adding and deleting records. And the updated information will be displayed on the fly.

As far as ColdFusion tools are concerned, Macromedia Dreamweaver UltraDev is one of the leaders, and it can be used to develop ColdFusion-based applications. Recently, Macromedia purchased Allaire and created a powerful database-driven application development tool: ColdFusion MX. This tool can help you to develop database access for finding and manipulating databases, such as Microsoft Access, Oracle, or MySQL. It can integrate with core Web technologies such as e-mail, HTTP, FTP, etc.; it can integrate with other Web-oriented technologies such as Flash, XML, and Java. It can also be used to develop an application framework including authentication and authorization services and session management.

ASP

ASP stands for Active Server Pages. It is Microsoft's solution to server-side scripting.

ASP is an object-oriented scripting environment that uses the VBScript language or JavaScript. Similar to ColdFusion, ASP is embedded in an HTML file for generating custom content based on a user's request. Often you will see a Web file that ends in the .asp suffix. This indicates that it is a text file that contains HTML and scripting that is configured to interact with ASP on the server.

ASP usually connects to an ODBC data source, handles SQL queries, and sends the results to the browser in HTML. The coded pages are put up and executed in Internet Information Server, a Microsoft Web server. In other words, in the client/server network architecture, the client computer sends a request for information to the file server, where special software interprets the request, takes the detailed steps needed to fill the request, and delivers the final results to the client computers.

Using ASP, the server can preprocess and change the file before sending it to the client browser. For every request for a file with an .ASP extension, the Web server runs the file through a special program called ASP.DLL, which parses the ASP commands. One feature of ASP is that it can be used across different systems. It can be connected to a database (SQL, Access, Oracle, or any ODBC-compliant database). Like PHP, ASP can be used for dynamic database-driven Web sites. Data from the databases can be put into your HTML pages and displayed as such. ASP allows designers to develop customizable Web sites and data entering/ retrieving systems operated over the Internet. To use ASP you need a Microsoft Web server. Microsoft provides some free Web servers. You can download them from Microsoft's Web site: *www.microsoft.com*. If you have a UNIX system, you can still use ASP with a third-party tool to translate ASP before it is sent to the client browser.

Alfred University Library's online reference database InfoIguana (*www.herr.alfred.edu/infoguides.asp*) is a database-driven Web site developed with the ASP technology. The online form is a regular HTML form. The form is executed with an ASP script sitting on the server. It retrieves the information from a database (Access) and presents the information in an organized way in HTML on the fly. The code calling action is as follows:

```
<form method="get" action="InfoIguanaResults.asp">
```

In this database, users select the subject they are researching, and pick the resources such as "Print Indexes," "Research Databases," etc. After they click "Fetch," they will be given a list of different resources related to their subject. This site interface is highly interactive and provides an effective research approach. Moreover, InfoIguana has a Web interface designed for library staff to update the database without messing up with HTML. Whenever a bibliographic resource such as a reference book, research database, or a Web site is added or edited in the ready-reference database, the corresponding research guide templates automatically show the changes. They need only be added or edited once in the database.

Figure 6–13 InfoIguana (ASP-Based Online Reference Database): Alfred University Library

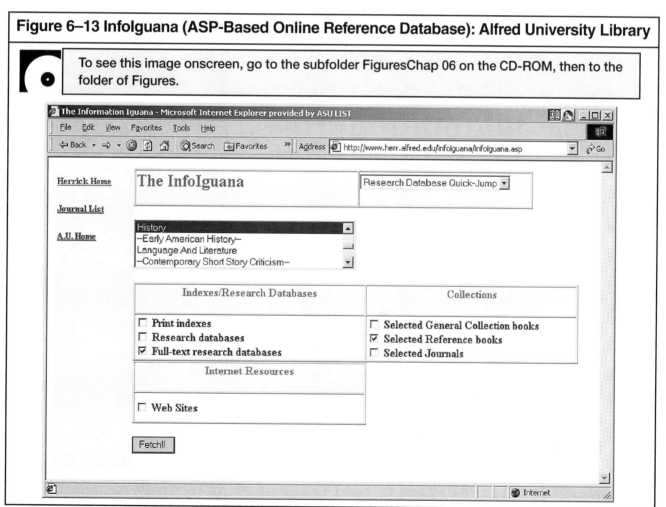

Figure 6–14 A Result Page of InfoIguana (ASP-Based Online Reference Database): Alfred University Library

To see this image onscreen, go to the subfolder FiguresChap 06 on the CD-ROM, then to the folder of Figures.

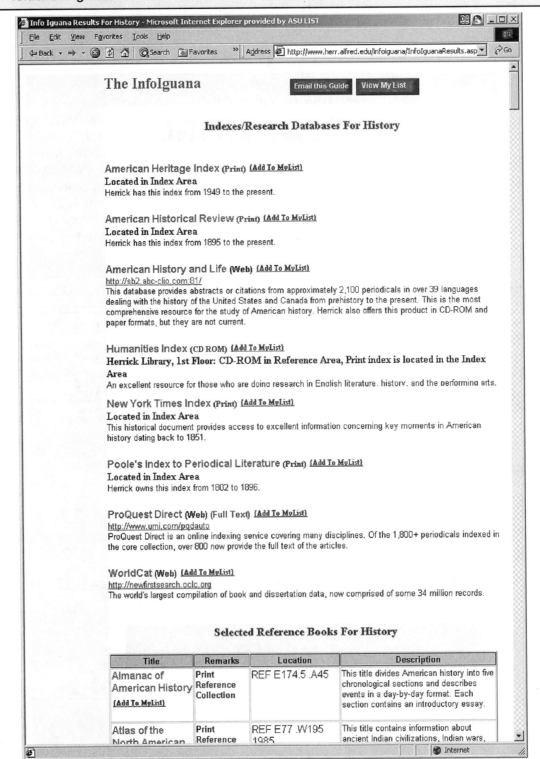

For more information about ASP, check the ASP101 site at: *www.asp101.com*. Another good source is: Microsoft Developer Network's page entitled "ASP from A to Z" at *http://msdn.microsoft.com/workshop/server/asp/aspatoz.asp*.

As far as ASP development tools are concerned, Dreamweaver UltraDev 4 and Microsoft FrontPage are very good. They can help you to easily connect your site to a database, build ASP applications, display personalized content, add searchable directories, and develop sites with data-rich online news and information. With FrontPage and UltraDev 4, you can quickly and easily interact with live server data and personalize user experience.

JSP

JSP stands for JavaServer Pages. Developed by Sun, this technology allows rapid development of Web-based applications that are platform independent. JavaServer Pages separates the user interface from content generation, permitting designers to change the overall page layout without altering the underlying dynamic content. In other words, it simplifies the process of creating pages by separating Web presentation from Web content. JSP acts dynamically; for example, it can process forms or read databases using Java as a server-side scripting language. Like ASP and PHP, JSP code is embedded directly in the Web page. And unlike ASP, JSP is a lot less platform-specific. In other words, it does not bind you to a particular computing platform.

JSP works in this way: a JSP engine interprets tags and scripts and creates the content required. It then sends the results back in the form of an HTML (or XML) page to the browser. The logic that creates the content is encapsulated in tags and beans (Java elements) processed on the server. JSP scripts enable developers to tie everything together, and to use ordinary HTML tags to control the formatting and display of the generated page.

For more information about JSP, go to *http://java.sun.com/products/jsp*.

If you are looking for a tool to create JSP applications, DreamWeaver UltraDev 4 is a good choice. UltraDev 4 provides excellent supports for development of JSP.

RESOURCES FOR CREATING A DATABASE-DRIVEN WEB SITE

Here is a list of resources you may want to use for developing a database-driven Web site:

- One of the database-driven Web site tools: PHP, ASP, ColdFusion, or JSP.

- An SQL server.
- Database application software such as Microsoft Access or Oracle.
- Application server such as ASP (Active Server Pages) or ColdFusion.
- Development tools such as Dreamweaver UltraDev or ColdFusion MX.

EXAMPLES OF DATABASE-DRIVEN LIBRARY WEB SITES

- University of Nebraska, Omaha (*http://library.unomaha.edu*) Research Wizard on this site is developed with the PHP technology. It provides a customized list of library and Web resources by subject areas and academic courses. The database contains selected indexes, library subject pages, and contact information.

  If you type a keyword (such as Newspaper, Stress, Computer Programming, HIST 3930) into the search box, the Research Wizard will retrieve listings of resources for that keyword. Take "Stress" for example; you will come up with Selected Electronic Indexes for Stress, Genisys (the library catalog) Searches for Stress, and Selected Internet Links on Stress. It is one-stop shopping that will get you related online journal databases, books, and Web links.

- Arizona Health Sciences Library (*www.ahsl.arizona.edu*) This site is created with the ColdFusion technology. For a given topic, listings can be dynamically generated based on the main resources such as Databases and Digital Collections, Journals, and Resource Guides drawn from many places on the site. The MultiFind search results in a single page displaying numerous links of electronic journals, databases, and Web resources on that particular topic. It shows descriptions of individual items representing each electronic resource in Arizona Health Sciences Library.

- Virginia Military Institute, JTL Preston Library (*www.vmi.edu/sourcefinder*)
  Built on the ASP technology, the SourceFinder offers selections of a general broad subject area. It helps users to focus on defined types of resources such as articles, biographical information, book reviews, encyclopedias, literary criticism, etc. It also helps users to limit sources to electronic, full-text, or nonelectronic (printed) format. To develop this site, the developers used FrontPage 98 to generate the Web site and an Access database to store the information.

  In this system, you can select a subject, source(s), and

limits them by clicking "Search" to create your custom study guide. The database-driven application takes the place of over 20 individual study guides and lists of resources' links, including lists arranged: by subject, format, and title. It allows the patrons to decide how to arrange resources, instead of forcing them to conform to lists created by librarians.

Focusing on centralization and ease of use, SourceFinder has a separate user-friendly interface for data entry and editing, which offers a consistent template for all Web pages created. The separate interface to the Web-based forms allows librarians to access and modify data in the SourceFinder database. Access to the database is password protected for security. Pages will automatically be made consistent in style and appearance, and librarians or content providers entering new resources or editing do not have to know any HTML.

- DePaul University Libraries (*www.lib.depaul.edu/Find_Resources*)
  Using ASP as the design tool, the developers created Find Databases (*http://apps.lib.depaul.edu/Eresource/database.asp*) and Subject Guides (*http://apps.lib.depaul.edu/eresource/subject_search.asp*). Both can display database-generated data.
- Dowling College Library (*www.dowling.edu/library/journaldb/jrnl.html*)
  Based on ASP, the Journal Locator functions as a database for identifying which databases index a particular journal, which databases offer the full text of a journal, and whether a journal is owned by the library. It also shows the dates available. If full text is available in a database, the words "Full Text" will appear bolded in the Holdings column.
- University of Illinois at Urbana-Champaign (*http://gateway.library.uiuc.edu/rex/selector.htm*)
  Article Database Advisor is designed with ASP to help users to locate useful databases for a particular topic. You can search it by keywords. This will bring up a list of good resources that librarians have selected.
- John Wesley College (*www.johnwesley.edu/erc/default.asp*)
  Using ASP technology, the developers designed E-Sources Electronic Resource Center, which provides dynamic retrieval of information from subject guides and lists of resources created and maintained by librarians. It has a consistent look and feel for Web pages generated.

- University of Minnesota (*http://research.lib.umn.edu*) Research Quickstart is developed with ASP. You can choose a research area from the drop-down list. A page will be generated with a description of the scope of the subject area and choices to search for current information from different resources including article indexes, Web sites, encyclopedias and dictionaries, bibliographies, statistics, and style manuals for citing sources.

CONCLUSION

By separating the page logic from its design and display and by supporting a reusable component-based design, the database-driven Web site technologies represented by PHP, ColdFusion, ASP, and JSP make it easier to create Web-based applications for libraries. All of the four technologies are still being developed. They have their own merits and demerits. It will take some time before we know which one is the best in this field. But for the time being, PHP seems to be very promising because it is an open source and freely available, and also because it is platform independent. It runs on Unix, Linux, Windows, and many other systems. Even if computer giants like Microsoft, Allaire, or Sun sank one day, you could still use PHP, which provides a great cross-platform migration strategy. With that said, you may still consider using ColdFusion, ASP, or JSP simply because IT giants such as Macromedia have developed powerful tools supporting development under the three environments of ColdFusion, ASP, and JSP.

7 PLANNING FOR THE FUTURE OF BUILDING BETTER LIBRARY WEB SITES

In August 1945, Vannevar Bush, a prominent scientist, published an article in the *Atlantic* magazine entitled "As We May Think." In his article, he made a proposal for "Memex," an imaginary machine, which would allow pieces of information to be accessed through random links. Since then his idea has inspired thousands of scientists in creating a system that would meet people's information needs. The Web in part realized Bush's vision. It serves as a powerful tool to boost people's thinking and to enhance the collective IQ of the social organisms represented by groups, institutions, organizations, and nations. It is helping to improve people's lives all over the world. Not only has it changed the way "as we may think," but it has also changed the way as we may work, play, cooperate, communicate, and apply knowledge and information. In general it has changed and will keep changing the way as we may live.

It is always risky to predict the future of the Web, but we can still do this because the change is already underway and a lot of the "future" of the Web exists today in its infancy. The ever-changing environment of the Web also enables everyone to be a visionary. Anything that we can imagine may become reality in the future. The future will arrive in two directions. One direction focuses on technology: hardware, software, and networks. No doubt they will become better, cheaper, and faster. The second direction involves applications: how the Web will be utilized. The applications will serve as the main impetus for the development of the "next" generation of Web technologies since applications concentrate on people. The following sections will examine both technologies and applications in the field of Web development.

NETWORKING

In the near future, there will be a convergence of telecommunications, networking, and broadcast media technologies. Radio and satellite technologies will provide a wireless environment for the Web. Continuously radiated information can be called up by messaging via satellite channels. The need of cabling will be eliminated; so will be the aesthetic, regulatory, or safety problems. With the obstacles of low speed, high cost, and limited range removed, a computer will communicate with other computers and peripherals via wireless connections. It will be easier to do collaborative writing, drawing, and designing in different places.

A PORTABLE WEB

Hand-held devices with Web access will become popular. Combined with electronic mail, fax, phone, and other applications, the digital agents will handle requests and perform tasks very efficiently. They can automatically create, save, and route information to users via the Web, phone, fax, or pagers. They can help you to perform search and communication tasks while you are on the road. The ultra-portability, the weight, and the wireless connection of the machine will provide great convenience to travelers and to people who enjoy beach reading or bathroom reading.

VERSATILE INTERFACE MODES

There will be versatile interface modes. Besides the conventional keyboard input, touch screen input and speech input may become alternative Web interface modes to fit the needs of users of different abilities, skills, and personal preferences. Children may like to use the touch-sensitive panel. The bedridden or visually handicapped will have easy access to the machine by using speech input. A user can order the voice-activated interface to perform various duties such as reading a document when he or she is driving a car. The development in this field will no doubt present a challenge for Web interface designers.

ARTIFICIAL INTELLIGENCE AND PORTALS

How to program Web sites to deliver customized information to individual users has been a hot issue since the beginning of the Web. With the development of artificial intelligence and the appearance of "push" media, content can be delivered to the personal computer and Web pages can be custom-tailored for each library patron based on the information gathered from the patron. This approach integrates patron profiles with Web server applications. It can become a form of one-to-one information delivery, which sends to prospective patrons useful information in individualized pages. However, the patron information should only be collected with his or her permission and can be accessed only by the library where the information is used.

There are two ways to get to know an individual's informational needs. One is through a traditional online survey: you fill out a survey that identifies your areas of interests. This survey becomes a profile for your needs. The other involves the use of intelligent agents or artificial intelligence software that monitors both your browsing and searching patterns and records the information in a database without being seen. For example, a patron who loves sports visits a library Web site. The intelligent agent software behind the scenes will monitor the patron's Web usage, record the information, and put it in a database. The next time that patron visits this Web site, the home page presents a custom-designed interface that highlights books, DVDs, or videos about the sports he or she likes. In other words, new Web pages will be created on the fly according to how a user responds to questions or moves through a Web site. Those digital agents can also make recommendations on new books or other library materials based on previous browsing, searching, and borrowing patterns, or on information gathered in profile questionnaires. Those user profiles could be tailored in terms of both content and presentation. After getting the information, the Web browser could use the tags such as XML tags to omit irrelevant portions and display only those portions of a document that the user thinks useful. This will certainly reduce information overload and speed up learning.

From the patron's point of view, the positive aspect of one-to-one information delivery is that it helps to provide useful information that fits users' interests. But it also raises concerns: this technology holds the potential for detailed monitoring and data-basing of patrons' individual tastes and Web usage. This may become controversial in the years to come.

Another approach is to let the users customize their pages with special software. This has been realized in commercial and educational sites (portals) such as MyYahoo, MyASU, MyUCLA, MyCornell, etc. In the last several years, a few academic and public libraries have been working on some very sophisticated models. MyLibrary is a Cornell University Library portal to provide many personalized library services to Cornell University students, faculty, and staff. It has MyLinks, a tool for collecting and organizing resources for use by a patron, and MyUpdates, a tool that keeps users informed of new resources provided by the university library. Interfaces such as MyLibrary@NCState, developed at North Carolina State University, are Web-based front ends to databases, which hold user and bibliographic information. These portal sites let users create personalized library Web pages, with links and information that are customized to their needs. After a user creates a personal profile, which is called a personal library interface (PLI) account, the system collects user information and puts it in a database. When the user logs in to the Web site, the system uses the user's profile to extract and present personalized bibliographic data. This technology helps the user to get information quickly without having to browse through many pages of extraneous information. Take a history student specializing in American History for instance; he or she will have a personalized Web page full of American History related resources.

In the future, more libraries may adopt this approach. People can get access to the library from any computer that is connected to the Internet. Not only can people get to the library's subscription-only online resources, but also they can add their favorite links from anywhere to create a page with the resources and sites they use most. It is technically feasible because each person will select a user ID and a password to obtain access to his or her own personalized page. No matter where they are, and no matter at whatever computer with Web access, they use that ID and password to sign in, and their individual page will pop up.

DATABASE-DRIVEN WEB SITES

The content-driven Web site or database-driven site technologies such as ColdFusion, ASP, PHP, JSP, and others will further enhance the developments of powerful interactive library Web sites. Right now, many library Web sites deal with static information. Future sites will have the ability to dynamically reconfigure the systems in response to changes in the network or its contents. Virtual structures (active objects) similar to dynamically generated views in relational databases will be created. Dynamic structures are possible only when current models of static information are changed to adapt to changing information.

DYNAMIC CREATION OF APPLICATIONS

Powerful online development tools will allow nonprogrammers to create useful applications and contents using a Web interface. The software Hot Potatoes (*http://web.uvic.ca/hrd/halfbaked/*) is a good example. The Hot Potatoes suite includes six applications, enabling you to create interactive multiple-choice, short-answer, jumbled-sentence, crossword, matching/ordering, and gap-fill exercises for the Web. It is free of charge for nonprofit educational users. What is neat is that users can develop interactive applications through an easy Web interface. The following are applications created with Hot Potatoes.

Figure 7–1 A Matching Exercise Created with Hot Potatoes

To see the Matching Exercise example created with Hot Potatoes, go to Chapter 7's Application Developed with Web-Based Tools folder on the CD-ROM and click on Matching.htm.

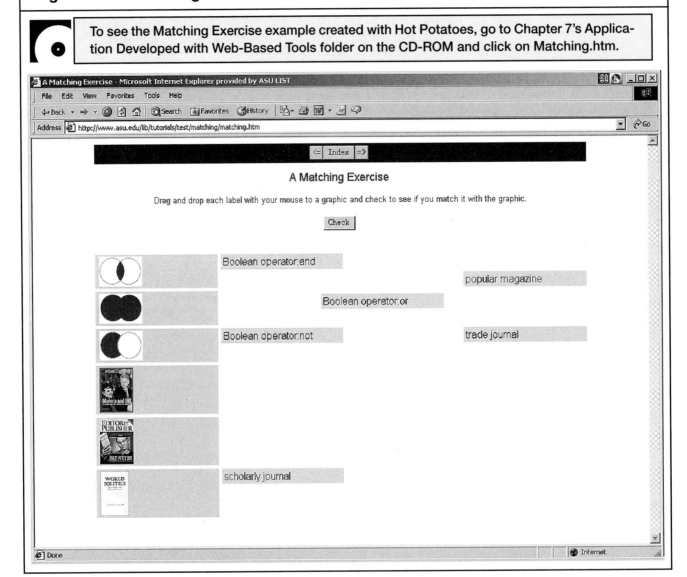

Figure 7–2 A Crossword Made with JCross of Hot Potatoes

To see this image onscreen, go to the subfolder FiguresChap 07 on the CD-ROM, then to the folder of Figures.

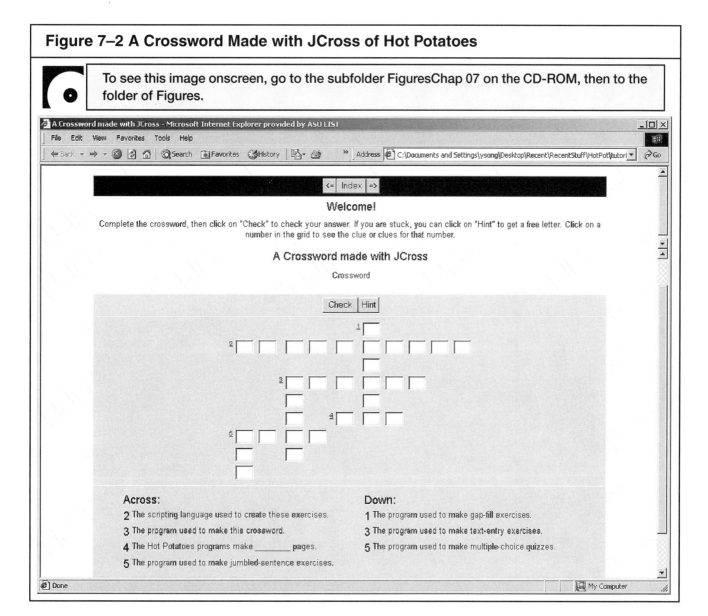

Figure 7–3 JCross Working Environment

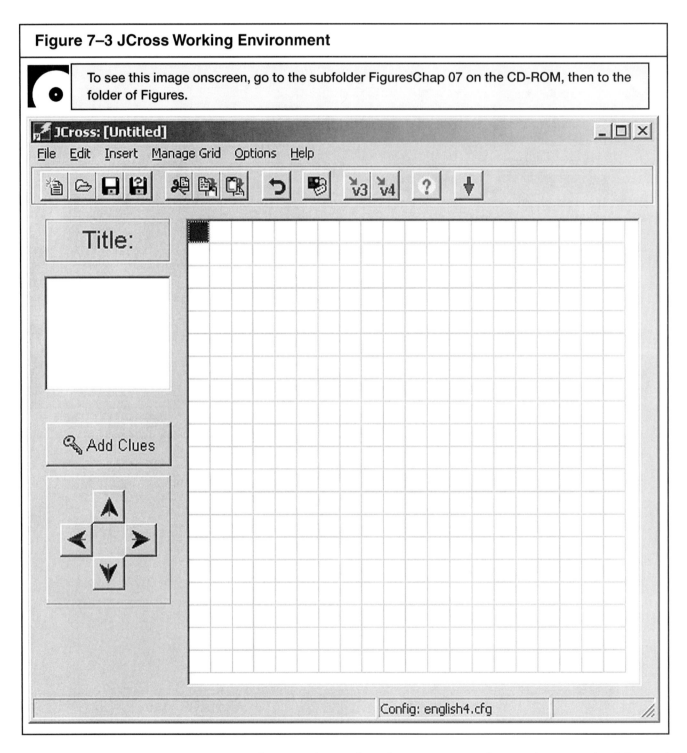

To see this image onscreen, go to the subfolder FiguresChap 07 on the CD-ROM, then to the folder of Figures.

Other online development tools such as Blackboard (*www.blackboard.com*) can also be used to create powerful applications. See Figures 7–4, 7–5, and 7–6.

Figure 7–4 An Application Created with Blackboard

To see these images onscreen, go to the subfolder FiguresChap 07 on the CD-ROM, then to the folder of Figures.

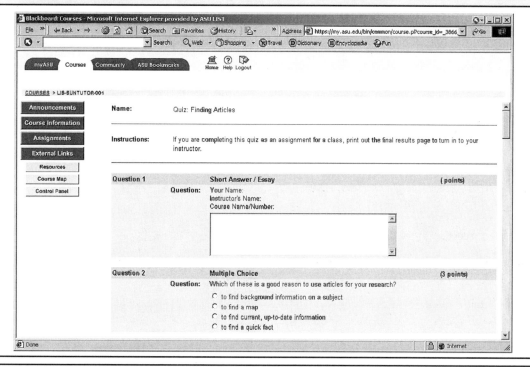

Figure 7–5 Blackboard Working Environment 1

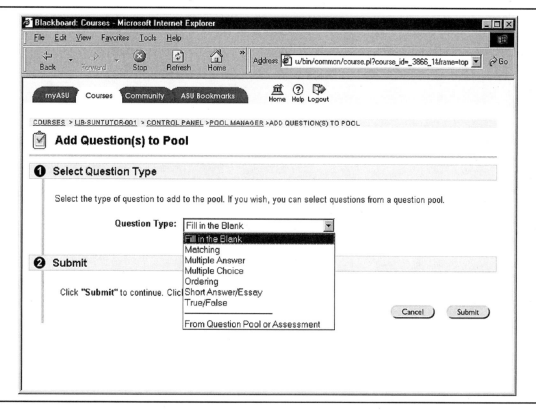

Figure 7–6 Blackboard Working Environment 2

To see this image onscreen, go to the subfolder FiguresChap 07 on the CD-ROM, then to the folder of Figures.

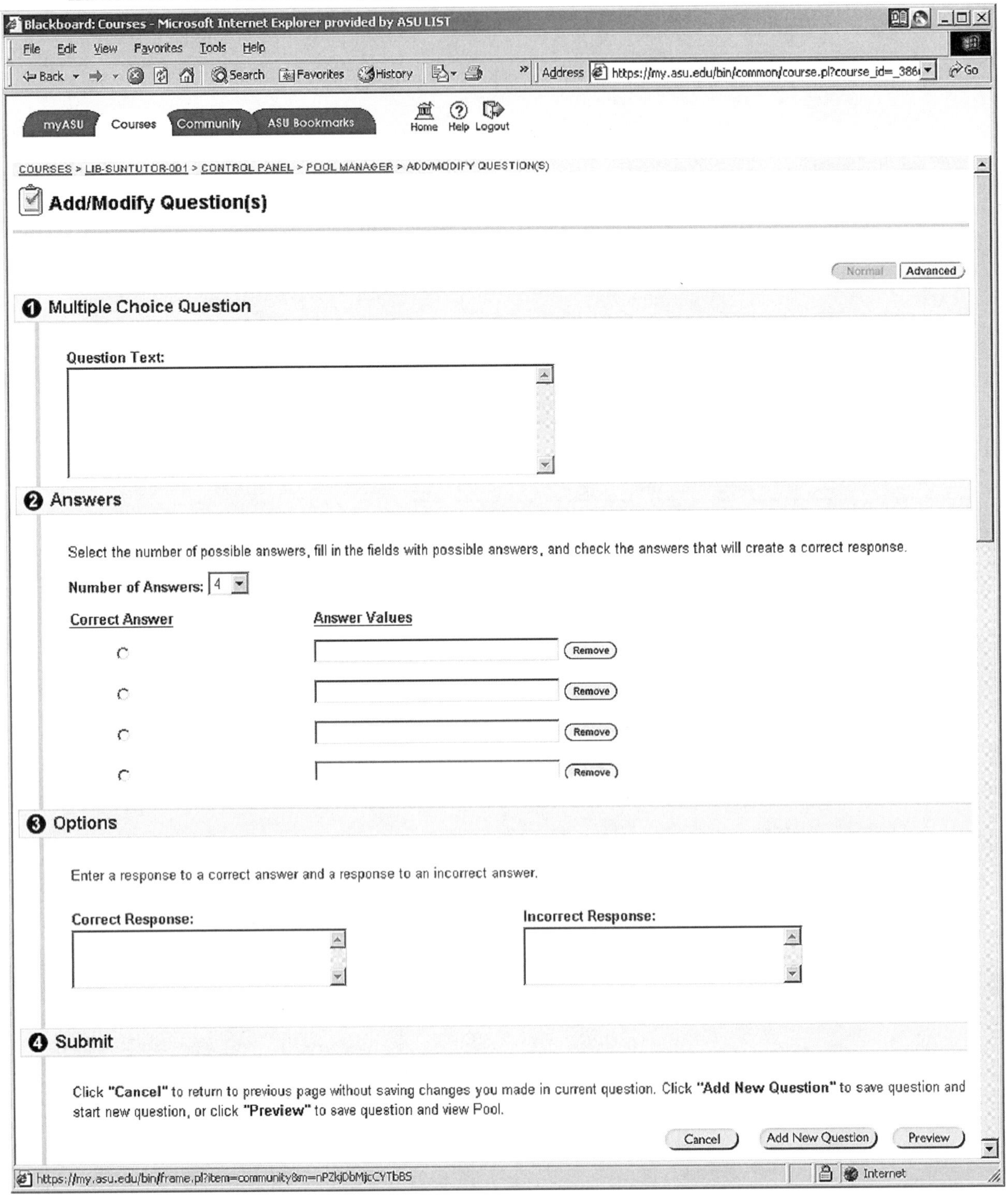

SOPHISTICATED SEARCH TOOLS

The future Web will provide more sophisticated tools for natural language searching, relevance ranking, fuzzy searching, adding synonyms, filtering, "find more like this" search, and other kinds of refined search. XML-based search tools will support different kinds of document type definitions (DTDs) such as Dublin Core for digital content, Text Encoding Initiative (TEI) for full-text content, and Encoded Archival Description (EAD) for archival materials. They can perform searching across disparate databases with different file structures and terminology, and produce an integrated display of the source information no matter what standards (MARC, EAD, TEI, or Dublin Core) are used to describe the data. With this kind of search tools, users will be able to go from a catalog record, a bibliographic citation, an abstract, even a footnote or an endnote, to the full text from different aggregators.

SUPPORT FOR MULTIMEDIA RETRIEVAL AND MANAGEMENT

New technologies will bring about changes in the multimedia world. The Web will be made easier for people to efficiently store, search, and retrieve different media such as pictures, audio, and video. The greatest challenge is how to deal with a one-direction, linear medium like audio or video.

Take video for example; if we are looking for relevant materials on a video clip, we have to watch the whole program from beginning to end. In other words, one must search through the video to find specific information. The traditional way to index video is to have indexers watch the entire video collection, provide short descriptions of the videos, and create a keyword database. The keyword data provided by a library or an archive such as the National Archives of the United States is a rough view of the content of any segment. The simple search page of those databases offers the ability for users to find preselected video content on demand. Still, we cannot really look for a specific segment without watching the entire video to see if it contains what we are looking for. One way out is the Web-based video content management system. The system provides many advantages that broadcast and traditional video archives cannot. It offers the capability of breaking video down into small segments, allowing searching and access to content, and offering customization, sharing, and book marking of video content.

Web-based video content management systems such as those developed by Virage (*www.virage.com*) can "watch" and "listen" to the video, find scene changes to generate key frame images, and use speech-recognition or closed-captioning to create a transcript. If trained properly, the system can even learn to recognize faces and voices, offering a clear clue to what the video contains. The system can produce data files that have information about start time, end time, and speaker, text, or image data for that time segment. If we put the data into a database, we can do more than a simple keyword search for video programs. For example, we can find more than the general stories of the reactions to the September 11 tragedy from the world; we can find all the specific references that the people in the world made about the event. We can find information about who said what and when. So the video will become an interactive archive of information instead of a linear clip. No doubt this system meets the need to have precise information accessed instantly.

Besides video retrieval, the new systems will make video content management easier. Before the development of this kind of systems, if you wanted to put video online you had to manually encode clips, manually track and manage video by opaque file names, and manually add video files one at a time to different Web pages. With the new systems, videos will be automatically encoded and indexed. Video is processed once but available to many. Browsing and managing large volumes of video can be easily done via a Web interface. Video is made available in digital format from a centralized location and quickly available with sophisticated search. Moreover, one can automate video publishing or link clips to the database.

On the whole, this new technology will possibly revolutionize retrieval and management of other multimedia materials. Gone will be the days when multimedia library or archive materials are difficult to apply to use.

Another development took place at Pennsylvania State University where computer scientists created software that responds to written questions by retrieving digital images and that has different kinds of potential applications such as streamlining museum curators' archiving of artwork. The ALIP (Automatic Linguistic Indexing of Pictures) system first creates a pictorial dictionary and then uses it for associating images with search keywords. Different from other content-based retrieval systems that compare features of visually similar images, ALIP uses verbal cues ranging from simple concepts such as "flower" or "grass" to higher-level abstract ones such as "rural" or "Asian." In addition to this, the ALIP system is able to classify digital images into a larger number of categories than other systems, and can be trained with concepts simultaneously and with images that are not visually similar.

MEDIA-BASED NAVIGATION

Media-based navigation provides a new way for online searching. It is a style of browsing in which the users employ the same kind of media for a query as the media they want to retrieve. During the navigation, interaction is done between the user and the system without translating the textual representation. In general, for hypermedia systems including the Web, media-based navigation is a useful interface for improving human-machine interaction. Its potential for future Web development is unlimited.

Developed by Japanese scientists in the early 1990s, the hypermedia system, "Miyabi," for instance, provides a useful paradigm for online information retrieval. This system has a set of tools for media-based navigation. In this system, the user browses through the whole system using specific information clues such as shape, color, construction for still images, motion for movies, and a tune for music data. Miyabi allows computers to understand images. In order to find pictures, the user can either sketch the approximate composition of the image or select an existing picture and use it to link to more of the same. For example, if the user wants to find a picture of Van Gogh, he can just draw a rough drawing of a painting by Van Gogh by using the system's drawing facility, and enter the search. The system can recognize the rough drawing and will match the image with indexed images. Then it will provide a couple of possible candidates from which the user can find the target image.

A different navigation scheme provided by Miyabi is the Online Tour Guide to Paris, in which the Eiffel Tower shows up as an existing picture. The user can tell the system to show all other images that look somewhat like the photo of the Eiffel Tower. The system displays miniatures of pictures of tall thin things and the user can select some of these images for full-scale display. The images again have hypertext links to the maps and to textual descriptions of the sights of Paris. Hypermedia navigation by image searching and retrieval is very useful for those who speak a different language other than a specific Western language when information to be searched is in that language.

Navigation by sound retrieval is another form of media-based navigation. Suppose the user wants to find Beethoven's Symphony No. 5, which he has listened to before but does not remember the name of the music. With the new system, he can just hum a tune of Beethoven's Symphony No. 5 to a microphone. The computer can recognize the sound and find it by matching the tune with the indexed music. Navigation by sound retrieval no doubt will also help the visually handicapped to find auditory data and information more easily.

ONLINE LANGUAGE TRANSLATION

Since the Web is a universal communication tool, how to translate Web pages on the fly has been a major issue for global communication. Generation of a target text language from a source language is another feature of the future Web. Translation memory programs will retrieve from pairs of matching words and phrases stored in a database, which serve as an electronic phrasebook. The future translation program will be combined with a voice recognition software. It can be used to translate major spoken languages in the world into a specified target language. Together with a scanner and handwriting recognition software, the program will not only be able to translate printed documents and hand-written materials, but also transmit the translated version on the fly via the Web as well.

There are now a few free online translation services. Search engines such as AltaVista have a translation feature that allows the reader to go to a foreign language page and do a seamless translation online. Translation choices include French, Italian, German, and Spanish from and to English. It is possible that the future development will integrate the online translation technology into the Web browsers. It will not only translate European languages, but also translate Unicode-based languages such as Chinese, Arabic, Japanese, and Korean in real-time. With a program built in your browser, the translation machine will enable the users to build their own custom dictionaries and grammars, and fine-tune the translation. More advanced translators will have voice recognition capabilities and be able to translate the input from a screen reader.

VIRTUAL REFERENCE AND LIVE BROADCAST

Virtual reference software will become popular. This kind of software includes "live output" features, which broadcast your screen over the Internet to the users in real-time during a reference session. It simulates a hardware PC camera and works with streaming media encoders, video conferencing, and Webcam applications. All of the special effects such as annotations, watermarks, and cursor highlighting will be available using the "live output" features. One company, ISSI (*www.virtualreference.net/virtual/*), has already developed powerful Virtual Reference Software. With this software, librarians may perform the following actions with any patron:

- Send Web pages to the patron in real-time, either one at a time, or through "escorting," where the patron's browser follows the librarian step-by-step.
- Preview any Web page before sending it. For patrons with advanced browsers (IE or Netscape 4.0 or better), do two-way browsing (meaning the patron can push pages to the librarian and vice versa) and use a form synchronization feature that allows librarians and patrons to fill in forms or search boxes together.
- Send "chat" responses to the customer's questions and statements.
- Send predefined scripted messages and answers to commonly asked questions.
- Capture and send screen shots from any application running on your computer.
- Walk the patron through slide shows and presentations.
- Transfer or conference the call to any of your other librarians on the system, or to any other library using the system.

Figure 7–7 shows Live.Brarian, the customized version of ISSI virtual reference product at Arizona State University Libraries.

Figure 7–7 Live.Brarian: Arizona State University Libraries

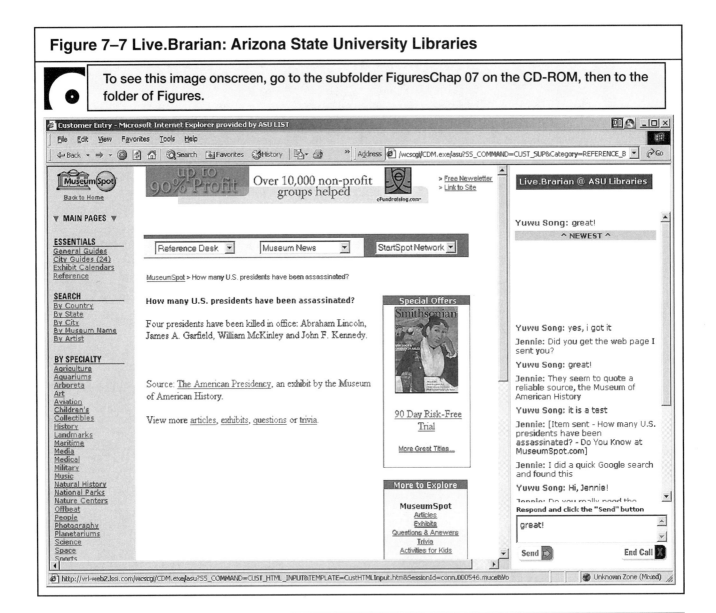

To see this image onscreen, go to the subfolder FiguresChap 07 on the CD-ROM, then to the folder of Figures.

DIGITAL LIBRARIES

Digital Libraries are organized collections of digital information. They combine the structuring and gathering of information, which libraries and archives have done, with the digital representation that computers have made possible. Digital information can be accessed rapidly around the world, copied for preservation without error, stored compactly, and searched very quickly. A true digital library also provides the principles governing what is included and how the collection is organized. The World Wide Web has been turned into many digital libraries by individuals or groups who select, organize, and catalog large numbers of pages. Technically, digital libraries deal with converting, constructing, indexing, storing, and retrieving the text and multimedia materials in online systems.

Digital libraries have been hot in recent years. Although their ramifications have not yet been fully appreciated, there is no doubt that they will play a big part in the future. The digital library concept has given birth to a revolution of changes that will occur in the library and the information world. Besides helping create digital documents, this new technology will convert large amounts of print and nonprint information into a digital format. When patrons want to access this information they will simply look up the subject desired, and they can print out what materials they need.

The digital libraries' values may not at first be what materials they have within their collections, but instead what materials people can access. This access to information is more valuable than the acquisition and the possession of hard copy materials. Today's conventional libraries are in the process of evolving into a more efficient information retrieval system. The traditional library institutions certainly will not disappear from our society, but they may have to restructure themselves and adapt to growing changes of technology.

Funded by the National Science Foundation, six universities are engaged in the development of some digital library projects. They include UC Santa Barbara's Alexandria Digital Library Project (*www.alexandria.ucsb.edu/*); UC Berkeley Digital Library Project (*http://elib.cs.berkeley.edu/*); Stanford University Digital Libraries Project (*http://diglib.stanford.edu/diglib/*); Carnegie Mellon University's The Informedia: Digital Video Library Project (*www.informedia.cs.cmu.edu*); University of Illinois' Digital Library Initiative: Federating Repositories of Scientific Literature (*http://dli.grainger.uiuc.edu/idli/idli.htm*); and The University of Michigan Digital Library Project (*www.si.umich.edu/UMDL*). At the same time the Library of Congress also plays a part in this field. In these projects, new standards and technologies such as Dublin Core and Z39.50 are experimented. Although it is still too early to say which standard and technology is the best, with further exploration we will reach our consensus for the ultimate solutions.

To predict the future is no easy task, especially when our horizons are limited by today's technology. In ten or twenty years, the library Web sites as we know them today will have evolved into something we can no longer recognize. The emergence of new technologies and inventions will provide important impetus.

At the same time new problems, technological, social, and economic, will appear. Hopefully, with collective efforts, we can rise to all the challenges to mankind to build a global electronic village.

APPENDIXES,

---

1. RESOURCES FOR THE FUTURE OF THE WEB

For further information about the Web's future, you can check the Web sites of a few governmental, educational, and private institutions that are involved in the ongoing development of the Web.

NATIONAL CENTER FOR SUPERCOMPUTING APPLICATIONS (NCSA)

The National Center for Supercomputing Applications is an organization that helps establish standards and coordinate the ongoing development of the Web. It also develops software programs for use on the Web.

> 152 Computing Applications Building
> 605 East Springfield Avenue
> Champaign, IL 61820
> Phone: (217) 244–0072
> URL: *www.ncsa.uiuc.edu*

WORLD WIDE WEB CONSORTIUM

The MIT World Wide Web Consortium is based at the Laboratory for Computer Science at the Massachusetts Institute of Technology. The consortium was created to support the CERN-MIT W3O initiative, set up standards, and coordinate activities for the development of the Web.

> 545 Technology Square
> Cambridge, MA 02139
> Phone: (617) 253–5851
> URL: *www.w3.org*

ELECTRONIC FRONTIER FOUNDATION

This organization is a nonprofit civil liberties organization that was created to defend people's rights to think, speak, and share ideas, thoughts, and needs using new technologies, such as the Internet and the World Wide Web.

1550 Bryant Street, Suite 725
San Francisco CA 94103 USA
Phone: (415) 436–9333
URL: *www.eff.org*
E-mail: *membership@eff.org*

INTERNET ENGINEERING TASK FORCE

The Internet Engineering Task Force (IETF) is a large open international community of network designers, operators, vendors, and researchers concerned with the evolution of the Internet architecture and its smooth operation. The organization establishes and approves protocols for the Internet.
URL: *www.ietf.cnri.reston.va.us/home.html*

INTERNET SOCIETY

The Internet Society is an international organization that provides leadership in addressing issues that confront the future of the Internet, and is the organization home for the groups responsible for Internet infrastructure standards, including the Internet Engineering Task Force (IETF) and the Internet Architecture Board (IAB).

12020 Sunrise Valley Drive, Suite 270
Reston, VA 22091
Phone: (703) 648–9888
URL: *http://info.isoc.org/home.html*

2. ESSENTIAL WEB FILE FORMATS

File Suffix (Extension)	Description & File Type	How to (Dis)Play
.aiff	A sound format (Binary)	Use QuickTime to play it.
.asf	Microsoft Advanced Streaming File (Binary)	Use Windows Media Player to play it.
.asp	Microsoft Active Server Page (Plain text file)	Use a Web browser to display it or a plain text editor to view it.
.au	A sound format found on the Web (Binary)	Use QuickTime to play it.
.cgi	Common Gateway Interface (Plain text file)	Use a plain text editor to view it.
.css	Cascading Style Sheet (Plain text file)	Use a plain text editor to view it.
.doc	A DOS/Windows program or a DOS/Windows Self Extracting Archive (Binary)	Use MS-Word to view it.
.exe	A DOS/Windows program or a DOS/Windows Self Extracting Archive (Binary)	Download and launch it in its own temporary directory; it may spawn a number of files and directories.
.fla	Macromedia Flash file (Binary)	Use Macromedia Flash to play it.
.gif	GIF (Graphical Interchange Format), the most commonly used graphics format found on the Web (Binary)	Use a browser or a graphics program to view the file.
.html .htm	Hypertext Markup Language, the code to create Web pages (Plain text file)	Use a Web browser to view the file.
.jpg .jpeg	JPEG/JFIF, a 24 bit graphic format (Binary)	Use a browser or a graphics program to view the file.
.js	JavaScript file (Plain text file)	Use a text editor to view the file.
.jsp	JavaServer Page (Binary)	Use a Web browser to view the file.
.midi	A sound format (Binary)	Use RealPlayer to play it.
.mp3	Music file (Binary)	Use Windows Media Player, QuickTime, RealPlayer to play it.
.mov .qt	QuickTime Movie, Apple's movie platform (Binary)	Use QuickTime to play it.
.mpg .mpeg	MPEG, the standard movie platform (Binary)	Use Windows Media Player, QuickTime, RealPlayer to play it.
.pdf	Adobe Acrobat Portable Document Format (Binary)	Use Adobe Acrobat Reader or Adobe Acrobat to view it.
.pl	CGI or Perl file (Plain text file)	Use a text editor to view it.
.rm	RealNetworks' video file (Binary)	Use RealPlayer to play it.
.rt	RealNetworks' text file (Plain text file)	Use a text editor to view it.

File Suffix (Extension)	Description & File Type	How to (Dis)Play
.smil	Synchronized Multimedia Integration Language (Plain text file)	Use RealPlayer or GriN.
.swf	Macromedia Shockwave Movie file (Binary)	Use Macromedia Flash player.
.tiff .tif	A large high quality image format (Binary)	Use Photoshop or other graphics software.
.txt	A plain Text File (Plain text file)	Use Microsoft Word, NotePad, WordPad, Apple's Simple Text to view it.
.wav	Windows sound file (Binary)	Use Windows Media Player to play it.
.wmv	Windows Media movie platform (Binary)	Use Windows Media Player to view it.
.xml	Extensible Mark-up Language (Plain text file)	Use Internet Explorer 5 or above to display it and use a text editor to view it.
.zip	A common DOS/Windows compression format (Binary)	Use WinZIP to view and extract archives.

3. QUICK GUIDE GLOSSARY

ACROBAT

Software developed by Adobe, Acrobat is used to create the PDF (Portable Document Format) files. Acrobat Reader (downloadable free from Adobe's Web site) is required to read PDF files.

ALIASING

A term in graphic design, aliasing takes place when a graphics file does not have a high enough resolution to represent a graphic image or font. An aliased image or font looks jagged.

ALIGNMENT

Alignment means the spatial placement of texts, graphics, applets, or multimedia elements on the Web page. These elements can be positioned to the left, right, or center of a page.

ALT-ATTRIBUTE

Part of the image source tag in HTML used for including text in image sources. For people who use text-only browsers, people who choose not to see graphics, or people who depend on text-reader software to access the Web, the ALT-attribute is always helpful.

ANIMATED GIF

A GIF graphic file with two or more frames or images displayed in a timed sequence to create the appearance of motion.

ANIMATION

A series of graphic images or frames displayed in a timed sequence. They are used to create the illusion of continuous movement. GIF and Flash animations are the most popular.

ANTI-ALIASING

A method or process to smooth the transition of pixels in graphics. It makes the edges in the image appear less jagged.

ASP

ASP stands for Active Server Pages. It is Microsoft's solution to server-side scripting and database-driven Web sites.

BANDWIDTH

Bandwidth refers to the data carrying capacity of the Internet connection. Telephone lines can carry 1K of data per second.

BITMAP IMAGE

Also called raster graphic, it is an image represented by pixel data, which defines a specific arrangement of colors of the screen dots. Most graphics on the Web are bitmap graphics. Bitmap graphics include GIF, JPEG, Photoshop, PCX, TIFF, Macintosh Paint, Microsoft Paint, BMP, and PNG.

BROWSER

The software used to access Web pages.

CACHE

Cache is a process in which images are downloaded by browsers and stored on a user's computer so the graphic images do not need to be downloaded more than once.

CGI

Common Gateway Interface. CGI is a programming language used for generating interactivity such as processing forms on the Web site.

CLIENT/SERVER COMPUTING

Client/server computing is a technique that allows computers to access a lot of information without taking computing power away from other active applications. In the client/server network architecture, the client computer sends a request for information to the file server, where special software interprets the request, takes the detailed steps (such as extensive indexing and sorting) needed to fill the request, and delivers the final results to the client computers. Using client/server techniques, applications running on client computers with modest processing power that are connected by slow long-distance circuits are enabled to obtain detailed and efficient access to large information databases.

COLDFUSION

ColdFusion is a technology integrated into the HTML coding of pages. It accesses the database via either a native database interface or using a standard protocol, open database connectivity (ODBC), and a common query language—SQL. It serves as a bridge between the database and the Web server. It handles client's queries to the online database and sends the results to the Web browser in HTML.

COMPRESSION

This is a technique by which video or image data is scaled down in size, consuming less storage space and requiring a narrower bandwidth or shorter download time. JPEGs and MPEGs are generally compressed files.

CSS

Cascading Style Sheets. Developed by the W3C, Cascading Style Sheets enabled Web developers to create style templates (sheets) that decide how text elements (paragraphs, headings, hyperlinks, etc.) are displayed on a Web page.

DHTML

Dynamic Hypertext Mark-up Language. DHTML is an HTML extension, which adds to HTML's functionality and interactivity on the client side. It gives the developers the ability to dynamically change content, style elements (text and graphic features), and a Web page's layout and structure.

DPI

Dots Per Inch. DPI defines the resolution of an output device such as a printer. Generally, print resolution is from 300–1200 dots per inch.

EXPORT

Export means to save a file in a different format rather than the default format in an application. For example, Fireworks' PNG files and Photoshop PSD files can be exported as GIF or JPEG files.

FLASH

Flash is graphic animation software developed by Macromedia.

FORM

A form is a page that includes areas for the reader to fill out. HTML form tags can be used to create text-entry boxes, check boxes, radio buttons, and drop-down menus.

FRAME

In video or animation, a frame refers to a single graphic image in a sequence of graphic images.

FRAMES

A frame is a rectangular region in the browser window that shows a Web page along with other pages in other frames.

FTP

File Transfer Protocol. FTP allows one to transfer files from one computer to another over the Internet.

GIF

Graphics Interchange Format. GIF is one of the two most popular Web graphic file formats. GIF images display up to 256 colors.

HEXADECIMAL

It is a computing system that uses a base of 16. Four binary digits may be represented with a single number or letter. The first ten digits are 0, 1, 2, 3, 4, 5, 6, 7, 8, 9 and the next six are A, B, C, D, E, F. Hexadecimal numbers are used for the color of Web graphics or background. The hexadecimal equivalent for the color white is #FFFFFF, while for the color of black it is #000000.

HTML

Hypertext Markup Language. It is a formatting language for creating Web pages that contain text, multimedia, and programming elements.

HYPERLINK
A hyperlink, also called a link, is an electronic connection between one page of a hypertext file and another.

HYPERTEXT
Hypertext is the text that allows the reader to jump around among onscreen documents or other resources by choosing highlighted keywords.

IMAGEMAP
An Imagemap is a graphic image on the Web that leads to multiple, clickable links, depending on which part of the image one clicks.

JAVA
Java is a Web-oriented programming language, developed by Sun Microsystems. It can be used to create complex applications or simple applications called applets, which can be downloaded into your computer for playback. Developers use Java to create animation, 3D effects, interactive games, etc.

JAVASCRIPT
A scripting language created by Netscape, JavaScript brings interactivity to the Web. It can be used to create special effects such as mouse-over and pop-up windows. It can also be used to develop interactive applications such as online quizzes or calculators.

JPEG
Joint Photographic Experts Group. It is a graphic file format for full-color and black-and-white graphic images. Images in this format allow for more colors than GIF images. Usually JPEG is used for photos.

LOSSLESS COMPRESSION
Lossless compression is a file compression technique, which does not rely on omission of pixel from the original and uncompressed images or videos. This technique is used for GIF images.

LOSSY COMPRESSION
A compression technique used to make file sizes smaller by casting away some pixel information or details from the original and uncompressed images or videos. By reducing the quality of a video or a picture when you save it, you can shrink the file size. Theo-

retically, it should lead to unnoticeable loss of image quality. JPEG and MPEG are good examples of lossy compression.

META TAG

Meta tags are HTML tags used for providing information about the author of a Web site or page, the HTML specifications, and the keywords or description of the Web site. The search engines usually search these keywords and descriptions and produce the search results based on them.

MODEM

A hardware device used for modulating and demodulating data transmitted over telephone or cable lines.

MOUSE-OVER

A special effect for Web graphics, usually used to change the color or appearance of an image or trigger pop-up windows when one places the cursor over the image.

MPEG

Moving Picture Experts Group. It is a compressed video format.

MULTIMEDIA

A term that can be applied to a system, a process, or a form of communication that combines text with graphics, video, audio, animation, interactivity, and so forth.

PATH

Refers to the location of a file (Web page, graphic, video, CGI, etc.) on a Web server or your computer's hard drive. Path comes in two types: absolute and relative. The "absolute" path means it contains the complete URL from beginning to end. For example: the complete path for the home page of Arizona State University Libraries is: *http://www.asu.edu/lib/index.html.* The "relative" path for the same page is: "/lib/index.html." The beginning slash orders the Web server to start from the first level (sometimes called "root") of its disk space. It will automatically fill in the "http://www.asu.edu" for the user.

PDF

Portable Document Format. Developed by Adobe Systems in its software program Adobe Acrobat, PDF files can be downloaded from the Web and viewed page by page with Adobe Acrobat Reader plug-in. Using the Acrobat Reader, one can view, navigate, print, and present PDF files. PDF documents are widely used because they retain the formatting used by the author. PDF documents ensure the information appears on the screen and prints on the printer the way the author wants.

PHP

PHP is a free server-side, platform-independent scripting language. It plays the role of middle-ware between the Web server and a database to support delivery of dynamic content to the browser. Like ASP, it interfaces well with the free MySQL database and others.

PLUG-IN

Software that adds functionality to an application. Take a browser for example; a plug-in for the browser might take the form of a video/audio playback feature. Plug-ins can also be used to save specially formatted files. One can download plug-ins free from the creator's Web page.

PNG

Portable Network Graphics. Pronounced as "ping." Used for lossless compression and displaying Web images, PNG supports images with millions of colors. PNG can create background transparency with no jagged edges. The cons are that older browsers do not support PNG, and PNG's file size is much bigger than that of JPG and GIF.

PORTAL

A portal is a Web site that users can personalize and customize. For example, MyLibrary is a Cornell University Library portal to provide many personalized library services to Cornell University students, faculty, and staff.

QUERY

A search request sent to a database to locate all records that meet the search criteria.

QUICKTIME

Developed by Apple, QuickTime is the multiplatform, industry-standard multimedia architecture used by software tool vendors and content creators to create and deliver synchronized graphics, sound, video, text, and music. Besides, QuickTime allows 3D and virtual reality to be viewed on the Web site.

SEARCH ENGINE

A program used to search words and phrases in Web documents. It returns a list of documents in which specified words or phrases are found. A search engine contains a spider and an indexer. The spider is the software that retrieves the documents, and the indexer reads the documents and makes an index in each document.

SERVER

A server is a computer connected to the Internet and has software, which "serve" out information to other users on the network. There are different types of servers: Web servers, e-mail servers, file servers, application servers, and so on. Generally, Web servers are used to host Web pages for access by users.

SMIL

Synchronized Multimedia Integration Language. A language developed by groups coordinated by the WWW Consortium, SMIL is a subset of XML. It is used for laying out multimedia elements and time control in a coordinated multimedia presentation.

SPIDER/ROBOT

A software program that searches every Web page, following all of the links and cataloging all of the text of every Web page.

TAG(S)

Tags refer to codes used in HTML to control layout functions on a Web page such as background colors, font specifications, image placement, forms, and multimedia elements.

THUMBNAIL

Thumbnail is a smaller version of a graphic. Usually a link connects the thumbnail to the larger version. By taking a glance at the thumbnail, the user can determine if the graphic with more detail is worth seeing.

URL

Uniform Resource Locator. It is an address of an electronic file, for example, an HTML document on the Internet. The URL is composed of the protocol (the communication language); the domain name (the exclusive name of a Web site); and the pathname of the file to be fetched, normally an HTML file.

VECTOR GRAPHIC

Vector graphics refer to images created in shapes and lines, called paths. The most popular vector graphic software includes Adobe Illustrator, Macromedia Freehand, and Flash. The graphics are exported in bitmap format. While retaining high quality, vector graphics' files are comparatively small.

WEB SITE

A Web site is a collection of electronic pages formatted in HTML. It usually can contain text, graphics, and multimedia elements such as audio, video, animation files, and other programming elements like CGI, Java, and JavaScript.

WYSIWYG

Acronym for "What You See Is What You Get." It refers to the abilities of Web authoring tools to hide the HTML code that was developed when a designer created a Web page.

XML

Extensible Markup Language, a subset of the Standard Generalized Markup Language (SGML). It is designed to make it more usable for distributing materials on the Internet. XML is different from SGML mainly in simplifying the complex formalisms of SGML in order to ensure that an XML parser is simple enough to embed in Web browsers. Like HTML, it is a mark-up language. But it is different from HTML in allowing the users to create new tags for describing data in a flexible and extensible way, making it possible for regular Web browsers to handle such user-made element types usefully.

4. A FREE DREAMWEAVER TUTORIAL

LESSON 1 INTRODUCTION

Macromedia's Dreamweaver is one of the most popular professional tools for visual Web site design. You can use Dreamweaver to create HTML pages without having to learn all the codes. Even if you do know the codes, Dreamweaver simplifies the process. One of the best features is that all of the codes created by Dreamweaver are cross-browser, so you don't have to worry about compatibility issues. Unlike many HTML editors, Dreamweaver preserves the format and structure of your codes created in other Web editors such as Adobe PageMill, GoLive, CyberStudio, NetObjects Fusion, Microsoft FrontPage, Claris HomePage, and Netscape Composer. Besides Dreamweaver's basic features for simple Web design, its built-in WYSIWYG tools are ideal for creating fantastic timeline-based animations, and for manipulating your page-using behaviors such as roll-overs, visibility changes, and sound. They are also good for adding your own customized behaviors, and even for defining your own customized objects and adding them to your pages. In addition, you can take advantage of advanced JavaScript coding, site management, and many more sophisticated features.

The Macromedia Dreamweaver Tutorial is designed for busy librarians who do not have much time to read a 400-page handbook about the tool. This tutorial gives the readers a brief introduction to the basics of Dreamweaver. Once you have familiarized yourself with these basics, you know well enough how to develop a powerful Web site. Dreamweaver 3 and 4 are the most widely used versions. The most current version is Dreamweaver MX. This tutorial is based on Dreamweaver 3; however, users of other versions can still use it since the software's major features, functions, and interface share a lot of similarities.

LESSON 2 WORKING ENVIRONMENT AND TOOLS
Working Environment

Dreamweaver has a graphical working environment for creating Web pages. The document window is the main editing window, which looks similar to the way a completed Web page would look. Dreamweaver provides other program features that publish the Web site by transferring files to a Web server and a place for typing in raw HTML codes if you wish.

Figure Appendix 4–1 Dreamweaver MX Working Environment

To see this image onscreen, go to the subfolder Appendix 4 on the CD-ROM, then to the folder of Figures.

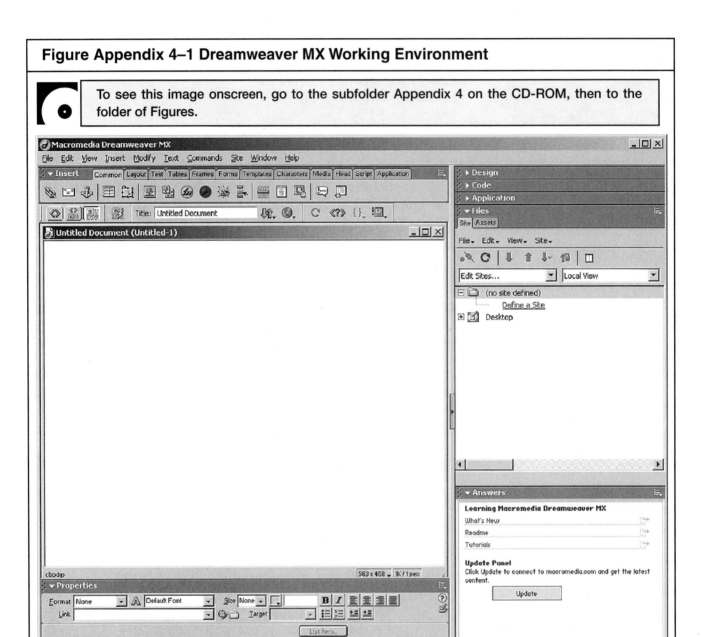

Figure Appendix 4–2 Dreamweaver 3 Working Environment

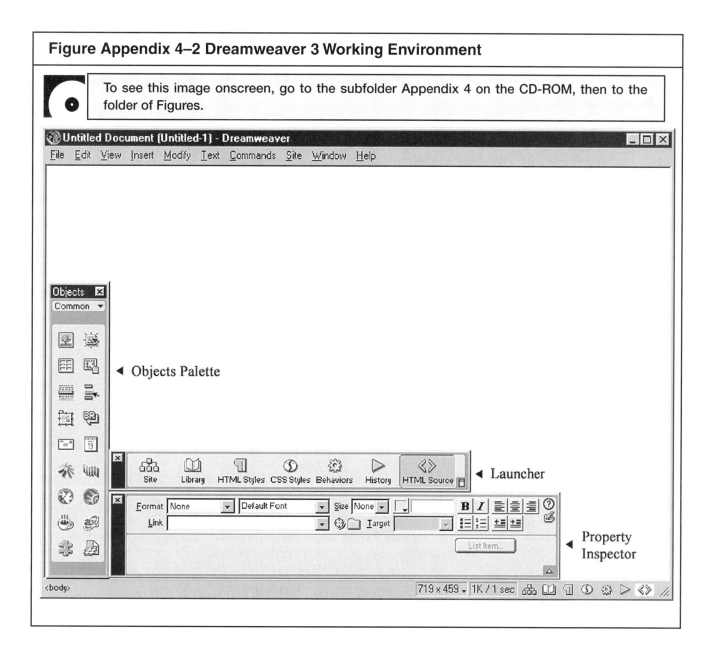

To see this image onscreen, go to the subfolder Appendix 4 on the CD-ROM, then to the folder of Figures.

Properties Inspector

Properties Inspector is a powerful tool for defining properties of various elements. To view it, select **Window > Properties** if it is not visible.

Figure Appendix 4–3 Properties Inspector

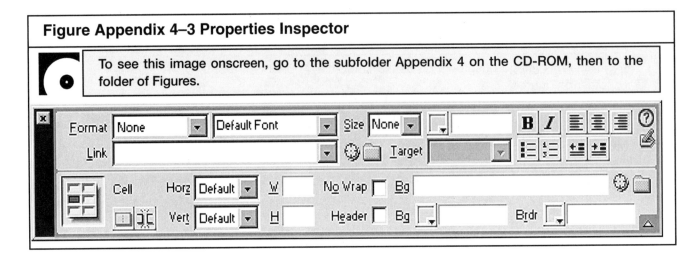

To see this image onscreen, go to the subfolder Appendix 4 on the CD-ROM, then to the folder of Figures.

Text Properties

Different elements have different properties. Take text for example; you can type a few words in the document window and highlight text to see available properties to apply to it such as lists, indent, font, font size, text color, bold, italic, link, and heading options.

Format

Format applies the selected tag to the text. Heading styles are used to apply a standardized hierarchical structure to formatted text. The smaller the number of the heading, the bigger the heading will be. For example, H1 describes the largest heading.

Font

Font applies the selected font combination to the text. Browsers render text using the first font in the combination that is installed on the user's system. **Default** specifies the default font for the HTML tag used for the selected text.

Size

Size defines either an absolute font size (1 through 7) or a font size, which is relative to the BASEFONT size (+/–1 through +/–7 with the default being 3). You can also enter an exact point size, such as 24.

Bold and Italic

Bold and **Italic** specify the respective style.

Left, Center, and Right

Left, **Center**, and **Right** define the respective alignment.

Link

Link makes the selected text a hyperlink to the specified URL. Type the URL or click the folder icon to browse to and select a page in your site.

Target

Target specifies a frame in which the linked page is loaded. The names of all of the frames in the current document appear on the list. If the specified frame does not exist, the linked page loads into a new window that has the name you specified. If this window exists, other files can be targeted to it. You can also choose from the following reserved target names:

> **_blank** loads the linked file into a new, unnamed browser window.
> **_parent** loads the linked file into the parent frame set or window of the frame in which the link is contained. If the frame containing the link is not nested, then the linked file loads into the full browser window.
> **_self** loads the linked file into the same frame or window as the link. This target is implied, so it generally need not be specified.
> **_top** loads the linked file into the full browser window, thereby removing all frames.

Text Color

Text Color renders the text in the selected color. Click the color box and select a browser-safe color by clicking the chip, or enter a hex value (for example #FF0000) into the adjacent text box.

List Item

List Item opens List Properties. The List Properties include numbered or bulleted lists with different styles.

Increase/Decrease Row/Column Span

Increase/Decrease Row/Column Span will add or remove cells from the current column or row. These buttons are available if the current selection is a table cell.

Indent and Outdent

Indent indents while **Outdent** removes indentation from the selected text by removing the <BLOCKQUOTE> tag. In a list, indenting creates a nested list and removing the indentation will undo the nested list.

Objects Palette

The third useful tool is the Objects Palette. Select **Window > Objects** to view the palette.

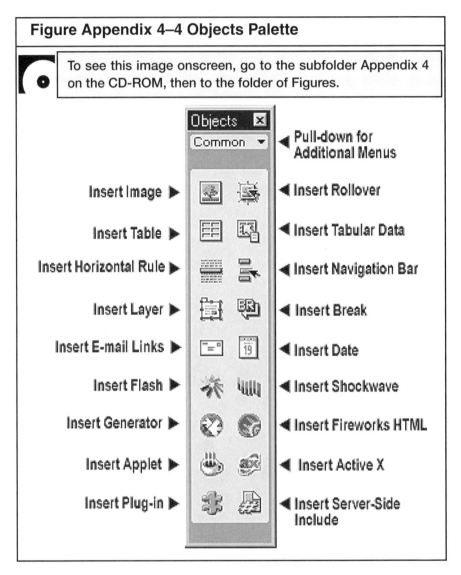

Figure Appendix 4–4 Objects Palette

To see this image onscreen, go to the subfolder Appendix 4 on the CD-ROM, then to the folder of Figures.

The Objects Palette contains buttons for inserting objects such as tables, layers, and images. Click any button to create the specified object. When inserting images, tables, or Shockwave movies, a dialog box prompts you for additional information. Use the Property Inspector to change object properties after the object has been inserted. Dreamweaver includes six panels in the Objects Palette: Characters, Common, Forms, Frames, Head, and Invisibles. Use the pop-up menu to switch between panels.

The Characters panel in the Objects Palette contains buttons for creating different kinds of characters. The Common panel has the most commonly used items: Images and Tables. The Form panel contains buttons for formatting forms. The Frames panel holds buttons for creating frames. The Head panel contains buttons for creating meta tags. The Invisibles panel has buttons for making invisible elements such as scripts, anchors, comments, line breaks, and so on.

Some Functions of the Most Useful Object Palette Buttons
Image

Image inserts a place holder for a graphic image at the cursor location. A dialog box appears so that you can specify a source file for the image.

Table

Table inserts a table at the cursor location.

Horizontal Rule

Horizontal Rule inserts a horizontal rule at the cursor location.

Layer

Layer creates a layer. Click the button and move the pointer into the Document window and drag to define the size and location of a layer. By default, Dreamweaver creates a Cascading Style Sheets layer defined by the DIV tag. Use the Property Inspector to select a different tag. You can change the default setting with Layer preferences.

Applet

Applet inserts a place holder for a Java Applet at the cursor location. Use the Property Inspector to specify a source file for the Java Applet.

ActiveX Control

ActiveX Control inserts a place holder for an ActiveX control at the cursor location using the OBJECT tag. Use the Property Inspector to specify a source file for the ActiveX control.

Plug-in

Plugin inserts a place holder for a plug-in at the cursor location using the EMBED tag. Use the Property Inspector to specify a source file for the plug-in.

Flash

Flash inserts a place holder for a Flash movie at the cursor location using the OBJECT and EMBED tags. Properties for tags have been preset with proper CODEBASE, CLASS ID, and PLUGINSPAGE values for Flash. Use the Property Inspector to specify a source file for the Flash movie.

Shockwave

Shockwave inserts a place holder for a Shockwave Director movie at the cursor location using the OBJECT and EMBED tags. Properties for tags have been preset with proper CODEBASE, CLASS ID, and PLUGINSPAGE values for Shockwave Director. Use the Property Inspector to specify a source file for the Shockwave Director movie.

Rollover Image

Rollover Image inserts a rollover image. A pop-up window will let you specify the rollover images.

Launcher

Select **Window > Launcher** to view the Launcher toolbar. The Launcher is an optional set of shortcuts to various functions of Dreamweaver. It is mirrored in the lower right corner of each Dreamweaver document. It has buttons to open and close various palettes, windows, and inspectors. They include Site, Library, HTML Style, CSS Style, Behavior, History, and HTML Source.

Note: To access floating toolbars and palettes use Dreamweaver Window Menu.

Using the Tools to Control Screen Size and Download Time
How to Control Screen Size

The reasonable size for Web pages is 536x192 (in pixels) for a regular 640x480 screen with the browser opened to its regular default size. Click the drop-down list for screen size at the bottom of the document window to see the preset size for browser windows. You can select a desired screen size from the list.

How to Control File Size and Download Time

The bigger the page gets the longer it takes to load in a Web browser. Generally 30K/30 sec. is a recommended size for a Web page. The calculation is based on the Dreamweaver setting in the **Preferences** found in the **Edit** menu. Clicking **Edit > Preferences >**

Status Bar allows the Web author to set the slowest common connection for their audience (28.8 modem connection). For an Intranet audience with high-speed connection, you may consider using 128 or 1500 connection.

LESSON 3 TEXT
Writing Text

To write text to your new page, start Dreamweaver and begin typing in the Document window just as you would use a regular word processor.

Saving Your Page

To save your page:
Click on **File>Save As.**

Naming the File and Choosing Save Location

If this is the first time to save the document, you will be prompted for a file name and location to save in. You should make sure to save your lead Web page document as index.html. This will be the first page that your viewers see when they go to your site. Name all other connecting Web pages with a short lowercase name (with no spaces or special characters) ending in the .html or .htm extension, for instance, renew.html, resources.html, or hour.html. You can create new documents by selecting **File > New**. To open documents for more editing, select **File > Open** and select the file. To format text, highlight your text and use the **Text** menu or Properties Inspector to make changes.

To See Your Page on the Web

You should upload your page to the server before you can see it on the Web. You can use an external FTP program to put your files on the server. Or you can use Dreamweaver's FTP program.

LESSON 4 EDITING TEXT
Changing the Font Size

The Properties Inspector can be used for editing text. Highlight the text you want to change and click on the Font Size pull-down menu on the Properties Inspector toolbar to make a selection. The default size is 3.

Figure Appendix 4–5 Text

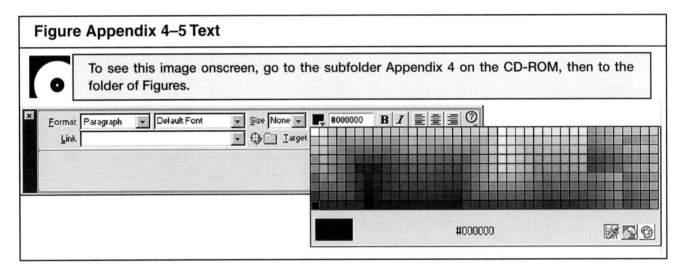

To see this image onscreen, go to the subfolder Appendix 4 on the CD-ROM, then to the folder of Figures.

Changing the Font Color

First, highlight the text you want to change, then click on the little arrow on Font Color Palette on the Properties Inspector and select a color. The default color is black.

Changing the Font Style

Highlight the text you want to change and click on the Font pull-down menu. The default font is Times New Roman, but you can also choose Arial (Sans-serif), Courier, Georgia, and Verdana.

Changing the Properties of the Text

To change the properties of the text (bold, italic, left, center, right), highlight the text you want to change and click on the appropriate properties button on the toolbar, just as you would in a word processor. The default is normal text and left justified.

Making Bulleted, Numbered Text, or Shifting Text

To bullet, number, or shift the text, highlight the text you want to change and click the appropriate button on the Properties Inspector toolbar. Shifting text is similar to indenting/tabbing the text.

LESSON 5 MAKING LINKS

Links provide a mechanism that leads you to other pages or locations on the Internet. Links can be connected to:

- WWW sites on the Internet (*www.asu.edu/lib*).
- Local HTML documents you make (*policy.html*).
- Images (*lib.jpg*).
- Multimedia (*sound.wav, movie.mov, realmovie.rm*).

- Application files for download (spreadsheet such as *databases.xls*).
- Mailto links: Contact e-mail links (*yuwu.song@asu.edu*).

Let's look at the four most important links:

Making External Links

1. Highlight the text Yahoo for the link in the Document window.
2. In the link box in the Properties Inspector type the entire URL (Web address) of the site: *http://www.yahoo.com*.
3. Click anywhere in the Document window to see the underlined link: *Yahoo*.

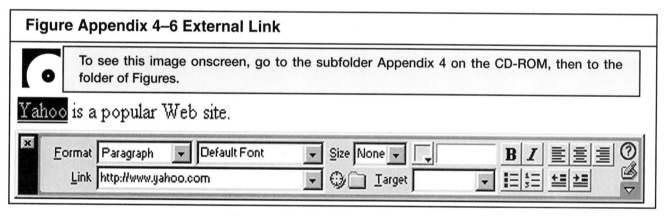

Figure Appendix 4–6 External Link

To see this image onscreen, go to the subfolder Appendix 4 on the CD-ROM, then to the folder of Figures.

To re-edit the link, select it in the page and make corrections through the Properties Inspector link box. If you have a very long URL, you can copy it from the Web browser location bar and paste it into Dreamweaver by two ways:

1. Highlight the URL, choose **Edit>Copy**, put the cursor in the link box, right-click your mouse, select **Paste**.
2. You can use shortcut keys.
   - Highlight the Web address in your Web browser location box.
   - On a PC, hold down the Control key and type the C key to copy the address (Control-C).
   - On a Mac, hold down the Command (Apple) key and type the C key to copy the address (Command-C).
   - Back in Dreamweaver, type the name of the site in your Dreamweaver document.
   - Highlight the text.
   - In the Link box of Property Inspector, click the cursor.
   - On the PC, use the Control-V combination to paste the address.

- On the Mac, use the Command-V combination to paste the address.

Making Internal Links

Internal links are clickable underlined text that links to content or files on your Web site. For example, a tutorial Web page called index.html contains a table of contents with a link to the introduction—introduction.html. Both Web documents are stored in the same directory/folder. The index.html page might also link to other local files for download such as assignment.xls (a spreadsheet file) or videoclip.mov (a video file format).

The following are the steps for creating internal links:

1. Create a new document by selecting **File>New**. Set the **Page Properties** for it and choose **Save As** and name it, for instance, calendar.html. Be sure the document or file you will link to is in the same directory as the document you are working on. It can also be in a subdirectory.
2. Type the link text in the Document window and highlight it. In the Properties Inspector, click the yellow folder next to link.
3. Navigate to the location of the file and click on it. Click the **Select** button.
4. The address that appears in the blank will be the file name (introduction.html) or a folder name followed by the file name (tutorial/introduction.html).
5. Click anywhere in the Document window to see the underlined text.

Figure Appendix 4–7 Internal Link

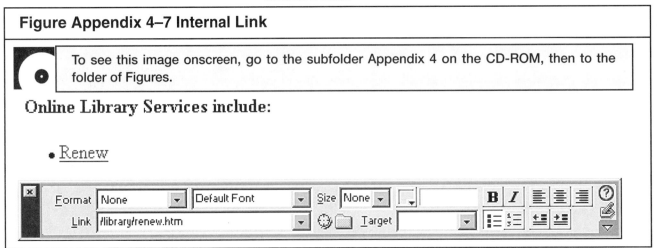

To see this image onscreen, go to the subfolder Appendix 4 on the CD-ROM, then to the folder of Figures.

Creating Mailto Links

Clicking this type of link will launch an e-mail program with a message box that can be filled in and sent to the e-mail recipient.

Keep in mind that a mailto link will only work if the browser supports e-mail and is set up to work with a local e-mail system. Otherwise, the e-mail link simply won't do a thing.

The following are the steps to create mailto links:

1. In the Document window, type the text for the contact link including at least the e-mail address. Highlight the e-mail address.
2. In the Properties Inspector type mailto, followed by the e-mail address. There are no spaces between the colon and the e-mail address. Example: *mailto:yuwu.song@asu.edu.*
3. Click anywhere in the Document window to see the underlined mailto link.

Figure Appendix 4–8 Mailto Link

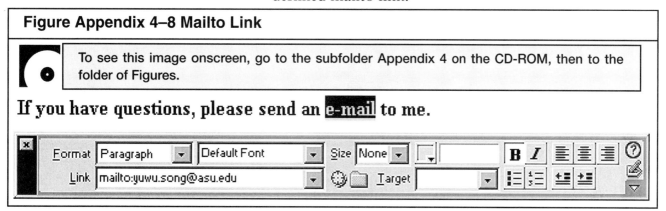

Creating Links to Page Sections (Anchors)

Clicking this kind of link will jump the user to a specific section of the page. To make links to sections of a Web page, you will need to use named anchors:

1. Place your cursor in the section (the part of the page that you have to scroll down to see) of the page you want to link with.

Figure Appendix 4–9 Anchor

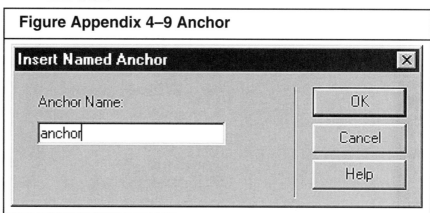

2. Choose **Insert > Named Anchor** and type a one-word, short, descriptive name (the name of the section) and click **OK**. A yellow anchor icon will appear. Click on the icon, if you need to re-edit the anchor.
3. Create a link to the anchor from the top of the same page by selecting text you want to be the hyperlink. Then, in the link box of the Property Inspector, type a # sign followed by the same name as you gave the named anchor.

Figure Appendix 4–10 Named Anchor

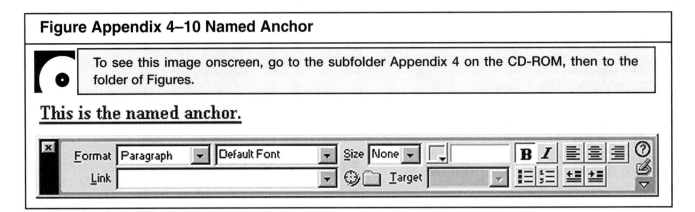

To see this image onscreen, go to the subfolder Appendix 4 on the CD-ROM, then to the folder of Figures.

If the named anchor was named Renew, the link would be #Renew, or as in the dialog boxes illustrated, anchor and #anchor respectively. To link across pages to a section on another page, the link name would be the name of the document it is in, followed by the # sign and the anchor name.

Checking Links Using Preview in Browser

This will open a copy of your Web page off the disk so that you can see it in a browser and check the links without publishing it first on the Web server. Choose: **File > Preview in Browser**, select a Web Browser and click through the links. To re-edit the link, select it in the page in Dreamweaver and make corrections through the Properties Inspector link box.

LESSON 6 INSERTING IMAGES AND HORIZONTAL RULES
How to Insert Images

Check and see if the image you want to insert is located in your Web directory. Put the cursor in the place where you want the image to be. Click on the **Insert Image** button on the Object Palette toolbar. After you click on the button, click on the name of the picture you want to insert and click **Select**.

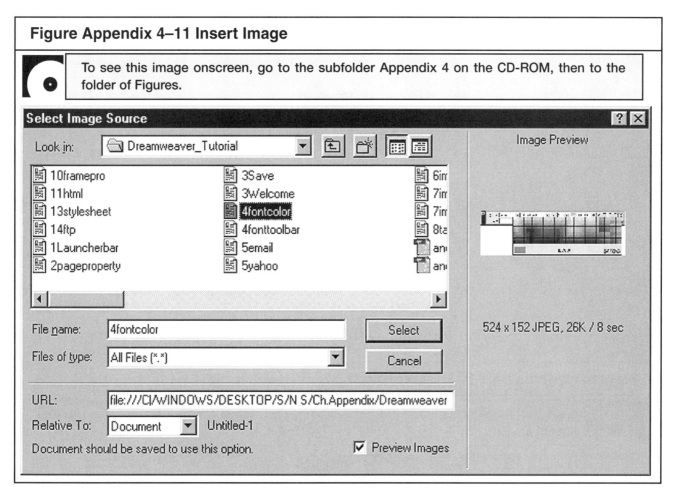

Figure Appendix 4–11 Insert Image

To see this image onscreen, go to the subfolder Appendix 4 on the CD-ROM, then to the folder of Figures.

Now you will see an image on your page. You can change the image's properties (making it larger, for example) by selecting the image and changing values in the property window that shows up. But be careful when you change values, it may make your images look distorted.

How to Insert Horizontal Rules

Horizontal rules are used to divide information up in a page. To insert a horizontal rule, put the cursor in the place where you want the horizontal rule to be and then simply click on the horizontal rule button. You can change the horizontal rule's properties (making it shorter, for example) by selecting the rule and changing values in the Properties Inspector window that shows up.

LESSON 7 VIEWING AND CHANGING HTML

Dreamweaver makes the exhausting coding tasks a simple matter of clicking, dragging, and dropping. Yet, if you are like most designers, there are times when you want to jump into your codes and hand-tweak little things. To give you complete control over the codes, Dreamweaver provides an HTML Inspector.

HTML Inspector

The HTML Inspector allows you to go back and forth between your document and the HTML source codes. You can have the Inspector open at all times to change or add codes or just to view the codes that Dreamweaver creates—this is a great way to learn HTML or JavaScript.

The Inspector also has a neat feature called "selection consistency," which means that it will simultaneously select whatever you select in your document. For example, if you type the words "Welcome to our library" and then select them in your document, they will also become selected in the Inspector.

To open the HTML Inspector, you can either click on the **HTML Source** icon on the Launcher toolbar, or click on **Window>HTML Source**.

The HTML Inspector window looks like this:

Figure Appendix 4–12 HTML Inspector

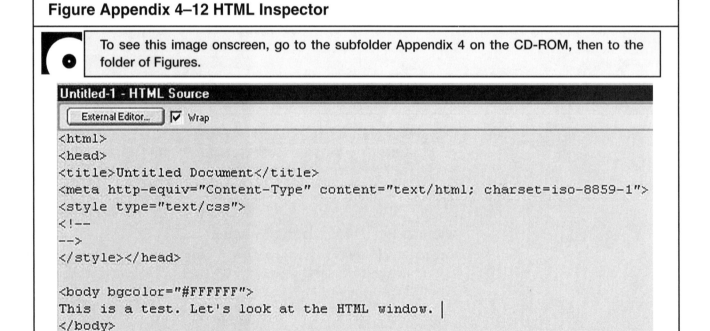

To see this image onscreen, go to the subfolder Appendix 4 on the CD-ROM, then to the folder of Figures.

LESSON 8 PAGE PROPERTIES

The Page Properties dialog box sets overall properties and the color scheme for the page. To create a new document file, you should select **File > New**. You can open an existing file by selecting **File > Open** and choosing the HTML file from your Web site folder. Next select **Modify >Page Properties** to access this dialog box. Click the **Apply** button after each choice to see the changes.

Figure Appendix 4–13 Page Properties Window

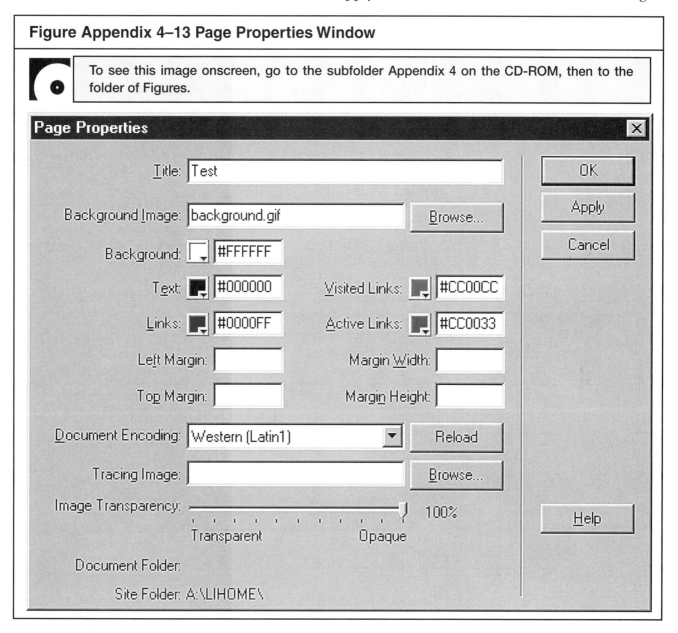

To see this image onscreen, go to the subfolder Appendix 4 on the CD-ROM, then to the folder of Figures.

Title Page

In the Title box, you should type in a title for the page. The title is used as the title of a site found in search engines, or marked in Bookmarks (Netscape) or Favorites (Internet Explorer) lists. The title usually shows up at the top of the Web browser window bar.

Select a Color Scheme

Choose **Commands > Set Color Scheme** to preview color schemes that set up the choices for you. Or Select **Your Own** as described below.

Color Scheme for a Web Page

There are 216 colors that are considered Web safe colors. Dreamweaver uses 212 of these colors in all the Dreamweaver color palettes for backgrounds, text, and link colors.

Background Image

To insert a background image, click the **Browse** button by Background Image and pick a GIF or JPG file stored in your Web site folder.

Background

Choose a color background by clicking in the color square from Background Color Palette. The color will be translated into a hexadecimal number such as #FFFFFF.

Figure Appendix 4–14 Background Color Palette

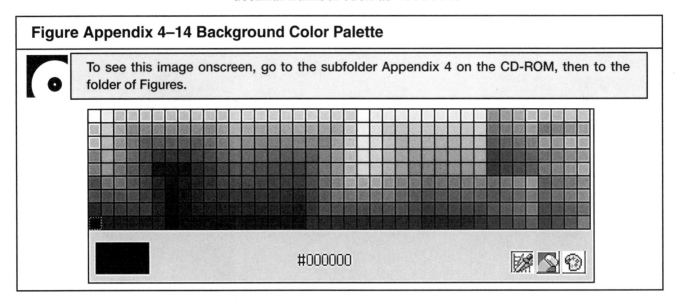

To see this image onscreen, go to the subfolder Appendix 4 on the CD-ROM, then to the folder of Figures.

#000000

Colors for Text and Link

Text is usually black. Individual lines of text color can be changed in the **Text > Color** menu. Traditionally links that are not clicked are blue. Visited or clicked links are purple. Active links, the flash color of the link the moment it is clicked is usually red. You can select a preferred color set by clicking on the color box in the Page Properties. You can also choose a color in the Properties Inspector.

LESSON 9 CREATING IMAGEMAPS

Imagemaps are used for sites that have images with clickable regions. The function of Imagemaps is to show the browser the coordinates of the clickable region of the picture so that it can turn it into a link. For instance, the library floor map below is an Imagemap. You can click on the various parts on the picture to go to the specified places.

Figure Appendix 4–15 Imagemap

To see this image onscreen, go to the subfolder Appendix 4 on the CD-ROM, then to the folder of Figures.

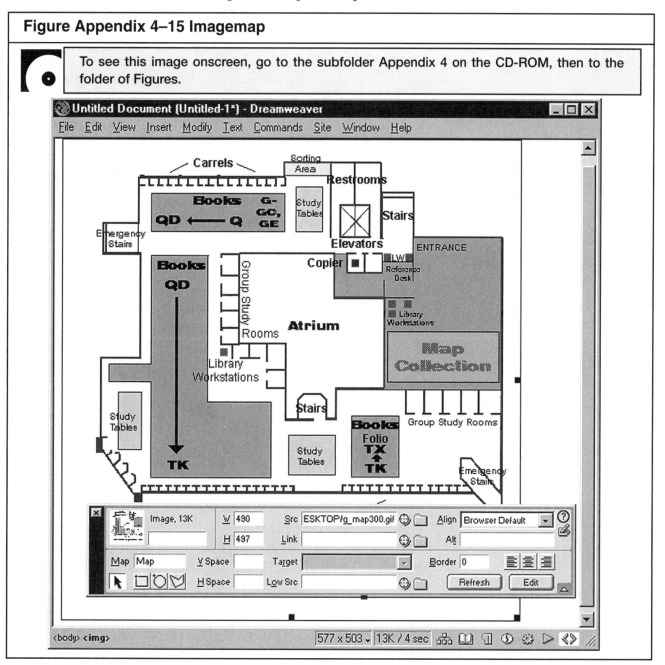

How to Create an Imagemap

To make an Imagemap, highlight the image to show the Imagemap Editor as part of the Properties Inspector. You can draw the hotspots for client-side images using the Imagemap Editor. First, put a name for your Imagemap. Then choose the shape (square, circle, or the irregular) you want your link on the graphic to be. Use the cursor to draw the link you want on the graphic. To make corrections, highlight the area you have selected, and press the Delete key on your computer. Once you finish drawing the link area, fill in the appropriate link information in the Imagemap Editor.

Note: Coordinates on an Imagemap are measured from the top-left corner of the image. If you resize an image after you create an Imagemap, you will need to rearrange the hotspots to match the new image size.

LESSON 10 CREATING TABLES
Why and How

You can create tables for storing information and also for page layout. Tables work well for dividing up information, or for indenting text, among many other options. They can be used to control where text and graphics appear in a page. Once you have created a table, you can modify it in the following ways:

- Format columns either in pixels or as a proportion of the entire table.
- Format text in a table, using the same formatting options you use to format text.
- Add or delete rows or columns.
- Format cells by adjusting their alignment and layout.
- Change the column width.
- Combine adjacent rows or columns.
- Create nested tables (add tables within a table when you need a more complex format).
- Put and position graphics in a table.

To insert a table, put the cursor where you want the table to be, then click on the **Insert Table** button on the Object Palette toolbar. The Insert Table dialog box will appear.

Figure Appendix 4–16 Insert Table Dialog Box

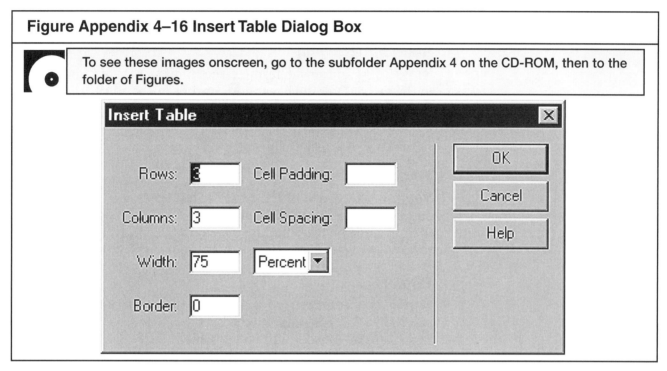

To see these images onscreen, go to the subfolder Appendix 4 on the CD-ROM, then to the folder of Figures.

Click OK. You will have a table with three rows and three columns. Highlight the table. You will have the Properties Inspector's interface changed: Table Properties boxes will show up in the Inspector. You can make necessary changes in the properties boxes.

Figure Appendix 4–17 Changing Table Properties

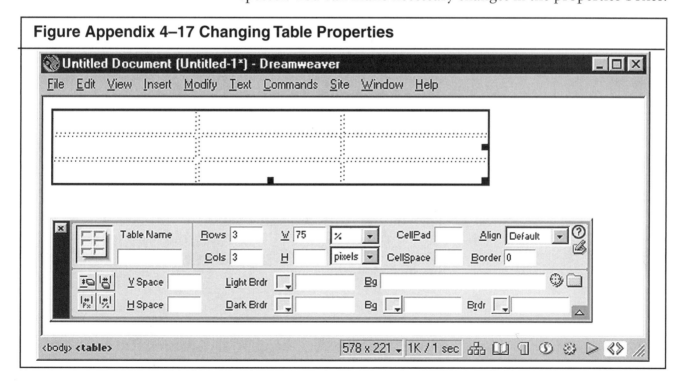

Table Structure Options
Rows and Columns

Rows and **Columns** determine the number of rows and columns in the table. Dreamweaver adds and removes rows from the bottom of the table, and adds and removes columns to the left. Dreamweaver does not warn you if you are deleting rows and columns that contain data.

Width

Width is the width of the table, specified as a percentage of the page width or as an absolute value in pixels. You can either set the width to be a set number, such as 600 pixels, or have it conform to the viewer's screen, such as 90 percent of the screen width.

Border

Border is how thick you want the table border to be. If you are using the table for page layout, specify a border value of 0. In the browsers, the border will be invisible.

Cell Spacing

Cell Spacing is the amount of space between a table's cells.

Cell Padding

Cell Padding is the amount of space between a cell's contents and its edges. Tables work very similarly to tables in word processors. You can select entire columns and rows and change the text individually inside each cell.

Table Properties

When a table is selected, the Properties Inspector shows the properties. To select a table, click its border. Dreamweaver offers a couple of additional options for dressing up your table. Add colors, change alignments, specify column span settings, and do much more with its simple interface. To change the column span, click the table cell of your choice, and then click the **Increase Column Span** button in the Properties Inspector. To add colors and alignments, right-click the table cell of your choice (Windows) or Control>click (Macintosh) and choose Cell Properties from the list. A dialog box appears giving you many options.

Align

Align aligns the table to the browser's default, left, or right. To center a table, select the table and choose **Text > Alignment > Center**. You can also do this using the Properties Inspector.

V Space and H Space

V Space and H Space add space in pixels around the top and bottom, and left and right of the table, respectively.

Color

Color options let you set the border and background colors for the entire table. In addition, the **Light** and **Dark** border options have a highlight and shadow effect, respectively, to give a three-dimensional appearance to the border. To reset colors to the default, delete the hex values in the color options.

Clearing Table Row Heights and Column Widths

Clearing Table Row Heights and Column Widths deletes all table row height and column width values, respectively, from the table.

Converting Table Widths to Pixels or Percent

The command of Convert Table Widths to Pixels or Percent converts the table width from a percentage of the page width to its current width in pixels; or converts its current width in pixels to a percentage of the page.

Resizing the Table

To make the table look just the way you want it, click and drag its borders. Add and delete rows and columns by right-clicking the table cells (Windows) or Control>click (Macintosh), which gives you a list of additional options.

Creating Nested Tables

Although the code can be complicated, Dreamweaver makes creating nested tables as easy as adding a regular table to your document. Just click the table cell of your choice, and start constructing a table as described above. If you look at the code, you'll find that it's cleanly formatted and easy to understand.

LESSON 11 CREATING FORMS

Forms require two components: the HTML describing the form and a server-side application to process the collected information. When the user completes the form (usually by clicking a Submit button), the collected information and the name of the processing application are sent to the server. The server activates the named application and passes to it the collected information. The server-side application is generally a Common Gateway Interface (CGI) script.

Form Objects Palette
Click the little arrow on the Object Palette. Then select **Form**. The Form Objects Palette shows up.

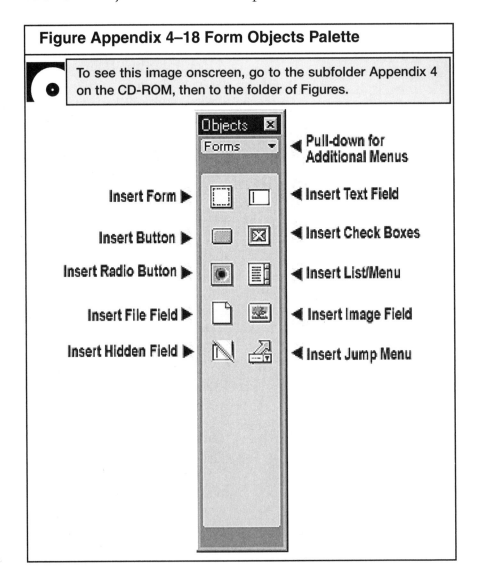

Figure Appendix 4–18 Form Objects Palette

To see this image onscreen, go to the subfolder Appendix 4 on the CD-ROM, then to the folder of Figures.

Major Form Objects
Buttons
Buttons perform standard tasks such as submitting or resetting forms, or perform a custom function. You can enter a custom label for a button, or use one of the predefined labels.

Check Boxes
Check Boxes allow for multiple responses in a single group.

Radio Buttons

Radio Buttons represent exclusive choices. Selecting a button within a group deselects all others in the group.

List Menus

List Menus list a set of values from which users can choose. The object can be a pop-up menu, in which values in the list appear only when you click the object (for a single response), or a list box that always displays the values in a scrolling list (for multiple responses).

Text Fields

Text Fields accept any type of text, alpha or numeric. The entered text can be displayed as a single line, multiple lines, or as asterisks or dots (for password).

How to Create a Form

Open the HTML file you want the form to appear in. Place the cursor where you want the form to appear and choose **Insert > Form** from the program menu (Or click the **Form** button on the Form Objects Palette. You can click corresponding buttons calling up other objects in the next few steps).

Note: A red dotted outline will appear on the screen indicating the area of the form. Select the Form Properties Inspector and type the following address in the **Action** field: h*ttp://www.domain/ library/cgi-bin/form.cgi.*

Figure Appendix 4–19 Form CGI

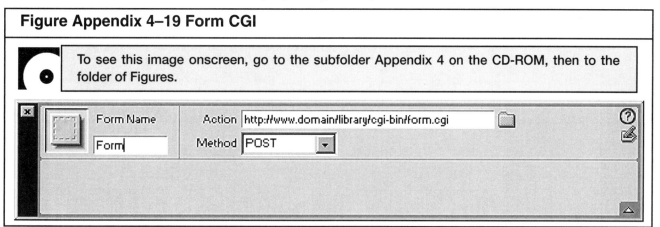

This information calls up a CGI script on your Web server, which processes the information.

To create form fields, place your cursor in the upper-left cell and type for instance: Please enter your name. Place the cursor in the next column, or just press to tab key to advance to the next cell, choose **Insert > Form Object > Text Field.** In the Properties Inspector, type: Name in the TextField box.

Figure Appendix 4–20 Form Text Field

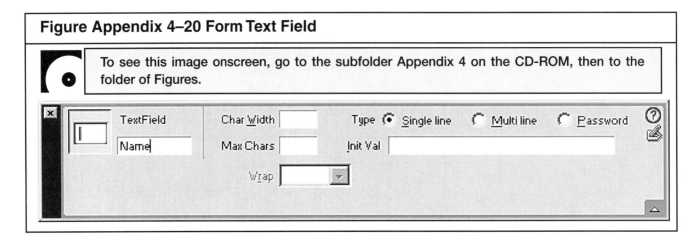

To see this image onscreen, go to the subfolder Appendix 4 on the CD-ROM, then to the folder of Figures.

Click the options in the Properties Inspector and make changes to suit your needs for the form. For example, you can create text fields for Name, Address, Phone, Comments, and so on. You can change the Type to Multi line, and set the Char Width, for instance, to 56 and the Num Lines to 4 (changing to a multi line field gives the user more than one line to enter information). You may want to put initial value in the box: In my opinion.

Figure Appendix 4–21 Form Multi Line

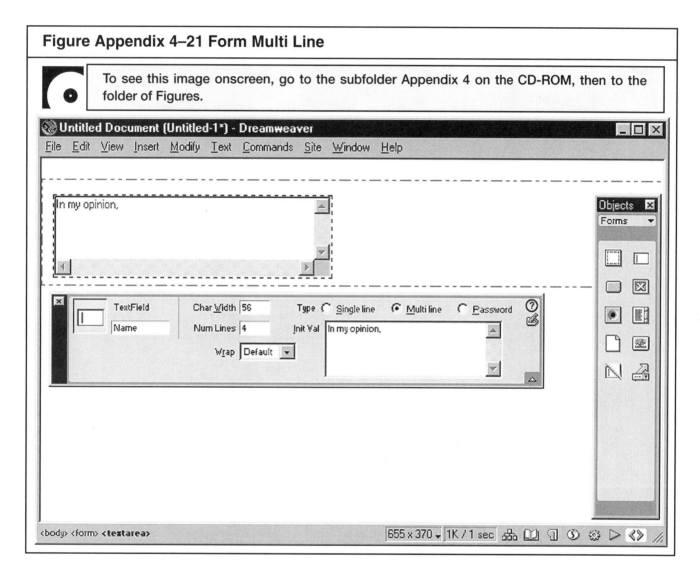

You need to create the button that will submit (send) the information to the Web server. Click the button icon in the Form Object Palette or choose **Insert > Form Object > Button**. Fill in the Label box with Send Info.

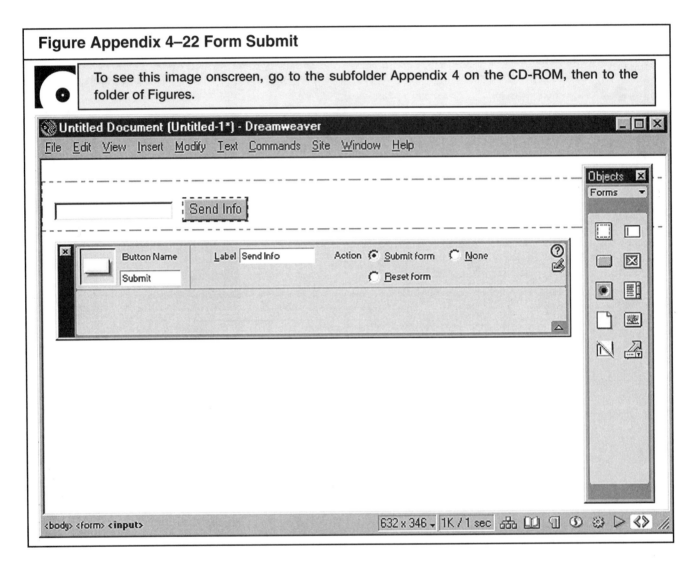

Figure Appendix 4–22 Form Submit

To see this image onscreen, go to the subfolder Appendix 4 on the CD-ROM, then to the folder of Figures.

Now you will insert some Hidden Fields. These fields are invisible on the Web page but allow you to control how the message is displayed when you receive it via e-mail. They can be inserted anywhere within the Form (the dotted red line). Click the Hidden Field icon in the Form Object Palette or choose **Insert > Form Object > Hidden Field**. Enter the e-mail elements in order for HiddenField. For the Value field, enter: Name, Address, Phone, Comments (This defines the order that the elements are listed in the e-mail). Make sure there are no spaces between the commas.

Figure Appendix 4–23 Form Hidden Fields

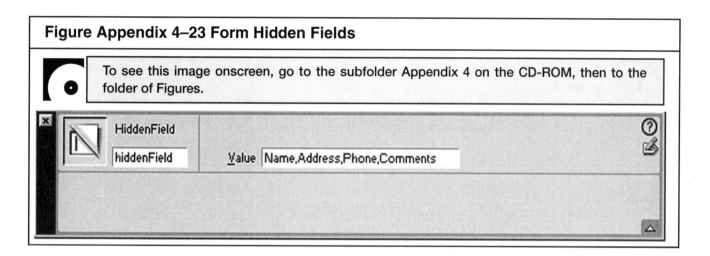

To see this image onscreen, go to the subfolder Appendix 4 on the CD-ROM, then to the folder of Figures.

To test your form, you should save your file, and press F12 to view the file in your Web browser. If you add your e-mail address to your CGI script, you will receive the message in your e-mail box.

LESSON 12 CREATING FRAMES
Why Use Frames?

Frames can be used to divide a Web page so that different files can be loaded into defined areas on the same page. Frames commonly define a navigation and content area for a page. A frameset is a file that defines a Web page with frames. A frameset stores information about the size and location of the page's frames along with the names of the files that should be loaded as the content for each of the frames. What a user sees as a single Web page with two frames is actually three separate files: the frameset file, and two files containing the content that appears inside the frames. You can change the properties of frames and framesets, resize frames, and use links to control their contents. Dreamweaver will automatically create a frameset when you divide a page into more than one frame.

Steps to Create Frames by Splitting a Page

1. Start Dreamweaver and open a blank window, if necessary.
2. From the Document Window menu bar, select **Modify > Frameset**. And then choose one of the following options: **Split Frame Up, Down, Left,** or **Right** from the Document window menu bar.

The **Split Frame Left** and **Split Frame Right** commands both split the current frame in half with a vertical frame border.

Figure Appendix 4–24 Frame Split Left/Right

To see this image onscreen, go to the subfolder Appendix 4 on the CD-ROM, then to the folder of Figures.

The **Split Frame Up** and **Split Frame Down** commands both split the current frame in half with a horizontal frame border (see Appendix 4-25).

Creating Frames by Dragging

You can also drag the frame border to create multiple frames on a page: **Choose View > Frame Borders** and Alt-drag (Windows) or Option-drag (Macintosh) a frame border into the document window to split the frame vertically or horizontally. Drag from one of the corners to divide the current frame into four new frames. Here are steps to create a frame by dragging:

1. From the Document window menu bar, select **View > Frame Borders**. A heavy outline will appear around the blank space in the window.
2. Hold down the Alt (Option) key and click on one of the borders.
3. Drag it to a new location and release the mouse button when you have positioned the border where you choose.

Figure Appendix 4–25 Frame Split Up/Down

To see these images onscreen, go to the subfolder Appendix 4 on the CD-ROM, then to the folder of Figures.

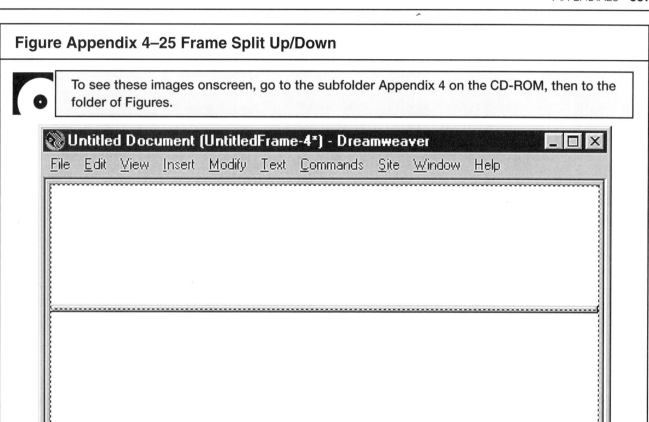

Figure Appendix 4–26 Frame Drag Left

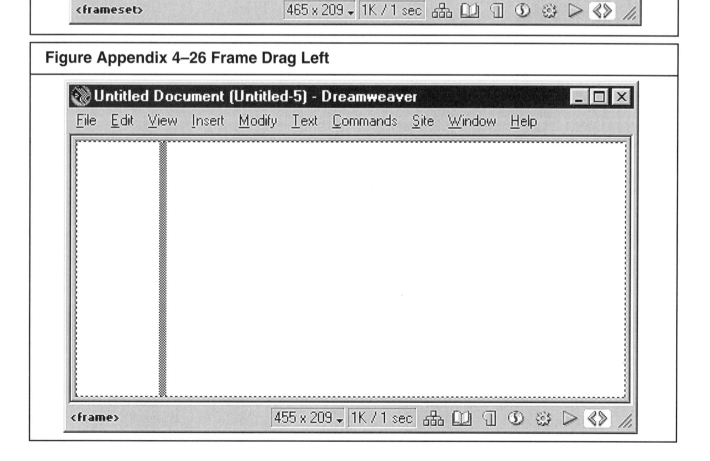

Let go of the mouse button when the frame border is where you want. You now have two frames.

If you hold down the Alt (Option) key and click the corner of a frame border, you can drag it to split the page into four frames.

Figure Appendix 4–27 Frame Drag from Corner

To see this image onscreen, go to the subfolder Appendix 4 on the CD-ROM, then to the folder of Figures.

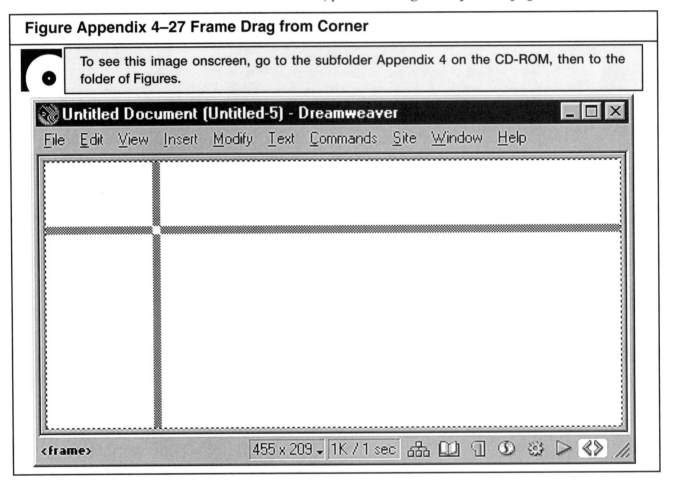

Nested Frames

To make a nested frame, click in an existing frame and choose **Modify>Frameset**. You will see a list that reads: **Split Frame Right, Left, Up,** or **Down**. When you make a selection, a new frameset, split according to your request, will be added to the original frame. When you look at the code, you will find it cleanly indented and easy to read.

Frame Properties

The Frame Inspector shows the framesets in the current document and allows you to select frames and framesets in the document to change their properties. You can specify border color, border size, source file, scrolling behavior, and more. To modify properties for the entire frameset, click any frame border and use the Properties Inspector. To modify a frame, Alt (Option)-click in the frame of your choice, and the Properties Inspector will display the options available for that frame. You can also choose **Window > Frames** to display the Frame Properties Inspector.

The Frame Properties Inspector

The following is the interface of the Frame Properties Inspector. You can change the values of the frame properties to suit your needs:

Figure Appendix 4–28 Frame Properties Inspector

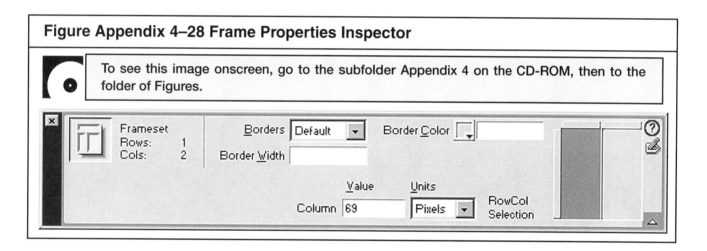

To see this image onscreen, go to the subfolder Appendix 4 on the CD-ROM, then to the folder of Figures.

LESSON 13 CREATING LAYERS
Advantages of Layers

Although tables provide a lot of control for positioning graphics, text, and other HTML objects at specific pixel coordinates, their capabilities are limited. With 4.0 browsers, you can create layouts using a new technology called Layers. You can use layers to position objects at precise pixel coordinates and overlap two or more objects (such as images). Layers also play a pivotal role in Dynamic HTML because you can modify their properties, such as visibility and location, after the page has loaded.

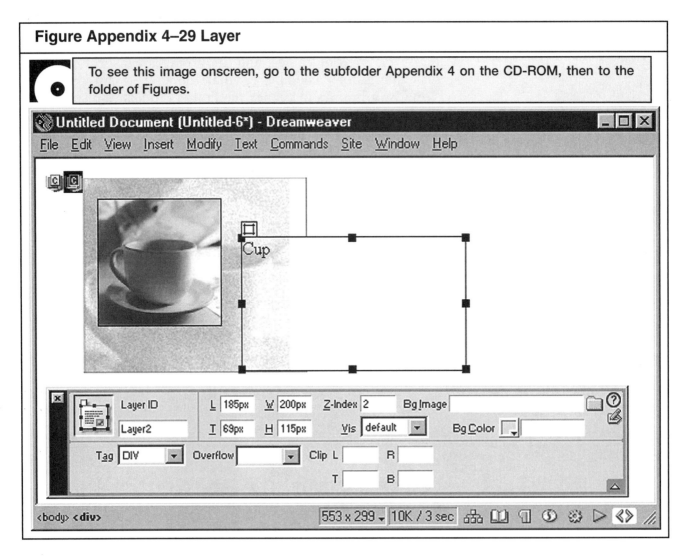

Figure Appendix 4–29 Layer

To see this image onscreen, go to the subfolder Appendix 4 on the CD-ROM, then to the folder of Figures.

This graphic shows overlapping and absolutely positioned two layers with Properties Inspector for layers.

Making a Layer

A layer can serve as a table in that it is a bounding box into which you can put images, text, and forms. Click the Layer icon in the Objects Palette. Then click anywhere in your document, hold the mouse down, and drag the box until it is the size you want. You have just created a layer.

Putting Content to a Layer

To add text to your layer, click in it and then begin typing—it works just like any other part of your HTML document. Add images, forms, text, or objects.

Positioning a Layer

Move the layer to any location simply by clicking its handle (at top left corner) and dragging it. When it is in approximately the right place, you can then use the up, down, left, and right arrows in your computer keyboard to move it one pixel at a time. You can also move a layer to specific pixel coordinates by using the Properties Inspector.

Changing Layer Properties

The Properties Inspector can be used to modify many layer characteristics, such as x and y coordinates, width and height, z-index (for changing stacking order), name, visibility, background color, and layer syntax. To view the Inspector, click the layer's handle. The fields L and T represent the layer's Left and Top coordinates (or x and y).

The Layers Palette

The Layers Palette lists all of your layers in Z-order. A Z-index defines a layer's stacking order. For example, a layer with a bigger number will overlay a layer with a smaller number: Z-index of 10 will be on the top of a layer with a Z-index of 2.

Figure Appendix 4–30 Layers Palette

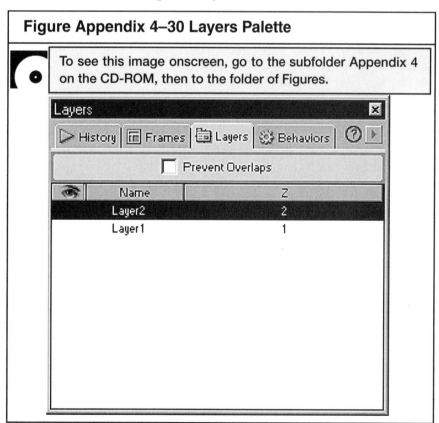

To see this image onscreen, go to the subfolder Appendix 4 on the CD-ROM, then to the folder of Figures.

LESSON 14 CREATING STYLES
Useful Style Sheets

A style sheet is used to specify a wide range of formatting options, such as font family, variant, weight, size, color, word spacing, letter spacing, alignment, indentation, line height, margins, and much more. The style sheet resides in the <HEAD> of your HTML document and with it you can apply styles to any text in your document. You can even create a single stand-alone style sheet for your entire site and then link to it from each HTML document.

Creating a Style Sheet

Style sheets provide you with many formatting options. Choose **Window>CSS Styles** to bring up the Styles Palette (or click **CSS Styles** button on the Launcher). This palette lists all of the available styles (It will be empty the first time you launch it). To create a new style, click the icon (New) at the lower right corner, name your customized style, and then use the interface to design it. The following image shows the Style Definition window. Use it to define a custom style. Options are divided into eight categories.

Figure Appendix 4–31 Style

To see this image onscreen, go to the subfolder Appendix 4 on the CD-ROM, then to the folder of Figures.

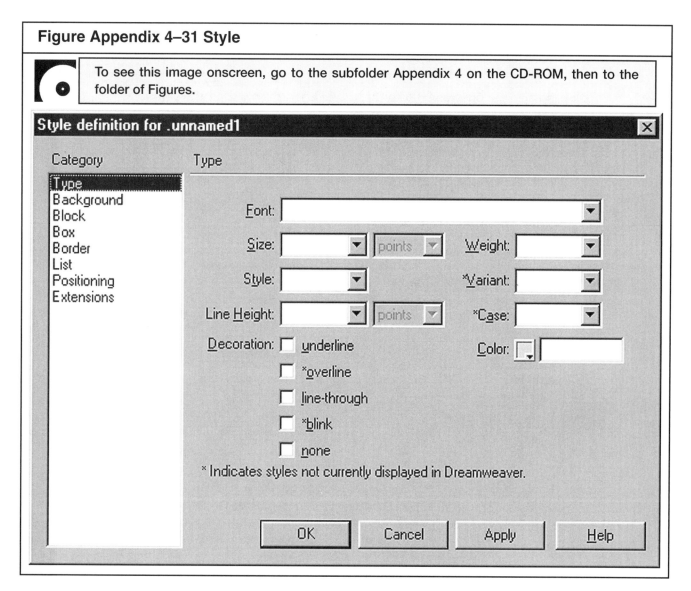

Applying a Style

Once you have designed a style, you can apply it to any text in your document. Simply select some text, choose **Window>CSS Styles,** and click the style of your choice. Dreamweaver will format the selected text in that style.

LESSON 15 FTP

Dreamweaver provides an FTP client that includes many useful features—especially for developers working in a collaborative environment. Click the **Site** button on the Launcher to get to FTP. Now you should fill in the FTP pop-up window with information about your local machine and your server. The FTP client after connecting to a remote server looks like this:

Figure Appendix 4–32 FTP

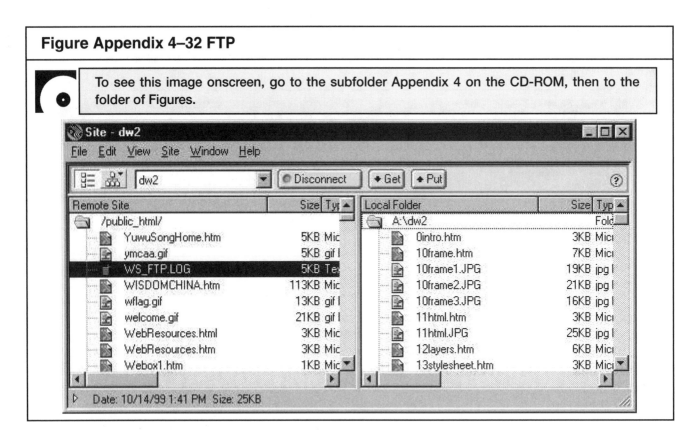

To see this image onscreen, go to the subfolder Appendix 4 on the CD-ROM, then to the folder of Figures.

FTP FUNCTIONS

The **Connect/Disconnect** button connects and disconnects to the remote Web server. The **Get** button gets files from the server and places them on your local machine. The **Put** button puts files from your local machine to the server. You can also transfer files back and forth between the server and your local computer simply by dragging them across the two windows. You can also use external FTP programs to transfer your files. After you put your files to the server, you can view it at the address you specified.

5. BIBLIOGRAPHY

CHAPTER 1 BUILDING AND MAINTAINING BETTER LIBRARY WEB SITES

Printed Sources

Andres, Clay. 1999. *Great Web Architecture: Top Architects Reveal Their Proven Techniques for Smart and Effective Sites*. New York: IDG Books.

Cohen, Laura and Julie M. Sill. 1999. "A Comparison of Research University and Two-Year College Library Web Sites: Content, Functionality, and Form." *College & Research Libraries* 60 (May): 275–289.

Cooper, Alan. 1999. *The Inmates Are Running the Asylum*. Indianapolis, Ind.: Sams.

Eager, Bill, Tobin Anthony, Donald Doherty, Michael Erwin, Noel Estabrook, Chris Feinstein, Galen Grimes, Molly W. Joss, John Jung, Eric Ladd, Jim O'Donnell, Joseph S. Risse, Nik Simpson, and Sarah G. E. Tourville. 1996. *Using the World Wide Web*. Indianapolis, Ind.: Que.

Ensor, Pat. 1997. *The Cybrarian's Manual*. Chicago: American Library Association.

Ensor, Pat. 2000. *The Cybrarian's Manual 2*. Chicago: American Library Association.

Ensor, Pat. 2000. "What's Wrong with Cool?" *Library Journal NetConnect* (April): 11–14.

Fisher, Scott. 1997. *Creating Dynamic Web Sites: A Webmaster's Guide to Interactive Media*. Reading, Penn.: Addison-Wesley.

Flanders, Vincent and Michael Willis. 1997. *Web Pages That Suck: Learn Good Design by Looking at Bad Design*. Alameda, Calif.: SYBEX.

Fleming, Jennifer. 1998. *Web Navigation: Designing the User Experience*. Sebastopol, Calif.: O'Reilly.

Garcia, Mario R. 1997. *Redesigning Print for the Web*. Indianapolis, Ind.: Hayden Books.

Garlock, Kristen L. and Sherry Piontek. 1996. *Building the Service-based Library Web Site: A Step-by-Step Guide to Design and Options*. Chicago: American Library Association.

Garlock, Kristen L. and Sherry Piontek. 1999. *Designing Web Interfaces to Library Services and Resources*. Chicago: American Library Association.

Junion-Metz, Gail and Brad Stephens. 1998. *Creating a Power Web Site: HTML, Tables, Imagemaps, Frames, and Forms*. New York: Neal-Schuman.

King, David L. 1998. "Library Home Page Design: A Comparison of Page Layout for Front-ends to ARL Library Web Sites." *College & Research Libraries* 59 (September): 458–465.

Kovacs, Diane and Michael Kovacs. 1997. *The Cybrarian's Guide to Developing Successful Internet Programs and Services*. New York: Neal-Schuman.

Krug, Steve. 2000. *Don't Make Me Think! A Common Sense Approach to Web Usability*. Indianapolis, Ind.: Que.

LaGuardia, Cheryl, ed. 1998. *Finding Common Ground: Creating a Library of the Future Without Diminishing the Library of the Past*. New York: Neal-Schuman.

Lilly, Erica B. and Connie Van Fleet. 2000. "Measuring the Accessibility of Library Home Pages." *Reference & User Services Quarterly* 40, no.2 (Winter):156–163.

Lynch, Patrick J. and Sarah Horton. 1999. *Web Style Guide: Basic Design Principles for Creating Web Sites*. New Haven, Conn.: Yale University Press.

Metz, Ray E. and Gail Junion-Metz. 1996. *Using the World Wide Web and Creating Home Pages: A How-To-Do-It Manual for Librarians*. New York: Neal-Schuman.

Murray, Laura K. 1998. *Basic Internet for Busy Librarians: A Quick Course for Catching Up*. Chicago: American Library Association.

Nielsen, Jakob. 1999. *Designing Web Usability: The Practice of Simplicity*. Indianapolis, Ind.: New Riders.

Rosenfeld, Louis and Peter Morville. 1998. *Information Architecture for the World Wide Web*. Sebastopol, Calif.: O'Reilly.

Siegel, David. 1996. *Creating Killer Web Sites: The Art of Third-Generation Site Design*. Indianapolis, Ind.: Hayden Books.

Siegel, David. 1997. *Secrets of Successful Web Sites: Project Management on the World Wide Web*. Indianapolis, Ind.: Hayden Books.

Stielow, Frederick. 1999. *Creating a Virtual Library: A How-To-Do-It Manual for Librarians*. New York: Neal-Schuman.

Still, Julie M. 1997. *The Library Web*. Medford, N.J.: Information Today, Inc.

Stoverm, Mark and Steven D. Zink. "World Wide Web Home Page Design: Patterns and Anomalies of Higher Education Library Home Pages." *Reference Services Review*, 24 (Fall): 7–20.

Stross, Charles. 1996. *The Web Architect's Handbook*. Harlow, England, U.K.: Addison-Wesley.

Tapley, Rebecca. 1999. *Who's Afraid of Web Design*. San Francisco, Calif.: Morgan Kaufmann.

Williams, Robin and John Tollett. 2000. *The Non-Designer's Web Book*. Berkeley, Calif.: Peachpit Press.

Young, Margaret Levine, Doug Muder, Dave Kay, Kathy Warfel, Alison Barrows, and William Steinmetz. 1999. *Internet: The Complete Reference*. Berkeley, Calif.: Osborne.

Web-Based Sources

Accessibility Home Page
www.microsoft.com/enable
This Microsoft site provides information and tools to make the Web more accessible to people with disabilities.

Bobby
www.cast.org/bobby

useit.com
www.useit.com

World Wide Web Consortium
www.w3.org/pub/WWW
W3C site provides a number of useful sections including Technical Reports and Publications, HTML 4.0 Specification, Cascading Style Sheets, W3C HTML Validation Service, which checks HTML documents for compliance with W3C HTML recommendations and other HTML standards and WAI Accessibility Guidelines.

WEB4LIB (Library Web Manager's Reference Center)
http://sunsite.berkeley.edu/Web4Lib

Developer Zone
www.projectcool.com/developer
Tutorials and reference on HTML and Web page design from Project Cool.

Digital Librarian Web Page Design
www.digital-librarian.com/web.html

Dr. Watson
http://watson.addy.com
This site checks HTML documents for compliance with W3C HTML recommendations.

Library of Congress World Wide Web Style Guide
http://lcweb.loc.gov/loc/webstyle

Library Webmasters Resources
http://librarysupportstaff.com/4libwebmasters.html

Net Mechanic
www.netmechanic.com

Net Notions for Librarians
http://dspace.dial.pipex.com/town/square/ac940/netnotes.html

Webomatic ToolKit from HotWired
www.hotwired.com/surf/special/toolkit/toolkit.html

Webmonkey.com
http://hotwired.lycos.com/webmonkey
The site regularly offers useful tips for Web designers.

Webreference: The Webmaster's Reference Library
http://webreference.com
The site provides Web site design tips and tutorials.

Web Techniques
www.webtechniques.com

Writing for the Web: A Primer for Librarians
http://bones.med.ohio-state.edu/eric/papers/primer/webdocs.html

Yale C/AIM Web Style Guide
http://info.med.yale.edu/caim/manual

CHAPTER 2 LEARNING AND MASTERING HTML BASICS
Printed Sources
Lemay, Laura. 1998. *Teach Yourself Web Publishing with HTML 4 in 21 Days*. Indianapolis, Ind.: Sams.
Musciano, Chuck and Bill Kennedy. 1998. *HTML & XHTML: The Definitive Guide*. Sebastopol, Calif.: O'Reilly.

Web-Based Sources
A Beginners Guide to HTML
www.ncsa.uiuc.edu/General/Internet/WWW/HTMLPrimer.html

Doctor HTML
www.imagiware.com/RxHTML/

WWW HTML
www.w3.org/hypertext/WWW/MarkUp/MarkUp.html

WWW HTML Editors and Converters
www.w3.org/hypertext/WWW/Tools/Overview.html

Guidelines for Web Document Style & Design from Berkeley Digital Library
http://sunsite.berkeley.edu/Web/guidelines.html

Style Guide for Online Hypertext
www.w3.org/pub/WWW/Provider/Style/Overview.html

Top Ten Mistakes in Web Design
www.useit.com/alertbox/9605.html

CHAPTER 3 MOVING BEYOND HTML

Printed Sources
Holzschlag, Molly E. 1997. *Designing with Style Sheets, Tables, and Frames*. Indianapolis, Ind.: Sams.
Knuckles, Craig D. 2001. *Introduction to Interactive Programming on the Internet: Using HTML & JavaScript*. New York: John Wiley.
Meyer, Eric A. 2000. *Cascading Style Sheets: The Definitive Guide*. Sebastopol, Calif.: O'Reilly.
Teague, Jason Cranford. 2001. *DHTML and CSS for the World Wide Web*. Berkeley, Calif.: Peachpit Press.

Wall, Larry, Tom Christiansen, and Jon Orwant. 1996. *Programming Perl.* Cambridge, Mass.: O'Reilly.

Web-Based Sources
JavaScript Source
http://javascript.internet.com

Matt's Script Archive
http://worldwidemart.com/scripts

MU Perl and Perl CGI Materials
www.cclabs.missouri.edu/things/instruction/perl

Randy's Column on Perl
www.stonehenge.com/merlyn/UnixReview/col13.html

The University of Florida Perl Archive
www.cis.ufl.edu/perl

Web Developer's Virtual Library
http://wdvl.internet.com
It has tutorials and reference for HTML, VRML, XML, CSS, CGI, Perl, Java, JavaScript, and much more.

Webreference
www.webreference.com

World Wide Web Tools for Web Authors
www.nas.nasa.gov/NAS/WebWeavers

CHAPTER 4 DESIGNING WEB GRAPHICS
Printed Sources

Webster, Timothy, Paul Atzberger, and Andrew Zolli. 1997. *Web Designer's Guide to Graphics: PNG, GIF & JPEG.* Indianapolis, Ind.: Hayden Books.
Weinman, Lynda. 1999. *Designing Web Graphics.* Indianapolis, Ind.: New Riders.

Web-Based Sources

Library Media and PR
www.ssdesign.com/librarypr/toolbox.html

Soo-Hyoung's Library Clipart
http://user.chollian.net/~sadrain1/clipart/index.html

Lynda's Web Site
www.lynda.com

CHAPTER 5 EXPLORING INVENTIVE WEB FORMATS AND MULTIMEDIA
Printed Sources

Alvear, Jose. 1998. *Web Developer.com: Guide to Streaming Multimedia*. New York: John Wiley.

Beggs, Josh and Dylan Thede. 2000. *Designing Web Audio*. Cambridge, Mass.: O'Reilly.

Gassaway, Stella, Gary Davis, and Catherine Gregory. 1996. *Designing Multimedia Web Sites*. Indianapolis, Ind.: Hayden Books.

McGloughlin, Stephen. 1997. *Multimedia on the Web*. Indianapolis, Ind.: Que.

Miles, Peggy. 1998. *Internet World Guide to Webcasting*. New York: John Wiley.

Novak, Jeannie. 1998. *Web Developer.com: Guide to Producing Live Webcasts*. New York: John Wiley.

Rose, Jay. 2000. *Producing Great Sound for Digital Video*. San Francisco, Calif.: CMP Books.

Web-Based Sources

Bouthillier, Larry. "Delivering Streaming Media."
www.webtechniques.com/archives/1999/12/bouthillier

MIT Media Lab
www.media.mit.edu

Powell, Adam. "Adam's Multimedia Tutorial."
http://hotwired.lycos.com/webmonkey/multimedia/tutorials/tutorial3.html

Apple QuickTime
www.apple.com/quicktime

Real Networks
www.real.com

Window's Media
www.microsoft.com/windows/windowsmedia/en/overview/default.asp

UC Berkeley: Berkeley Multimedia Research Center
http://bmrc.berkeley.edu/index.html

CHAPTER 6 INVESTIGATING ADVANCED WEB TECHNOLOGIES
Printed Sources

Bryan, Martin. 1988. *SGML: An Authors' Guide to the Standard Generalized Markup Language*. Wokingham, England: Addison-Wesley.

Desmarais, Norman. 2000. *The ABCs of XML: The Librarian's Guide to the eXtensible Markup Language*. Houston, Tex.: New Technology Press.

Feiler, Jesse. 1999. *Database Driven Web Site*. San Francisco, Calif.: Morgan Kaufmann.

Flanagan, David. 2002. *Java in a Nutshell: A Desktop Quick Reference*. Sebastopol, Calif.: O'Reilly.

Gulbransen, David. 1996. *Creating Web Applets with Java*. Indianapolis, Ind.: Sams.net.

Kennedy, Tim. 2002. *SMIL: Adding Multimedia to the Web*. Indianapolis, Ind.: Sams.

Morrison, Mike, and Joline Morrison. 2000. *Database Driven Web Site*. Cambridge, Mass.: Course Technology.

St. Laurent, Simon. 1998. *XML: A Primer*. Foster City, Calif.: MIS Press.

Stanek, William R. 1996. *Web Publishing Unleashed: HTML, CGI, SGML, VRML Java*. Indianapolis, Ind.: Sams.net.

Web-Based Sources

World Wide Web Consortium XML Site
www.w3.org/XML

XML.com XML Site
www.xml.com/resourceguide/index.html

Innovative Applications in Libraries
www.wiltonlibrary.org/innovate.html

Macromedia: Director—"Shockwave Technology"
www.macromedia.com/Tools/Shockwave/index.html

SGML/XML Web Page
www.oasis-open.org/cover/sgml-xml.html
This site contains reference information and software pertaining to the Standard Generalized Markup Language (SGML) and its subset, the Extensible Markup Language (XML).

CHAPTER 7 PLANNING FOR THE FUTURE OF BUILDING BETTER LIBRARY WEB SITES
Printed Sources

Bush, Vannevar. 1945. "As We May Think." *Atlantic Monthly* 176, No.1 (July): 101–108.

Hirata, Kyoji, Yoshinori Hara, Hajime Takano, and Shigehito Kawasaki. 1996. "Content-Oriented Integration in Hypermedia Systems." *ACM Hypertext 96 Proceedings*: 11–21.

International Essen Symposium. 1997. *Towards a Worldwide Library: A Ten Year Forecast; 19th International Essen Symposium, 23 September–26 September 1996*. Essen: Universitätsbibliothek Essen.

Lesk, Michael. 1997. *Practical Digital Libraries: Books, Bytes & Bucks*. San Francisco, Calif.: Morgan Kaufmann.

Web-Based Sources

Digital Library
www.dlib.org

Library-Oriented Lists and Electronic Services
www.wrlc.org/liblists

Buildings, Books, and Bytes: Libraries and Communities in the Digital Age
www.benton.org/Library/Kellogg/buildings.html

C|Net: the computer network
www.cnet.com

Electronic Frontier Foundation
www.eff.org

Libraries for the Future
www.lff.org

World Wide Web Consortium
www.w3.org/hypertext/WWW

ZDNet
www.zdnet.com
Provides access to computing magazines such as ZD Internet, PCWeek, and FamilyPC.

Internet World Online
www.internetworld.com

Web Review
www.webreview.com

MSDN Online Web Workshop
http://msdn.microsoft.com/workshop
This Microsoft site provides the latest information about Internet technologies, including reference material and in-depth articles on all aspects of Web site design and development.

National Center for Supercomputing Applications (NCSA)
www.ncsa.edu

INDEX

ABOUT THE AUTHOR

Dr. Yuwu Song serves as Web developer/Instruction Librarian at Arizona State University Libraries. His major duties include library instruction and Web development. In this position, he teaches students to use the library information systems and develops Web sites related to library instruction. In addition, he consults with library subject specialists to create, revise, and digitize library publications. He is interested in experimenting with new Web technologies to develop effective library Web sites in general and library instruction Web sites and tools in particular. Actively involved in professional development activities, he has presented papers and workshops in several professional conferences. He has also published quite a few articles, book chapters, and reference book entries in the past few years.

Dr. Song received his B.A. in English from Luoyang Foreign Studies University in China, his M.L.I.S from the University of Texas at Austin, Texas, and his Ph.D in History from the University of Alabama at Tuscaloosa, Alabama.